ABOUT GUIDEPOSTS MAGAZINE

Guideposts magazine, with a circulation of over 3½ million and an average monthly readership of more than 15 million, is America's most beloved magazine of spiritual help and encouragement. It features true first-person stories written by people who, with God's help, have found answers in their most difficult crises.

Founded by Norman Vincent Peale, *Guideposts* counts among its contributors the greatest inspirational writers of our day, including Catherine Marshall, Marjorie Holmes, Kathryn Kuhlman and Billy Graham.

ABOUT THE GUIDEPOSTS TREASURIES

These volumes, each one a hardcover bestseller, have long been sold only in hardcover, and only through the pages of *Guideposts* magazine. Now, by special arrangement with Bantam Books, all five are available in paperback at bookstores everywhere, or will be coming soon:
THE GUIDEPOSTS TREASURY OF HOPE •
THE GUIDEPOSTS CHRISTMAS TREASURY
• THE GUIDEPOSTS TREASURY OF FAITH
• THE GUIDEPOSTS TREASURY OF INSPIRATIONAL CLASSICS • THE GUIDEPOSTS
TREASURY OF LOVE

The
Guideposts
Treasury
of
Hope

BANTAM BOOKS
TORONTO · NEW YORK · LONDON

*This low-priced Bantam Book
has been completely reset in a type face
designed for easy reading, and was printed
from new plates. It contains the complete
text of the original hard-cover edition.*
NOT ONE WORD HAS BEEN OMITTED.

THE GUIDEPOSTS TREASURY OF HOPE

*A Bantam Book / published by arrangement with
Doubleday & Company, Inc.*

PRINTING HISTORY

THE GUIDEPOSTS TREASURY OF HOPE *published by
Guideposts Associates in 1976.*

Doubleday edition published August 1979

Serialized in Junior Teachers Quarterly,
August 1979; Catholic Digest, *October 1979;
and* National Enquirer, *November 1979*

Bantam edition / August 1980

ACKNOWLEDGMENTS

*Permission to quote material from the following sources is
gratefully acknowledged:*

*"The Day the Band Left Me"—Reprinted with permission
from the book* Wunnerful, Wunnerful! *by Lawrence Welk with
Bernice McGeehan, © 1971 by Lawrence Welk. Published by
Prentice-Hall Inc. "Walking Where Dragons Live" by Keith
Miller from* Habitation of Dragons © 1965 by Keith Miller—
used by permission of Word Books. "How to Love Coura-
geously" by Norman Vincent Peale. Adapted from* Overcoming
Anxiety and Fear, *a booklet © 1967 by Norman Vincent Peale.
Published by the Foundation for Christian Living. "Let Go and
Let God" by Helen Steiner Rice, from the book* Someone
Cares © 1972 by Fleming H. Revell Co. Used with permission.
"My Christmas Miracle" by Taylor Caldwell. Reprinted by
permission of* Family Weekly, *December 24, 1961.*

ISBN 0-553-13678-X

Published simultaneously in the United States and Canada

PRINTED IN THE UNITED STATES OF AMERICA

0 9 8 7 6 5 4 3 2 1

Contents

1.

HOPE FOR PEOPLE WHO ARE LONELY AND DISCOURAGED

2.

HOPE FOR PEOPLE WHO NEED HEALING

6.

HOPE FOR PEOPLE WITH UNFULFILLED DREAMS

7.

HOPE FOR PEOPLE WHO NEED FORGIVENESS

8.

HOPE FOR PEOPLE SEEKING A DEEPER FAITH

Introduction

Blessed is the man that trusteth the Lord and whose hope the Lord is.

JEREMIAH 17:7

A Guideposts reader once wrote us that a popular mail order catalog was her wish book, that the Bible was her faith book and that Guideposts was her hope book. Over the years—30 now—thousands upon thousands of others have written to tell us that Guideposts has been a very special instrument of hope to them, often at some crucial, pivotal moment in their lives, when things were bleak and prospects discouraging.

The staff of Guideposts, those who edit and write the magazine which is now read by approximately six million people each month, believes that one of its prime missions is to give realistic hope. In fact we consciously strive to incorporate that element into every page of the magazine. It is therefore not difficult to understand why we decided to prepare this book themed on the word hope when we laid plans to observe our 30th year of publishing.

The book you now hold in your hands is the fourth in our "treasury" series, having been preceded by *The Guideposts Treasury of Faith, The Guideposts Christmas Treasury* and *The Guideposts Treasury of Inspirational Classics*. Like its forerunners *The Guideposts Treasury of Hope* offers what we believe to be significant and lasting spiritual help. The stories in this volume represent some of the most memorably inspiring that we have published in recent years. We know that to be so, because of the response the offerings drew from you, the readers. (One thing for which we always are grateful is the warmth with which Guideposts subscribers write and express their opinions about "their" magazine.)

People ask us, "Where do we find testimonies of faith and hope in a world that sometimes seems an arid desert of faithlessness and hopelessness?" The answer is that we learn of many of them from people such as yourself, and once we have a story lead, our writers and editors check it out thoroughly. Our chief criterion for material which appears in Guideposts is that the story is true. Second, we ask, is it helpful? Does it offer something positive which the reader can *take away* from the story and apply to his or her life. In a word: does it offer hope?

In this book, we present the kind of stories that have become the hallmark of Guideposts, stories that illustrate God's healing power, His inexhaustible caring, His limitless love, His saving grace. The selections are divided into eight chapters, one each for people who are lonely and discouraged, for people who need healing, for people whose courage needs shoring up, for people who hope to change some negative pattern in their lives, for people who face crises, for people with elusive hopes and dreams, for people who need forgiveness and for people who fervently desire a deeper, more meaningful faith. Also, we have included throughout the book little nuggets of inspiration— fragile moments of hope, prayers of hope, Scripture verses of hope and poems of hope. Each in its own way offers uplifting words from people who have had their faith tested in the laboratory of life and found it indomitable.

The people who speak in these pages come from all walks of life; they are ministers and housewives, astronauts and doctors, athletes and businessmen, actors and students. Each has a story capable of renewing and recharging people who are defeated, lonely, sick, tired, afraid or filled with doubt. We pray in confidence that this book will find its way into the hands of those who need its message. We hope that *The Guideposts Treasury of Hope* becomes one of your treasured books, one worthy of repeated readings in the years ahead.

THE EDITORS

1.

Hope for People Who Are Lonely and Discouraged

Come unto me, all ye that labor and are heavy laden, and I will give you rest.

MATTHEW 11:28

A Man Alone
by Don Fay

The touching story of a young father who was
suddenly forced to become a mother, too.

I left five children at home the evening I went to the hospital with Mary. This would be our sixth child.

When I returned, I woke our eldest girl to tell her that she had a new brother. And then, before her happiness became too great, I told her that her mother had died.

I held her close while she cried quietly. Then I went to bed to wait for the morning and the day I wished would never come. There were still four more children to tell, then my family, Mary's family, our friends.

Somehow I managed to get through the day. The house was so busy with friends coming by that at first I hardly had time to feel alone. But eventually the living room, the kitchen emptied, the last of the well-meaning people were gone. My mother would soon arrive to do all she could to help feed and care for my large family. It was time I began trying to put the family back together. A place had to be made for both my mother and the baby. Everything, it seemed, had to be changed.

The baby lay asleep in my lap. A bit of formula I had prepared trickled from the corner of his small mouth. His tiny fingers were drawn up in a tight fist as he slept. Holding his warm, frail body close, I had relaxed and had, for a moment, forgotten those persistent problems. But they came back and I began to sort them through my mind. The girls needed new dresses before school started. Mary had been a wise shopper and she had also made beautiful dresses for the girls. How would I ever keep them looking loved?

3

Lesana came in crying, so I reluctantly put Nathan back in his crib. I washed the blood and dirt from her knee and then the tears from her face. I held her close until the sobbing stopped. Then I watched out the window as she limped across the lawn to join the others.

Even if I had the money to hire a housekeeper, even if I didn't have to go to work the next day to make a living, how would I ever find the time to hold, love, guide and teach six children? I tried to remember how Mary had managed to give the children so much love.

She had a way of giving each child just the kind of love needed. She would have known how to love Nathan. I wondered if she had known it was a boy before she died. How do you teach an infant? I wondered. I had always believed it was a woman's responsibility. Now it was mine.

How was I to get up in the morning, fix the formula, dress and bundle the baby, comb and braid the little girls' hair? Who would see to it that teeth were brushed, that socks matched, that coats, hats, mittens and boots were found and that the children were up, fed and ready for school?

There just wasn't time to think through the many decisions I had to make. I made them the best I could and then went on to the next problem, confident of God's ability to keep me from bad mistakes. When I came home at night I had to decide who got to go to visit a friend, who could go to what activity, how they were to get there and how they were to get back. I had to find time to repair the all-important washing machine and unclog a perpetually clogged drain.

Most difficult was settling disputes between the children and grandma. What was fair for grandma wasn't fair to the children. What was fair to the children wasn't fair for grandma. I thanked the Lord for children to whom I could say, "I know it isn't fair, but there's nothing else I can do."

Most important, I realized ever more clearly that I needed to make God as real to the children as Mary had done. How I missed hearing her read to them from the Scriptures. I used to listen as the sound of her voice came floating down the stairs. It was some time before I realized that the King James version she read came alive because she changed the difficult wording that added understanding as she read.

There were the nights when the children were sick and I only half slept listening to every sound. It was Mary who used to miss the sleep. Now I had to go to work too tired to give the job the quick thinking it required. There were nights that were endless and empty without Mary. There were the times I needed somone to talk things over with, the times I needed somone to encourage me and the times I needed someone to lovingly, carefully, rebuke me.

God began to take on a new dimension to the whole family. As we leaned more and more on Him, our confidence grew. As problems seem to get worse, God seems always to become greater. I came to understand that God was working in two ways. He either gave me what I needed—strength, wisdom, understanding, love and occasionally a little extra money—or He sent people to me with those abilities I did not have myself.

How I thanked God for Margaret Filler, for example. My mother was with us only a few months before she had an eye operation. She was in the hospital and then home in bed for months. Margaret took Nathan each day. I dropped him off before work and picked him up each evening.

Margaret's whole family gave Nathan such love and care that my guilt at leaving him with a baby-sitter was taken away. Margaret was never just a baby-sitter. She was a God-supplied mother to him. Her love and concern for Nathan were as great as they would have been for her own child. She was never willing to take any money for all she did and yet she eased my pride by almost convincing me that I was doing her a favor by letting her share Nathan.

When my mother went to the hospital for her operation, meals were prepared, frozen in disposable containers and put in our freezer by friends. Neighbors saw to it that the children were taken to school activities and brought home again. When I was faced with the problem of buying underclothing for growing girls, some understanding women came to my rescue. Most important were the people who had the time to befriend my children and listen to their problems.

Then one day months after Mary died, I stopped and looked around me. I saw all that God had done. There hadn't been any earthshaking miracles. His wisdom had come to me in the still small voice of His word and in the

loving concern of His people. His wonders had come
through people who had learned how to give the best—
themselves.

Yet as I looked, I saw that important things had
slipped away. Everywhere the evidences of a loving
mother and wife were being worn into nothingness. I had
known for some time what was needed. I knew that
strength and wisdom could never provide it. I knew that
loving Christian friends could never bring it.

The wild plums were in bloom. I picked a large bou-
quet not thinking that Mary wasn't at home to put them in
a vase. I arranged them myself and set them on the table.
The children were thrilled and I realized how important
the things were that had slipped away. I needed someone
who would treasure a gift of wild plums. I needed someone to give myself to.

As I prayed I knew that somewhere there was a
woman God had chosen. I wondered what sort of woman
God would choose to be a wife to a very tired, lonely
man. What kind of woman would He find to be a mother
to six children?

One thing I did know. She would be the very best,
for God always gave His best.

Editor's Note:

Two years passed as Don Fay tried to be both father
and mother, holding a full-time job at the same time.
Meanwhile, his children, who had been taught to sing as a
group by their mother, gave concerts at nearby churches.
Occasionally, out-of-town churches also asked the Fay
children to come sing for them. During one of those appearances they were photographed, and the photo was
published, along with some information about the family,
in *The Christian Standard*, a national publication of the
Church of Christ, among whose readers was a woman who
was disturbed by the story. So much so that she wrote a
letter to Don. Following is her version of what happened
as a result.

'Something Should Be Done About Those Children'

It really wasn't like me to write a letter like that. But when I read about that father taking his children around the country, the idea of his exploiting their singing ability stirred up my old-maidish indignation. The picture showed six beautiful children; the youngest a baby. The widower wasn't in the picture. "Probably over fifty, bald and fattish," I said to myself.

So I did something completely out of keeping with my usually careful, conservative self—I wrote to the father, Don Fay, expressing my concern and gently taking him to task for pushing his children into situations for which they might not be ready. I was polite and objective. But, at age 38, having been active in youth work and serving as music director of our church in Bloomsburg, Pennsylvania, I felt I knew what I was talking about.

A letter came back from him. I was a bit flustered when I saw it, for I had not really expected an answer. I took it up to my room in the house where I lived with my parents and read it. His answer was kind and direct and carried no hint of resentment at what he might easily have considered my meddling.

No, the children didn't suffer from the extra attention, he wrote. He explained that it was impossible for him to give the children all the love and closeness they needed. The trips were at best a poor substitute for all they had lost, he continued, pointing out that the children were not professionals and every effort was made to keep the programs from becoming polished. In closing, he expressed the hope that if the children should appear in my area, I would come and hear them.

Well, I thought, perhaps I had been a bit presumptuous. So I wrote and thanked him for taking time to answer. I felt a strange sensation as I mailed the letter. His next letter was polite and restrained, but . . . was there

7

something between the lines? I rushed to my older sister with it. I felt that she, having five children, could better understand what Don might be saying.

My sister was noncommittal, but she smiled at my question.

Several more letters passed between us during the next three months. Soon mother was giving me knowing looks when I asked about the mail.

Then I wrote a letter that I worded very carefully, even prayerfully. I sincerely felt that everything that had transpired thus far was God's doing. Even so, it took a whole pad of paper before just the right words emerged.

Don's answering letter this time was very restrained but it did include an invitation to stop and meet the children if I should ever be up that way. I quickly decided it was time to visit a girl friend in Watertown, New York, about 140 miles from Caledonia, where Don lived. So I wrote him and said I would like to visit on my way through.

I was surprised when he phoned me. His voice was deep, and he chose his words cautiously. He invited me to dinner and then pointed out that since it would still be a long way to my friend's place, perhaps I should plan to spend the night with them. I could have his daughter's room.

You should have heard my mother! She let me know in no uncertain terms that visiting a man whom one did not know was absolutely wrong. But something deep inside me urged me to go anyway.

The Fays lived a few miles outside of Caledonia. As I stepped out of my car that June evening and surveyed the large old farmhouse, I hesitated. *What am I getting into?* I wondered. At that moment a blue van pulled to a stop behind my car. A small man with a dark beard jumped lightly to the ground. He wore work clothes and obviously did something that got him quite dirty. He walked quickly to me, smiled, held out his hand and introduced himself. It was Don Fay, and he was neither 50 nor fattish.

---

*Hope never spread her golden wings
but in unfathomable seas.*

—RALPH WALDO EMERSON

We walked to the front door, which was rapidly filling with children, all dancing with excitement. I marveled at his ability to hear them all at once. Sweeping the toddler into his arms, he led me to the kitchen where he introduced me to his mother. I was surprised—he had not mentioned her in his letters.

Don helped her with several things, excused himself and reappeared in a remarkably short time—washed, clothes changed, and again ready to help his mother. He took over and the chaos ended.

The children sang for me after dinner. They were simply children singing. Their voices were good but untrained.

After the children were in bed, I sat on the worn sofa. Don sat across the room. I learned that he was a printer and also ran a used-book shop. *How old is he?* I wondered. *He must be over 30 because of the children.* He looked younger. We talked well into the night, sharing our thoughts on life, our philosophies, our beliefs. The next morning I was sorry I had to leave to drive on to see my friend in Watertown. That's the trouble with excuses.

I returned home so excited I could hardly wait to talk with my sister. "There is so much love in that home!" I marveled. "They have lost so much, yet have kept their love for God."

Don soon found a reason to invite me back in July. He asked me to attend a community "opera under the stars" program with him and the children.

What a wonderful weekend it was! All the neighborhood youngsters were rounded up for the opera and we were well-chaperoned on our first date by ten children.

In the evenings he would patiently see the children to bed until only the older ones were still up. He would let them share in our conversation for a while and then send them off to bed. He seemed to get strength from those long evenings of just talking. I wondered at his ability to make me feel loved without any outward expression on his part.

In late August, a month later, I invited him and the children to visit my home. Mother, dad and my sisters loved him and his children from the first. My parents and younger sister helped keep the children occupied while Don and I spent time alone. Don suggested we walk across the college campus nearby.

It was a balmy August Saturday evening, pungent with the scent of growing things. We sat down on a garden bench overlooking the town below, its lights twinkling like diamonds set in black velvet. And as we sat, Don drew me close to him and asked me to be his wife, and mother to his children.

I sat there for a long time, not able to answer. I wanted to do what God wanted. But I was worried. After living so many years alone, would I be able to meet the needs of so many people? Most of all, would Don be willing for us to have a child? He already had a large family. His wife had died during childbirth. Would he be willing to go through it all again?

Don said he was.

Don and the children left that Sunday. And I had not yet given him an answer.

Alone, I began to doubt. Looking at all the problems that would face me, I concluded that I had neither the wisdom nor the strength to handle them.

I cried over my weakness, and then, turning to God, I prayed, "If You want me to take on this responsibility, then my lack will not matter. I *know* You will provide."

The next weekend was Labor Day. I drove toward Caledonia, turned at the Shell station and drove out Route Five to the big white house under the trees. Don was standing under the honey locust sorting books, his children helping him. I stepped from the car, and the children turned and waved, laughing. Don looked up, then stood there looking at me, seeing my answer in my smile.

We planned the wedding (November 11, 1972) to be an expression of our gratitude to God for His part in bringing us together. And, of course, the children were a very important part of it. In addition to my vows to Don, I exchanged vows with the children. As the words of the recessional rang out, "Joyful, joyful, we adore Thee, God of glory, Lord of love," the whole church seemed caught up in the thrill of what God was doing.

That was two years ago, two years of good times and some difficult ones. On special occasions I received six baby roses from Don, one for each of the children. When Jonathan was born, there were seven and a note which read, "And one makes seven."

The Lord has blessed our family and home. No matter how great the problem, no matter how tired I might be, He has been there, with just the right amount of wisdom and strength—and always with love, overflowing love that heals and restores and makes us all a family.

—BETSY EUNSON FAY

DAY OF FAITH

However long and dark the night,
Day is sure to break,
And children rise to laughter,
And birds to rapture wake.

However long the winter,
Spring will surely come,
Bringing gold of jonquil,
Silver of flowering plum.

However deep the sorrow,
However great the pain,
Be sure that peace will follow,
As sunlight follows rain.

ELIZABETH NEAL WELLS

When I Found a New Beginning

by Helen Hayes

A famous actress recalls how she rebounded from deep sorrow.

When you have lost someone who is dearer to you than life itself, the gaiety and heedlessness of a fiesta crowd is bewildering. You wonder how anybody can possibly be so elated when it is plain to you that this is a lonely world. When a close loved one died some years ago, my son and I tried to weather a siege of loneliness and bittersweet memories by going to Cuernavaca, Mexico. We arrived at the start of the Christmas season.

But I was just not ready for the fiesta spirit that surged over the walls and in through my open windows. I was an alien and I knew it, an alien alone on an island of grief.

For a place of solace I found a beautiful old Franciscan church on the cathedral square. I discovered I could pray in that church; and when I could not pray, it was comfortable just to sit there, watching the brilliant sunshine streaming through the old Spanish door and reflecting on the griefs and joys that had come through it in two and a half centuries.

After a few visits to the church, I began hearing a lot about one of its young priests, Father Wasson, a man with a very large heart. I made it a point to see him for myself.

Father Wasson is large, shy and guileless-looking. He is accomplishing a quiet revolution in Mexico. Well, not exactly quiet—boys are not the stuff that quiet is made of, but quiet in the sense that there is no fanfare. About 15 years ago he started taking in boys who had been in trouble with the law. Now he has cared for well over a thousand.

Exactly how he clothes and feeds all those children not even he is sure. Except that he has many friends—in Mexico, in the United States, Canada and in heaven. The friends are, indeed, part of the miracle—they prove that goodness is contagious.

Once he had to borrow money from the sewing woman to buy tortillas for the week. Another time when there was absolutely nothing in the cupboard, he got a large check from a stranger. When he really needs something, when the need is tangible and desperate, he doesn't go to the local bank, he *prays* for what he needs. Somebody promptly comes along and gives him just enough money. To him this is an admirably simple system.

Just when you have decided that he is a nice uncomplicated soul, left over from the early Franciscans, you discover that he is also a college professor and a psychiatrist. I know these things now, but I didn't then. He struck me, as he does many people on first acquaintance, as someone who has wandered out of a story book and should not be allowed to bruise himself on our sophisticated problems.

Father Wasson took me to see his children, and I saw them at their best, all scrubbed and shining for Christmas season. In Mexico, Christmastime is a totally religious holiday, with no gifts. It actually begins with an event called a posada on the evening of the 16th. In the Latin custom, this is Christ's birthday and He should get the gifts. This I found very beautiful.

My anguished heart was soothed by the look in the children's eyes; this world was still magic for them, cold or no cold, hunger or no hunger. When you see the great, solemn, shining eyes of the children, you reach out, you think, *Heaven is still there, if only I can touch it.* I reached out timidly, gropingly, and found a small warm hand that was little-boy grubby but magnificently understanding. And so I met Rudi.

Someday Rudi will break somebody's heart with those great limpid eyes. He was a little rascal whose time in the streets had not been wasted, and he had the face of a Murillo cherub.

Rudi escorted me through the posada. Each evening, just as the stars began to push through the curtain of a green and lavender sky, we all lined up and began the posada, a sort of pageant right out of the middle ages where you go from door to door unsuccessfully seeking a lodging for José, a poor carpenter, and his wife Maria. Four little boys carry the litter with the statues of San José and his wife Maria. And down the centuries came the litany of excuses.

"I cannot let you in, Lord, because important people would be embarrassed by you."

"I cannot let you in because I am so busy grubbing for some wealth to leave behind me."

"I cannot let you in because you have no social standing."

"I am too busy. I am too busy. Go away."

"I cannot let you in because hate has sealed the door."

Rudi as gallant as any knight of old Castile, escorted me from door to door, looking at my face from time to time to see how I was taking it. As we walked along, singing the endless verses of the old chant, I could not have stopped if I had wanted to. Neither of us knew the other's language, but I heard him loud and clear. The grand, sonorous prayers I had said as a child came back to me.

At the very summit of the Christmas season is the Day of the Kings, the day of gifts for the children. Rudi's uncontained excitement fizzed over into the silent gardens of my heart. Alerted by his great zest for living, I too began to scan the horizon for those three mysterious figures to come riding out of the East to bring gifts: Caspar on his fine Arabian horse, Melchior on a stately camel, and Balthasar the Ethiopian on a great gray elephant. All my life I had lived with the make-believe of the theater and a world shaped with the magic of words. Now, wordless, a fantastic little actor was weaving around me a world of make-believe that was part and parcel of this great fiesta of light. You had to be a child to fully comprehend, but with Rudi's help I did pretty well.

Every step I took in the posada was a going back; every drop of my Irish blood reminded me that I had once been a citizen of Rudi's world of unquestioning trust in an all-provident Father in heaven.

Over the next days I reflected that God had been very good to me through the years of an interesting life. God gave and He took away and I had not been as meek as

Job about it. Finally I asked Father Wasson to instruct me for my return to the church from which I had drifted years ago.

Like others of father's earthly friends, I tried to help him get some money for the ever-growing needs of his family. We talked a beautiful station wagon out of the Rotary Club of Cleveland, Ohio. We sought by a dozen means to pull together the poles of supply and demand. Sometimes this was sad work and sometimes we got angry. But I remember these enterprises most for the lovely laughter. We laughed in a beautiful knowledge that He is already doing the completely impossible.

All that was some years ago. But still, going back to Cuernavaca now is like going home. The wriggling, bright-eyed boys who smiled at me that first Christmas are gone now—most of them are teaching, some are married. And though their places have been taken by others of Mexico's beautiful children, Rudi and his friends—including wonderful Father Wasson, who still labors on—are not forgotten. They never can be. For they brought me a special gift that Christmas—not in a sack, tucked in with toothbrushes and new clothes and sugar cane. My gift came as an oasis of peace in a time of sadness—a gift of new love given me at a time when I desperately needed to love.

There is the time in every life, I think, a time of the star, a moment very dark when one must look up and—if he is wise—follow the light as the Magi did, a light that leads to love and hope.

Fear not for I am with thee: be not dismayed for I am thy God: I will strengthen thee; yea, I will help thee; yea, I will uphold thee with the right hand of my righteousness.

ISAIAH 41:10

I Was the Man Nobody Saw

by John Westbrook

> *"We don't have any black athletes on the team," the coach told me. "You'd be a great guy to break the ice."*

A golden butterfly poised on a branch at our back fence, and as my five-year-old eyes feasted on it, a scrambling sounded through the fence boards. I knew it would be the white boy who'd just moved in next door.

Another kick and he stared down in that open frankness between children. "Are you a nigger?"

"No," I said, "are you?"

He puzzled: "I don't know—but I heard my folks say you were one." Then he saw the butterfly.

"Hey, a beauty!" he hollered, and came tumbling down my side of the fence. The butterfly fluttered into the sunlight, and the two of us chased it until it was lost in the blue.

Butterflies—one of His love notes to us. Love was about all I knew in those days—and for years afterwards. Love was the message my father preached in his little Baptist church in Marlin, Texas, and what he acted out with every human being he knew. Love was in my mother's voice as she read to my brother and me out of the Bible, and in her hands as she nursed me through pneumonia.

And it was love, ultimately, that spoke to me the night I decided to take my life. At the time I was attending Baylor University in Waco, Texas. Dad had advised me against going to Baylor. "You're just laying yourself open to grief," he cried. "There're practically no black people there." The university had voted to integrate the year before.

Yet all through my growing years dad had taught me: "You are a son of God, John. Always remember that and hold your head high."

Moreover, I had already decided to become a minister like dad and his father and his father before that. Baylor was not only the largest Southern Baptist university in the world, but offered the religion and psychology courses I wanted.

Along with my savings from after-school jobs and a student loan, I was able to enter Baylor in 1965. Of 7000 students seven of us were black. When one of the football coaches, Jack Thomas, talked to me about going out for the team, it seemed a natural thing to do. Before becoming a minister, dad had been a high-school coach. Sports to us boys was as much a part of life as prayer meetings. After school hours we'd tossed a basketball at an old wheel rim nailed up by the parsonage, or tried to outdo each other at the homemade high-jump pit.

When Coach Thomas talked to me, he told me, "We don't have any black athletes on the team. You'd be a great guy to break the ice," he said.

Well, I wasn't so much interested in breaking any ice as I was in playing football. During my freshman year mom and dad came out to see every game, even though I played only a total of two and a half minutes that season.

I made the varsity when I was a sophomore, and became the first black football player to compete in the Southwest Conference.

Out on that field it was great. Sure I had my share of the rough part, all the way from brain concussions to knee and ankle injuries. But I was part of a brotherhood in which we fought one for all and all for one. If I was in a spot to receive, the passer didn't stop to consider if I was black or not, but only saw a Baylor man in position to make the most of it.

But off the gridiron, it was different. Most of the students weren't overtly antagonistic—but most just looked through me as I walked across campus.

Others acted like black was catching. In the cafeteria, they'd watch where I picked up my silverware from the tray, then reach clear across to take theirs from the other side. All the little cuts like this began to fester. On top of this, a knee injury had put me back on the fourth team for spring training. There were personal things, too, deaths of people close to me.

Then I found out my own mother—the warmest, most unselfish person I'd ever known—was dying of cancer. If mom wouldn't be there to see me graduate, what was the sense in sticking it out?

It was around the time of the assassinations of Martin Luther King and Robert Kennedy that I began to feel that the whole world wasn't worth sticking around for.

One morning shortly after Dr. King's death, I went down to the stadium early to work out as I always did and I ran into a grounds keeper who'd given me a hard time before. "Hey, boy!" he hollered. "I see they finally got Martin Luther Coon! 'Bout time, boy."

For some reason that senseless remark stayed with me. Coach had sent me to a number of doctors for my knee, and in the process I'd accumulated some pain pills, tranquilizers and sleeping tablets. A few nights later I poured them all into my hand and took them.

I awoke the next morning with a throbbing head and a determination to do it right next time. I thought about Lake Waco, where I could drive in and just let my car sink.

Was that why I took the road to the lake—or was it because that road led past the home of Riley Eubank? Mr. Eubank was pastor of the Seventh and James Baptist Church where I was serving my student ministry. He didn't say much when I rapped on his door, just told me to come in and get it off my chest.

And out it came. The rage, the hurt—everything I had against people. When it was all out, Mr. Eubank went and picked up his Bible. "I don't read," he said "that a Christian's supposed to love people because they're great. I read it like this. . . ." He handed me the book, open to a passage in John: "This is my commandment; that ye love one another, as I have loved you." *(John 15:12)*

As He had loved me. For the first time in my life I really thought about that love, the love underlying all the other loves I had known. What about the kind of folks I had, how had I deserved them? How about the ability to play football, the brains to go to school? Even the food I'd taken for granted—what was anything except the love of

God poured out on me, not because I was great, but because *He* was.

Well, of course, I didn't drive into the lake; I drove back to the campus, determined to see if I could love like this. Not much changed around me, but bit by bit I changed. I began to open up more to other people. I realized I'd been doing some ducking of my own—holding back my hand, for instance, letting the other guy stick his out first.

In a way, too, I came to see I'd brought all my own prejudices to campus. All the time I was growing up, in the segregated grade school and high school, white kids had been held up as the shining example. White boys didn't talk back to their teachers. White boys didn't run in the hall. I guess I'd grown up thinking white people were some kind of angels—and when I met the reality, I couldn't take it.

One day I was surprised with an invitation to speak on the Baylor Religious Hour, a college radio program. They wanted my impressions on being a black man at a southern college. I thought a long time about it; it would be easy to say what people wanted to hear—no problems, everyone's been swell. But instead I told the truth as I saw it—of my loneliness, of the sin of stereotyping a man, either way. Too many people didn't look at me as John Westbrook, I said. They didn't ask me my aims in life or what I thought. When they looked at me, all they saw was black—and their thinking ended right there.

The moderator's face turned red; the program was being broadcast over a wide area. But I ended up getting a big pile of congratulatory letters from white people, and not a mean note from anyone.

I graduated from Baylor in 1969 with a lot to be proud of. I'd been elected president of Sigma Tau Delta, an English honorary fraternity, and for three years led the Baylor Bears in yards gained per carry.

But the biggest plus wasn't anything that showed up on the record. It was a truth I'd learned about love. Love—the kind of love Christ demands—doesn't depend on the other guy earning it. It's that simple, and everytime I begin to forget it I just have to remember—John, you big jerk, doesn't *He* love *you?*

The Widow
by Maida Dugan

---

*Suddenly, she felt old and purposeless and
most of all, alone.*

I had become a widow after 40 years—stunned,
feelingless, moving about as in a bad dream from which I
could not arouse myself.

Of the two weeks following Earl's death I recall little
except the robotlike action of greeting friends, sitting
through the service, then being wth our two sons at home.

After a week the boys went back to their homes and
work in other cities. They reluctantly left me alone to start
a new pattern of living.

I did not want to sell the big old house that had been
our home for 25 years and take an apartment, as some
friends suggested. There was room for my two sons and
their families to come home to visit in comfort. So I made
my decision to stay.

But I was afraid. The sudden death of my husband
had unnerved me. Creaks and crackles which I had never
heard before came from the joints of the old stairs and
floors and terrified me in the night. I balked at coming into
the silence when I unlocked the door at night. Friends
telephoned me to relieve my loneliness in the evening. But
I kept my fears and feelings to myself. I felt so suddenly
old, a person left behind, purposeless. I thought of the old
dry leaves blown along the sidewalk by the November
wind on that last evening with Earl. I felt a kinship with
them.

One Friday night about a year after Earl died, I was
gone from the house until late and came home over-
fatigued. I answered two phone calls while I was eating a

small supper in the kitchen. I had promised to call a friend to say whether I would do a community service committee job. This should have been a brief call, so I thought I would get it out of the way. But the conversation went on and on, so I asked the friend to let me use the phone in the study where I could relax as we visited. I snapped off the kitchen light. When the call was finished a half hour later I went upstairs. I was so tired that I fell asleep as soon as my head hit the pillow.

About 12:30 A.M. I was awakened suddenly by men's voices in the hall outside my bedroom door. I sat up alert, terrified. I reached for the phone by my bed. I had memorized the police department's number long before. But before I dialed I mustered up the courage to ask, "Who is out there?" A man's voice replied, "The police."

I did not believe that the police had broken into my house and thought this was a ruse to get me to unlock my bedroom door.

With phone in hand I knew I could push-button the number before they could break through my door. So I made one more try with, "What do you want?"

"Lady, your son Dick in Madison has been trying to call you and getting a busy signal for three hours. He called your next-door neighbor and she couldn't rouse you. He finally called us and asked us to break in and investigate."

Then came the trembling voice of my next-door neighbor confirming the story. "It's Dorothy, Maida. I called to you from the porch, but you didn't answer. We have all been terribly worried."

I put the bedside phone back on the hook and remembered the phone I had left off the hook in the kitchen when I went into the study to finish the conversation earlier in the evening. I unlocked my bedroom door and went out.

There they stood—two big policemen, and a sergeant who had to be there if they broke in without a search warrant, and dear little Dorothy Phillips, my neighbor of 25 years. She was crying.

Downstairs were the Reeds, two of our oldest friends. My son had also called them. They had dressed at midnight and driven across the city to be there when the police broke in. All were quiet, stilled by the strain of waiting.

This was the way it would have been if they had found me as they feared—on the floor with the phone knocked off the hook as I had gone down trying to call out before I slipped into eternity.

I told the sergeant I was embarrassed and sorry. I went down to the kitchen and showed him the phone where I had left it on the table. He smiled and assured me that there was no need for embarrassment or apologies. They were just glad to find me safe and sound, he said, but sorry they had to break two doors to be sure. Then, with a twinkle in his eye, he added that I really didn't need to worry much about burglars breaking in because breaking in was really quite a job with all my double locks.

My son had stayed on the telephone line next door to wait for the police report. My neighbor ran back home to tell him I was all right. He wept with relief.

When everyone had left, I called my son. He showed no irritation with my carelessness. He simply said, "You don't know what we've been through, mom. We thought you had gone like dad."

I went back upstairs and sat for some time by the window looking out on the old familiar houses and the street. Something was happening inside my lonely heart. My life still had deep meaning to my children. Even the policemen, who were strangers, after all their work of breaking in due to my carelessness, had been happy. They had shown no impatience with an older woman who had caused a dozen people to spring into activity and wait in suspense in the middle of the night because she had left a phone off the hook.

I went back to my bed and slept soundly the rest of the night. There would be no more complaining to God about the futility of my widowhood. I would put my spirit back to work with my mind and body.

Once more I became a grateful mother, an interested neighbor, an eager friend. The dead dry leaf has become a part of the rich soil that feeds the tree of life again.

My Christmas Miracle
by Taylor Caldwell

---

*One of America's favorite novelists tells the
story of her own most wondrous Christmas.*

For many of us, one Christmas stands out from all the
others, the one when the meaning of the day shone clearest.

Although I did not guess it, my own "truest" Christmas began on a rainy spring day in the bleakest year of
my life. Recently divorced, I was in my 20s, had no job,
and was on my way downtown to go the rounds of the
employment offices. I had no umbrella, for my old one
had fallen apart, and I could not afford another one. I sat
down in the streetcar, and there against the seat was a
beautiful silk umbrella with a silver handle inlaid with
gold and flecks of bright enamel. I had never seen anything so lovely.

I examined the handle and saw a name engraved
among the golden scrolls. The usual procedure would have
been to turn in the umbrella to the conductor, but on impulse I decided to take it with me and find the owner myself. I got off the streetcar in a downpour and thankfully
opened the umbrella to protect myself. Then I searched a
telephone book for the name on the umbrella and found it.
I called, and a lady answered.

Yes, she said in surprise, that was her umbrella,
which her parents, now dead, had given her for a birthday
present. But, she added, it had been stolen from her locker
at school (she was a teacher) more than a year before.
She was so excited that I forgot I was looking for a job
and went directly to her small house. She took the umbrella, and her eyes filled with tears.

The teacher wanted to give me a reward, but—

23

though $20 was all I had in the world—her happiness at retrieving this special possession was such that to have accepted money would have spoiled something. We talked for a while, and I must have given her my address. I don't remember.

The next six months were wretched. I was able to obtain only temporary employment here and there, for a small salary, though this was what they now call the Roaring Twenties. But I put aside 25 or 50 cents when I could afford it for my little girl's Christmas presents. (It took me six months to save $8.) My last job ended the day before Christmas, my $30 rent was soon due, and I had $15 to my name—which Peggy and I would need for food. She was home from her convent boarding school and was excitedly looking forward to her gifts the next day, which I had already purchased. I had bought her a small tree, and we were going to decorate it that night.

The stormy air was full of the sound of Christmas merriment as I walked from the streetcar to my small apartment. Bells rang and children shouted in the bitter dusk of the evening, and windows were lighted and everyone was running and laughing. But there would be no Christmas for me, I knew, no gifts, no remembrance whatsoever. As I struggled through the snowdrifts, I just about reached the lowest point in my life. Unless a miracle happened I would be homeless in January, foodless, jobless. I had prayed steadily for weeks, and there had been no answer but this coldness and darkness, this harsh air, this abandonment. God and men had completely forgotten me. I felt old as death, and as lonely. What was to become of us?

I looked in my mailbox. There were only bills in it, a sheaf of them, and two white envelopes which I was sure contained more bills. I went up three dusty flights of stairs, and I cried, shivering in my thin coat. But I made myself smile so I could greet my little daughter with a pretense of

---

He who carries a candle of joy
Will light the path for a brother
And furnish the spark to start the flame
Of hope in the heart of another.

JOSEPHINE MILLARD

happiness. She opened the door for me and threw herself in my arms, screaming joyously and demanding that we decorate the tree immediately.

Peggy was not yet six years old, and had been alone all day while I worked. She had set our kitchen table for our evening meal, proudly, and put pans out and the three cans of food which would be our dinner. For some reason, when I looked at those pans and cans, I felt broken-hearted. We would have only hamburgers for our Christmas dinner tomorrow, and gelatin. I stood in the cold little kitchen, and misery overwhelmed me. For the first time in my life, I doubted the existence of God and His mercy, and the coldness in my heart was colder than ice.

The doorbell rang, and Peggy ran fleetly to answer it, calling that it must be Santa Claus. Then I heard a man talking heartily to her and went to the door. He was a delivery man, and his arms were full of big parcels, and he was laughing at my child's frenzied joy and her dancing. "This is a mistake," I said, but he read the name on the parcels, and they were for me. When he had gone I could only stare at the boxes. Peggy and I sat on the floor and opened them. A huge doll, three times the size of the one I had bought for her. Gloves. Candy. A beautiful leather purse. Incredible! I looked for the name of the sender. It was the teacher, the address simply "California," where she had moved.

Our dinner that night was the most delicious I had ever eaten. I could only pray in myself, "Thank You, Father." I forgot I had no money for the rent and only $15 in my purse and no job. My child and I ate and laughed together in happiness. Then we decorated the little tree and marveled at it. I put Peggy to bed and set up her gifts around the tree, and a sweet peace flooded me like a benediction. I had some hope again. I could even examine the sheaf of bills without cringing. Then I opened the two white envelopes. One contained a check for $30 from a company I had worked for briefly in the summer. It was, said a note, my "Christmas bonus." My rent!

The other envelope was an offer of a permanent position with the government—to begin two days after Christmas. I sat with the letter in my hand and the check on the table before me, and I think that was the most joyful moment in my life up to that time.

The church bells began to ring. I hurriedly looked at

my child, who was sleeping blissfully, and ran down to the street. Everywhere people were walking to church to celebrate the birth of the Saviour. People smiled at me and I smiled back. The storm had stopped, the sky was pure and glittering with stars.

"The Lord is born!" sang the bells to the crystal night and the laughing darkness. Someone began to sing, "Come, all ye faithful!" I joined in and sang with the strangers all about me.

I am not alone at all, I thought. *I was never alone at all.*

And that, of course, is the message of Christmas. We are never alone. Not when the night is darkest, the wind coldest, the world seemingly most indifferent. For this is still the time God chooses.

A Fragile Moment of Hope

A friend of mine, whose wife died tragically and suddenly, almost went out of his mind with shock and grief. His doctors recommended a trip abroad, and he went to Italy. But travel was not the answer, and one day he climbed a famous mountain pass with a single thought in mind. He was going to commit suicide.

As he stood at the edge of the precipice, ready to jump, he suddenly heard music. At the edge of a cave, by the side of the mountain path, a barefoot lad was playing a harmonica.

"I had felt completely alone," my friend told me afterward, "all reason stifled by the depth of my grief. But somehow that music, so pure and simple and unexpected in that wild place—somehow it got through to me. It made me realize how much beauty and goodness life still had to offer—and how ungrateful and selfish I was being in my grief. It proved to me that when you need a miracle most, God will be with you, standing by, ready to reach out and touch you with His hand."

OLIVE BRADSHAW

How to Handle
a Lousy Job
by David Parsons

A Guideposts Youth Writing Contest winner describes a turning point in his life.

Life had suddenly gone sour on me. I was almost 18 years old and had nothing to look forward to. My senior year at Edsel Ford High School, which had just started, should have been a time of excitement. Instead, I was filled with the dread certainty that I would not graduate with my class. I lacked the necessary credits and had only myself to blame.

Naturally that realization didn't remove the sting of disappointment. It only made my part-time job at the gas station seem less bearable. If I had graduation to look forward to—if only I knew I could enroll in a college next fall . . . Now I had to go to night school (which I hated the thought of) and continue to work at the station (which I hated the thought of even more).

My job helped me financially, but it sure wasn't helping me to like people. Let's face it, you don't see people at their best when you're a gas pump jockey. People are always in a hurry, blowing their horns and yelling out orders.

You get these guys who drive up in a Lincoln Continental or a Cadillac and order two dollars' worth of gas on a charge. Or there's the dude who comes in during a driving rainstorm, and you stand dripping wet by his window (which he barely rolls down so *he* doesn't get wet) and try to understand his garbled speech while he barks out orders through a fat cigar.

27

Or the young drunks who flock in around 2 A.M. with their old junk cars—so misshapen they defy description. All they want is 50 cents' worth of gas and they have to take up a hurried collection for that! Or the housewife in for a grease job, completely oblivious to the fact that her kids are running rampant through the station—so you hurry to get her car serviced before they tear up the place.

Yes, I hated the thought of night school; but, heck, I had to graduate or I might end up pumping gas for the rest of my life and putting up with all these crazy people. I shuddered at the thought, jerking the nozzle carelessly out of the car's gas well. "Hey, buddy, watch the paint job, will ya!" The guy jutted his head through the open window as he yelled at me, and I had the greatest urge to grab him and yank him the rest of the way.

All my evenings were filled with similar hateful thoughts. At the end of each evening I would go home spent and depressed. I had decided that I really didn't like people and, even worse, I didn't like myself!

What had happened to me? Why had I changed? I tried to think things through as I lay sleeplessly in bed. I hadn't prayed for a long time. God, like my schoolwork, had been sloughed off—forgotten—for better things. "Oh, God," I prayed in earnest, "I need Your help. I want to change. Help me to like myself—and people—again."

God has funny ways of helping people. Sometimes it's all done so subtly we don't recognize that it's His providence.

"Dave—Dave Parsons!" The fellow in the car looked familiar, but I couldn't place him. "Bob Stone," he said with a warm smile.

"Gosh, Bob, I didn't recognize you. How're things going?" I didn't have to ask that. I knew how things must be going for Bob. We had gone to high school together but Bob had become all fouled up on drugs. He was expelled from school and had barely survived death from an overdose.

Yet as we talked now, somehow I knew that this down-and-out character understood my problem. I found myself telling him the whole bit—all my complaints, my frustrations, my fears.

Was I ever in for a shock! "I guess you would still call me a freak," he said with a broad grin. "But now I'm a Jesus freak. I'm what I call an ambassador of God."

He went on to explain that when he had nearly died, he had prayed to God that if He would spare him, he'd spend the rest of his days making up for the tragic mess he had made of his life. So now he was helping other kids kick drugs.

I mentally compared myself to Bob Stone. Bob had lived through some hard knocks, but instead of going around with a chip on his shoulder and feeling sorry for himself as I had in the past, he had reached out to others and given of himself. He had turned his defeats into victories with the help of God. He had found the one thing that makes life worthwhile—a purpose in being through Jesus Christ.

It was that very night that I made my commitment to Jesus Christ. From now on, I vowed, I was going to live like a Christian—not just practice verbal religion—and try to be an example to others of what Christ can do with us.

What a wonderful opportunity I had on my job to be an ambassador of God. Think of all the people I came in contact with!

Needless to say, I didn't change right away. But those words of Bob's, "ambassador of God," stuck with me. Without realizing it, I was becoming a different person. My faith in myself and my attitude toward people improved day by day. I became enthusiastic about my job and began to whistle and laugh more.

I talked to the customers. They loved it! But, more important, I began to see people as just that—people. People with the same doubts, fears and frustrations as I had; people with the same need for love and understanding.

The fellows with their flashy cars, too busy to be nice, were to be pitied. The housewife hadn't meant to be irresponsible. She was probably a loving wife and mother who appreciated a few moments of adult conversation. The young drunks were kids like myself—searching for a meaning in life.

Once in a while I bump into a person now who snaps at me, "What are you so cheerful about?" And I say to them, "I've got a lot going for me, thanks to God. And to me life is just wonderful."

Some go away frowning—but then there are all those who leave the pumps smiling. It's so good to help people smile!

The Cold, Cold World of Mary Brittain

by Mary Brittain

She had no heat, no job, no money. What could ever lift her from her hopelessness?

The most terrible time of my life was when I had to move my whole family into the bathroom.

It all started when my husband decided he wanted a divorce. That left me in a small apartment with three small children.

I got a job working in a doughnut shop but the salary was low and there were no fringe benefits. The kiddies missed their daddy and would cry and ask about him. He was supposed to pay me weekly child support. But he skipped and missed and mostly missed.

Whenever I ran short of money, which was most of the time, I would phone Alice, my oldest sister, and ask for a loan. She had a wonderful husband, Paul, who would fix things for us, and three children too.

The real hassle started when winter came. The apartment was heated by stoves. But I couldn't find any way to connect my big heater in the living room. A tiny gas heater was installed in the bathroom. I kept it burning and kept the kitchen oven on to keep us from freezing when the thermometer was teasing zero.

Then the doughnut shop went out of business. I also got a huge electric bill and since I couldn't pay it they shut off our service. I had to use candles for light. Then Alice's husband Paul died of a heart attack. I cried and cried, reproaching God for taking a good man like him.

We attended the funeral and then came home to

more problems. I certainly couldn't ask Alice for help. She had plenty of her own problems now. The few other relatives I had all held on to their nickels so tight it's a wonder the buffaloes didn't bite.

Our money was gone and we had no food. I managed to arrange credit with a local grocer and bought only enough food to sustain us from day to day. I couldn't cook it with the electricity turned off so we lived on cold soup and sandwiches. When the children and I arose each morning, we all made a beeline for the bathroom. The temperature continued to linger close to zero most of the time and the bathroom with its wall heater was the only warm place.

That was when, in a manner of speaking, we moved into the bathroom. After the two girls left for school, four-year-old David, my youngest, and I would stay in the bathroom all day to keep from freezing. I would rush into the bedroom long enough to make our beds. That was the limit of my housework.

When the girls came home from school they too headed for the bathroom and there we all remained every night. At first the children would play, but after a while they grew tired of being cooped up like chickens and they'd pick at each other and cry. It would get on my nerves so bad I could have pulled my hair out by the roots.

After they tired of annoying each other, they would lie down on the floor and go to sleep. Then I would pick them up one at a time and carry them to the cold bedroom and cover them with every blanket we had. After I put the children to bed, I would go back to the bathroom and cry and pray and wonder what to do.

During this time, a young couple named Georgia and Bill Graves brought us food and some money. They invited me to go to church with them, but I didn't feel up to going. Georgia spoke of how close she felt the Lord was to everyone, but I never felt that.

Each day and night seemed worse than the last. No one could locate my former husband. Our grocer, landlord and other bill collectors were pressuring me for their money.

One night after two months of living like this I felt I just couldn't stand it any longer. I was going to do away with all of us. I would let the children fall asleep on the bathroom floor and then blow out the flame in the little wall heater. But then I began to think of other people in the apartment building. I thought the gas might cause an explosion and hurt some of them. So I didn't have the heart to go through with it.

I went back to the bathroom, sat on the floor by the heater, and cried and drank tap-water coffee. It came to me what Georgia had said about feeling the Lord was so close. I got down on my knees and prayed to the Lord to forgive me of my sins. Then I asked Him to show me He was with us. I felt that if He was with us, then I could endure our problems knowing He would help us out of our prison. I waited till my bottom felt paralyzed from sitting on the floor. I finally thought He would not do it because I had been wicked. I gave up and went to bed.

The next morning I heard someone knocking at our kitchen door. A little girl friend of Sharon's asked if she wanted to go to Sunday school with her. Sharon said yes, then got up and ran to the bathroom to dress. As I stepped into the bathroom with her, Sharon happened to raise her eyes to the ceiling. She gasped and said, "Look, mommy, there is a picture of Jesus on the ceiling." I looked up and nearly fell over. She was right.

At first it frightened me. Then my mind went back to the night before and my praying for Him to show me He was with us.

I sat down on the floor and kept staring at the portrait. The best description I can give is that it was from the top of His head to His waist. His beard and hair were long and black; His face was pale with dark features. He held a long rod in His right hand.

I sat there a long time trying to figure out how He had painted it there. Then it dawned on me. The little gas heater gave off a lot of carbon because I kept it turned up so high. Our ceiling had turned a dirty gray color from the heater. During the night the Lord must have guided the soot from it to just one area to paint His portrait.

When Sharon came home from Sunday school, I explained to her and the other two children why the portrait was there. I called my sister and Georgia Graves and told them about it. After a few days the picture slowly started to fade as the dirt from the heater gradually spread over it.

But it had served its purpose. I was a changed

woman. I told Georgia and Bill I wanted to go to church with them. I dug out my Bible and dusted it off and read the New Testament to the kids in the bathroom every night. The children ceased to fuss and we were all happy and at peace for the first time in months.

One day the rain was pouring down and it was not fit for man or beast to be out, but still I heard knocking at my door. There stood my attorney. He said he had a present for me and handed me a check for $300. My former husband's attorney had mailed it to him. I thanked him from the bottom of my heart for bringing it to me all the way in the rain. I don't believe any better attorney ever walked in shoe leather. Not even Perry Mason.

I grabbed my coat and broken-down umbrella and ran out into the rain. I cashed the check and paid the electric bill. Then I stopped at the grocery and paid our food bill and bought food and goodies for the children. When I got home the electricity was back on. I cooked us supper, the first good hot meal we had eaten in months.

After supper I felt so good I turned on the electric light in the living room and started to clean the room. As I was moving the sofa to another part of the room, I saw a little white pipe running along the top of the baseboard. It was a gas pipe! I ran next door and my neighbor came and hooked up our large heater to the connection.

So all in one day we have been given money, food, electricity, heat and televison. We were so happy! A couple of weeks later I got an office job with good pay and fringe benefits. Thanks to the generosity of the good Lord, life was finally coming up roses for us. I guess the Lord had to put me in the dark to make me see the light.

Delight thyself also in the Lord; and he shall give thee the desires of thine heart. Commit thy way unto the Lord; trust also in him; and he shall bring it to pass.

PSALM 37:4,5

When Your Prayers Run Dry

A Guideposts Spiritual Workshop to help with a problem we've all faced.

That dry period in our spiritual life—when the reality of God seems to evaporate and we seem unable in any real sense to pray—is a condition experienced by everyone. In fact, this situation often follows a period of marked spiritual growth and enlightenment.

It was just after his magnificent victory over the prophets of Baal at Mount Carmel that Elijah lost his courage and ran from the fury of Jezebel. He hid in the desert, the Bible's traditional setting for spiritual as well as literal dryness.

"This condition is a state of fatigue; a reaction sometimes from excessive devotional fervor, sometimes from exacting spiritual work which has exhausted the inner resources of the soul," says Evelyn Underhill in her book, *Concerning the Inner Life.** She also points out that at other times the source of the wilderness experience is God Himself. It was the Holy Spirit, after all, who led Jesus in His desert sojourn.

In either event, such is the pattern which all praying people experience. We reach heights of spiritual awareness and dedication; then we descend into the valley where like Elijah, we want only to sit under a tree and sleep.

What we can do about our dry periods is the subject of this Spiritual Workshop, based on Miss Underhill's writings.

STEP ONE: *Don't worry.* Accept the situation quietly. Don't aggravate it, don't worry, don't dwell on it.

---

*E. P. Dutton & Co., New York City.

Ego sometimes enters our dry periods. We feel that we ought to be able to live on high planes forever. If we slip into a normal (and even necessary) time of inactivity, we accuse ourselves of backsliding.

STEP TWO: *Turn to secular interests.* Instead of fretting, turn to some relaxing activity. "Many a pastor," Miss Underhill says, "ends every Sunday in a state of exhaustion in which he cannot possibly say his own prayers—in which, as one of them observed, the only gift of the Spirit in which he was able to take any interest was a hot bath."

Gardening, travel, sports, a concert or movie, a book—all of these can be recreation. If we try to keep ourselves spiritually productive and growing at every moment, it will be a forced growth, like one of those leggy plants that is all stem and no bloom.

STEP THREE: *Experiment.* Once you realize that your dormant periods are nothing to worry about, you may even discover that they are good times to experiment with ingrained religious habit-patterns.

A farmer, when it comes time to protect his soil against exhaustion, has two alternatives. He can let the land lie fallow or he can plant a rotation crop.

A field, for instance, that has been producing corn can be planted in alfalfa. Change not only rests the soil, but the legume increases the land's productivity by adding nitrogen.

You can handle your own need for rest in a similar way. While waiting out your dry period, try some changes. Use a different daily devotional if you have stayed with the same one several years. Volunteer for a completely different kind of church or community work.

And try a different type of prayer. One Christian leader in Westchester County, New York, distinguishes between mental prayer and acted-out prayer. During his dry periods he does not attempt mental prayer except as a deliberate routine. Instead, he practices prayer-in-action. These are the times when he goes out of his way to take a lonely person to a ball game, to visit a shut-in, or to find special occasions to give himself to others. All of these activities he considers prayer. They are his alfalfa crop, his way of putting nutriment back into his spiritual soil.

Finally, it is important to realize that dry periods are the result of *our* exhaustion, not God's. Most people who are experienced in prayer maintain their regular devotions right through such times, realizing that the *feeling* of contact with God is not important—it is the *reality* of contact with God that is essential.

To keep a check on the reality of prayer, keep a prayer diary. Mark the beginning of your dry period with a colored ink, then watch the results of your seemingly dead, "routine" prayers. Write out your prayer request and the date; then later write the date the prayer was answered.

It will probably surprise you, as it has many, to discover that there is no substantial loss of effectiveness during these periods. A prayer offered without feeling during a time of dryness, when there is no sense of the reality of God, can be every bit as acceptable as the same prayer offered with the wonderful emotion of close fellowship with God.

Summing up: "It is one of the most distressing aspects of personal religion," writes Evelyn Underhill, "that we waste so much of the very limited time we are able to give to it through distraction and dryness. No one escapes these wastes, but it concerns us all to reduce them as much as we can."

And not only to reduce them, but to commit them to Him, so that at the end all things—even the desert places of our lives—may be seen to have worked together to the glory of God.

2.

Hope for People Who Need Healing

And he said unto her, Daughter, be of good comfort: thy faith hath made thee whole.

The Healing of Maude Blanford

by Catherine Marshall

She was dying of cancer until she uttered the most powerful of prayers.

This is a story of a healing, one of the most remarkable I have ever encountered. And yet—to me—the physical miracle is not the chief thing the experience has to say to us.

Healing through faith remains a mystery to me. I have been part of prayer campaigns where it was gloriously granted, others where, at least in this world, it was not. As a young wife and mother I myself was wonderfully healed. At the time of Peter Marshall's first heart attack, he was brought back from the brink of death, yet went on into the next life three years later. And despite all-out prayer effort, the baby daughter born last summer to my son Peter John and his wife Edith lived on this earth but six weeks.

Why? There are no glib answers. I sense that my own questions about healing are shared by scores of honest seekers. Yet in my experience, as God has closed one door, He always has opened another.

So even as I was parting tenderly with my tiny granddaughter last summer, a new friend from Louisville, Kentucky, came through an open door on another side of this difficult question, by telling me of Maude Blanford's healing from terminal cancer 12 years ago. In the end, I was intrigued enough to fly to Louisville and get the details from the former patient herself.

The woman across the dining table from me had no trace of gray in her reddish hair, though she is past middle age now, a grandmotherly type, comfortable to be with. "How did your—ah, illness begin?" I asked, feeling foolish even asking the question to someone obviously in such radiant health.

"My left leg had been hurting me," Mrs. Blanford replied. "I thought it was because I was on my feet so much. Finally, when I couldn't stand it any longer, my husband and I decided that I should go to the doctor."

When her family doctor examined her, his eyes were solemn as his hands gently probed several firm tumor masses on her left side. When he spoke words like "specialist" and "biopsy," the patient read the unspoken thought: *malignancy.*

Mrs. Blanford was referred to Dr. O. J. Hayes. He examined her on June 29, 1959, and prescribed radiation treatment. The treatment began July 7, and was followed by surgery on September 29. After the operation, when Mrs. Blanford pleaded with Doctor Hayes for the truth, he admitted, "It *is* cancer and it's gone too far. We could not remove it because it's so widespread. One kidney is almost nonfunctioning. The pelvic bone is affected—that's why the pain in your leg. I am so sorry. I *am* sorry."

Maude Blanford was put on narcotics to control the by-now excruciating pain, and sent home to die. Over a six-month period, while consuming $1000 worth of pain-relieving drugs, she took stock of her spiritual resources and found them meager indeed. There was no church affiliation, no knowledge of the Bible, only the vaguest, most shadowy concept of Jesus.

The first week in January, 1960, she suffered a cerebral hemorrhage and was rushed back to the hospital. For 12 days she lay unconscious; her husband was warned that if she survived the attack it would probably be as a vegetable.

But Maude Blanford, oblivious to the world around her, was awake in a very different world. In her deep coma a vivid image came to her. She saw a house with no top on it. The partitions between the rooms were there, the furniture in place, but there was no roof. She remembered thinking, *Oh, we must put a roof on the house! If it rains, all the furniture will be spoiled.*

When she came out of the coma, Mrs. Blanford's mind was very much intact, but bewildered. What could the roofless house have meant? As she puzzled over it, a

Presence seemed to answer her. Today she has no hesitation in calling Him the Holy Spirit. "He seemed to show me that the house represented my body, but that without Jesus as my covering, my body had no protection."

I leaned forward, excited by an insight: Wasn't this what I had always been taught about the Spirit—that His role was to show us Jesus and our need of Him?

"At that time," Mrs. Blanford went on, "I didn't know *how* to get the roof on my house."

From then until July, 1960, her condition worsened. Heart action and breathing became so difficult she was reduced from normal speech to weak whispers. Even with the drugs, the suffering became unbearable.

By July she knew she no longer had the strength to make the trip for radiation treatment. "On July first I told the nurse I wouldn't be coming back."

But that day, as her son-in-law helped her into the car outside the medical building, she broke down and wept. "At that moment I didn't want anything except for God to take me quickly—as I was. I said, 'God, I don't know who You are. I don't know anything about You. I don't even know how to pray. Just, Lord, have Your own way with me.' "

Though she did not realize it, Maude Blanford had just prayed one of the most powerful of all prayers—the prayer of relinquishment. By getting her own mind and will out of the way, she had opened the door to the Holy Spirit, as had happened during the period of unconsciousness in the hospital.

She did not have long to wait for evidence of His presence. Monday, July 4, dawned beautiful but hot. That afternoon Joe Blanford set up a cot for his wife outdoors under the trees. As the ill woman rested, hoping for the relief of a bit of breeze, into her mind poured some beautiful sentences:

"Is not this the fast that I have chosen? To loose the bands of wickedness, to undo the heavy burdens, and to let the oppressed go free, and that ye break every yoke. . . . Then shall thy light break forth as the morning, and thine health shall spring forth speedily. . . . Here I am."

I stared at Maude Blanford over the rim of my coffee cup. "But I thought you didn't know the Bible?"

"I didn't! I'd never read a word of it. Only I knew

this didn't sound like ordinary English. I thought, *Is that in the Bible?* And right away the words came: *Isaiah 58.* Well, my husband got a Bible for me. I had to hunt and hunt to find the part called Isaiah. But then when I found those verses just exactly as I had heard them—except for the last three words, 'Here I am'—well, I knew God Himself had really spoken to me!"

Over the next weeks Maude Blanford read the Bible constantly, often until two or three o'clock in the morning, seeing the Person of Jesus take shape before her eyes. It was an amazing experience, without human assistance of any kind—no Bible teacher, no commentary, no study guide—simply reading the Bible with the Holy Spirit.

Along with the hunger to meet Jesus in the Word, the Holy Spirit gave her an intense desire to be out-of-doors, close to His world. "Joe," she told her husband one day, "I want to go fishing."

This made no sense to him. The terrain to the lake was rough. She would have to be carried down and then back up a steep hill.

But then some kindly neighbors offered to take her, and her husband acquiesced. She could not fish, of course, but she could look—at a breeze rippling the water, at the wheeling birds and the distant hills. And as she looked, a response grew in her, a response which is another of the Holy Spirit's workings in the human heart: praise. All that first day she praised Jesus for the world He had made. That night she slept like a baby.

After that, the lake trip became routine. A month or so later, Maude Blanford was walking up the hill to the road by herself. At home she had begun very slowly climbing the stairs, praising Jesus for each step attained. Or she would sit in a chair and dust a mahogany tabletop, saying, "Thank You, Jesus. Isn't this wood beautiful!"

Next she tried putting a small amount of water in a pail. Sitting in a kitchen chair, she would mop the floor in the area immediately around her, scoot the chair a few inches, mop again. "Thank You, Jesus, for helping me do this!"

Her daughter-in-law, who was coming over almost daily to clean house for her, one day asked in great puzzlement, "Mom, how is it that your kitchen floor never gets dirty?"

The older woman twinkled. "Well, I guess I'll have to confess—the Lord and I are doing some housework."

But their chief work, she knew, was not on this building of brick and wood, but on the house of her spirit, the house that had been roofless so long. Gradually, as her knowledge of Him grew, she sensed His protective love surrounding and sheltering her. Not that all pain and difficulties were over. She was still on pain-numbing narcotics, still experiencing much nausea as the aftermath of the radiation.

"The will to live is terribly important," she commented to me. "It takes a lot of self-effort just to get out of bed, to eat again after your food has just come up. This is when too many people give up."

One Saturday night, when the pain would not let her sleep, she lay on her bed praising God and reading the Bible. About two A.M., she drifted off to sleep with the Bible lying on her stomach. She felt that she was being carried to heaven, traveling a long way through space. Then came a voice out of the universe: "My child, your work is not finished. You are to go back." This was repeated three times, slowly, majestically, and then she was aware of her bedroom around her again.

The rest of the night she remained awake, flooded with joy, thanking God. When her husband woke up in the morning, she told him, "Honey, Jesus healed me last night."

She could see that he did not believe it; there was no change in her outward appearance. "But I knew I was healed and that I had to tell people." That very morning she walked to the Baptist church across the highway from their home and asked the minister if she could give a testimony. He was startled at the unusual request from someone who was not even a member of the congregation, but he gave permission, and she told the roomful of people that God had spoken to her in the night and healed her.

A few weeks later she insisted on taking a long bus trip to visit her son in West Virginia. Still on narcotics, still suffering pain, she nonetheless knew that the Holy Spirit was telling her to rely from now on on Jesus instead of drugs. At five o'clock on the afternoon of April 27, 1961, on the return bus journey, as she popped a painkilling pill into her mouth at a rest stop, she knew it would be the last one.

So it turned out. In retrospect, physicians now consider this sudden withdrawal as great a miracle as the remission of cancer cells to healthy tissue.

It took time to rebuild her body-house—nine months for her bad leg to be near normal, two years for all symptoms of cancer to vanish. When she called Doctor Hayes in 1962 over some small matter, he almost shouted in astonishment. "Mrs. Blanford! What's happened to you! I thought you were—"

"You thought I was long since gone," she laughed back.

"Please come to my office at once and let me examine you! I've got to know what's happened."

"But why should I spend a lot of money for an examination when I'm a perfectly well woman?" she asked.

"Mrs. Blanford, I promise you, this one is on us!" What the doctor found can best be stated in his own words:

"I had lost contact with Mrs. Blanford and had assumed that this patient had expired. In May of 1962 she appeared in my office. It was two and a half years following her operation and her last X ray had been in July, 1960. . . .

"The swelling of her leg was gone. She had full use of her leg; she had no symptoms whatsoever, and on examination I was unable to ascertain whether or not any cancer was left. . . .

"She was seen again on November 5, 1962, at which time her examination was completely negative. . . .

"She has been seen periodically since that time for routine examinations. . . . She is absolutely asymptomatic. . . . This case is most unusual in that this woman had a proven, far-advanced metastatic cancer of the cervix and there should have been no hope whatsoever for her survival."

No hope whatsoever. . . . No hope except the hope on which our faith is founded.

The miracle of Maude Blanford reminds me again of that scene on the night before His crucifixion when Jesus spoke quietly to His despairing disciples, "Ye have not chosen me, but I have chosen you. . . ." (John 15:16) He is still saying that to us today, while His Spirit—always working through human beings—sometimes confounds us, often amazes us and is always the Guide to the future Who can bring us joy and exciting fulfillment.

Three-Day Pause

It was a beautiful spring day, and a sense of peace stayed with me as I left the cathedral on the Monday morning after Easter. I paused for a moment on top of the steps leading to the avenue, now crowded with people rushing to their jobs. Sitting in her usual place inside a small archway was the old flower lady. At her feet corsages and boutonnieres were spread out on a newspaper.

The flower lady was smiling, her wrinkled face alive with joy. I started down the stairs, then on an impulse turned and picked out a flower.

As I put it in my lapel, I said, "You look happy this morning."

"Why not? Everything is good."

She was dressed so shabbily and seemed so very old that her reply startled me. "No troubles?" I responded.

"You can't reach my age and not have troubles," she replied. "Only it's like Jesus and Good Friday." She paused for a moment.

"Yes?" I prompted.

"Well, when Jesus was crucified on Good Friday, that was the worst day for the whole world. And when I get troubles, I remember that. And then I think what happened only three days later—Easter and our Lord arising. So when I get troubles, I've learned to wait three days—and somehow everything gets all right again."

And she smiled good-bye. Her thoughts still follow me whenever I think I have troubles: "Give God a chance to help—wait three days."

PATT BARNES

The Woman Who Couldn't Cry

by Susan Holliday Beaudry

A story of how faith and love turned a tragedy into triumph.

By the time I turned 22, I was pretty much of a snob. I was mainly interested in good times. Appearances meant a great deal to me. In evaluating possible dates, I can remember confiding to my friends, "He's not tall enough," or, "I don't like the color of his hair—blonds are my type." My boyfriends also had to be athletic because I was crazy about sports. A new bowling ball was helping me edge up toward a 200 game. In high school I played on a girls' football team.

The pace of my life accelerated after I finished school. Knowing I'd get bored sitting behind a desk in an office, I took a job in an aircraft factory. I was on my feet all day helping the mechanics, and I loved it. My spare time was devoted to whirling around dance floors, watching ball games played by my company teams on weekends and vacationing in Europe.

I went to church, too, but that was mostly because I had got into the habit and liked to be around the other young people who also attended.

One Sunday morning in June, 1969, I walked out of my apartment, climbed into my car, buckled my seat belt and headed for church. I really don't remember getting into the car, however. I don't even remember going to bed the night before.

My knowledge of the events of that day comes from my family and newspaper accounts I read later. I was driv-

46

ing toward the Boulevard Park Presbyterian Church, a
half mile away from my apartment. As I went through an
intersection, a car driven by another young woman sped
toward me. I had the right of way, but that was little con-
solation for what happened next. The other driver
slammed into me broadside on the passenger's side. I was
wrenched from under the seat belt and thrown free of the
car into a rocky wall on the side of the road.

For the next three and a half months I was in a
coma. Suffering from multiple fractures and internal
bleeding, I needed electric shocks to keep my heart
beating, and in one day I received a transfusion of 11
pints of blood.

"If Susan does live," the doctors told my parents,
"you should be prepared to see considerable brain damage." At best, they suggested, I would likely be a physical
cripple and a mental vegetable.

But I guess God had other ideas. For some medically
unexplained reason, I pulled out of the coma mentally
alert. But even though my mental powers were intact, my
body had undergone a radical change. I had lost about 40
pounds, I couldn't speak and I was unable to stop my legs
from involuntarily thrashing against the hospital-bed
railings.

For several days I kept thinking that I must be having a long nightmare—that I'd soon wake up and find I
was the same old Susan Holliday. Then I'd blink and blink
again, but the white hospital room would still be there.

Screams of frustration welled up inside me. *I've got
to say something or even moan or grunt!* I'd think as I
strained my throat and moved my lips. But no sound came
out.

A month of desperately attempting to mutter just one
syllable passed, and the maddening silence still held me.
The doctors were pessimistic; they told me that because of
damage to my vocal chords, I probably would never speak
again.

Emotionally and physically drained, I finally decided
to try prayer. Then I discovered that I didn't know how to
talk with God. I fell back on an example I remembered
from the Bible. All day long I repeated in my mind the
first two words of Psalm 12: "Help, Lord . . . Help, Lord
. . . Help, Lord. . . ."

Dozens, hundreds of times that day I turned those

words over in my thoughts. Finally, that very evening, God responded. As I sat outside my room in my wheelchair, I saw my doctor at the nearby nurses' desk and I somehow softly rasped my first words in more than four months. "Hello, Doctor Nelson."

From that wonderful moment on, the incredible power of simple prayer became an everyday reality to me. Hardly an hour went by when I didn't talk to God about something.

As I slowly learned to speak again, I found my vocal cords wouldn't always work. The words were there in my head, but by the time they had passed through my throat to my lips, the sound was often an unintelligible, slurred croak or grunt. And because I could only manage one monotoned syllable for each breath, it was hard to find anyone with enough patience and imagination to sit around and absorb what I was trying to say.

Friends from my church and members of my family did their best to communicate with me. But of them all, John Beaudry, a young man I'd known slightly from my high-school days, became my most concerned and understanding companion. He surprised everyone by continuing to visit me almost every day. He'd come into the room and, like a big friendly bear, plant a brotherly kiss on my forehead. Then he'd say quietly, "How're you feeling?"

Although I usually had to repeat each sentence several times to others, John seemed to comprehend everything immediately. We talked about trivial things—I can't even remember most of the conversations. But I can recall clearly how those tender, brown eyes of his would search my face.

In a way he seemed almost unaware of the seriousness of my injuries; he made it clear he regarded them as temporary problems. It was always, "When you go back to work . . ." or, "After you get back on your feet again. . . ." His confidence in my recovery was infectious, and I began to find myself thinking the same way.

For some reason I couldn't explain at the time, I began to look forward to our comfortable visits more eagerly than any party or athletic event I had known before my accident. Still, I wasn't prepared for his words one afternoon soon after my late November discharge from the hospital. He came into my room at home and, looking very serious, said, "I love you, Susan, and I want to marry you."

My ears started ringing, and I caught my breath and shut my eyes. He had never hinted at romance. Except for those little pecks on the forehead, he'd never even kissed me. For a few moments I was silent as conflicting thoughts rushed in and out of my mind. More than anything else, I had always wanted to get married; but since the accident a gnawing feeling had made me doubt whether any suitable young man would ever want to take responsibility for someone with injuries and disabilities like mine.

Confused and upset, I responded lamely, "I can't be sure right now, John. Give me some time to think."

Thinking—and praying—became my primary occupation during the next two weeks. The accident may have changed me on the outside, but God was changing me even more radically on the inside. Even if I had wanted to, I knew I could no longer judge a person by his face or hair color. John's loving nature obviously made him someone special.

Finally I said yes. Then things began to happen so fast that I could hardly keep pace with them. Strength slowly returned to my weakened arms and back as physical therapy taught me to roll over, sit up and crawl. And as summer approached, all my attention turned to preparations for the wedding.

Our church was packed that July day in 1970 when my dad rolled me down the aisle in my wheelchair. It was a beautiful wedding, and a lot of eyes were wet—but not mine. You see, another side effect of my accident was that something had gone wrong with my tear ducts. I couldn't cry.

And as I embarked on my challenging but frequently frustrating new career as a handicapped housewife, I often wished I could fall back on the emotional release that tears can provide.

One day not long after we were married I was sitting by the stove watching some meat simmer when I suddenly realized I had forgotten to add a sauce. I unlocked the brakes on my wheelchair, tediously wheeled myself to a cupboard, locked the brakes again and then, shakily, stood to get the sauce.

Then I slowly reversed the routine to get back to the stove, hoping all the time that the meat hadn't burned. At the same time a pot of water started boiling over and yet I could only watch it helplessly as I struggled, with rising despair, to position my wheelchair in front of the stove again.

Peeling a potato sometimes took five minutes or more—peel, pause, peel, pause, pick up the dropped potato. Cleaning our house was an even more humbling experience. I would slide to the floor from my wheelchair and crawl as well as I could, dragging the vacuum cleaner behind me.

Making the bed was another major project. Sometimes I'd collapse into a heap on the floor, overwhelmed with my physical handicaps. Unable to cry, I could feel the emotions boiling up inside until I thought I was about ready to explode.

But God was always there, and He supported me and relieved my anxieties when I prayed: "Lord, I'm so frustrated! Please help me. Give me a sense of peace, a confidence that Your will is being done in my life."

John's faith helped me too. As he watched me try to bring a bowl of salad to the table one evening in my wheelchair, I could see he was quietly confident that I was eventually going to make it. I had dropped the bowl before, and he knew I might drop it again. But he didn't pity me. He had the wisdom to be just firm enough to make me try to do things on my own instead of trying to do everything for me.

After I had placed the bowl carefully on the table, he said, "I knew you could do it." The affectionate look in those brown eyes—the eyes I had thought would have to be blue—helped me understand how deeply he loved me despite my physical limitations. It gave me the incentive to try to clear the next obstacle, and the next, and the next.

Gradually strength and flexibility began to return to my legs and increase in my arms. I found that I could hobble along haltingly behind a walker, then walk by leaning against a wall for support. Before long, I was able to carry large bowls with both my hands.

But most wondrous of all, despite the predictions of medical experts that I could never become pregnant, I did.

Our daughter Janine was born a year and a half after our marriage, and not even the painful pregnancy I endured could cast a shadow over the joy I felt when I looked into her sparkling blue eyes and fondled her soft hair. As I was recuperating from the delivery, John gave me a little book called, *How Much I Love My Wife*. The sense of my blessings overwhelmed me as I sat there holding that volume. And suddenly, for the first time in more than two years, I cried—not tears of frustration, but tears of total joy.

I know now that the car accident that I thought had ended my life was the best thing that ever happened to me. I'm a different person—and all the changes have been for the better. Whenever I start to get blue, I think about the miracles God has performed in my life. I'm alive, I'm speaking much better and I'm very much in love with the father of our own beautiful daughter. I seldom need a wheelchair or any other support to walk, and I see marked improvements in my condition almost every day.

All of that has been the result of trusting prayer. I truly have cause to shout Psalm 40:5: "Thou hast multiplied, O Lord my God, Thy wondrous deeds and Thy thoughts toward us; none can compare with Thee!"

THE NEWER HOPE

I see a thousand miracles
With each new holy dawn.
A swiftly fading memory
Of yesterdays now gone.
I shall not dwell upon the past,
I must be moving on.

I feel God's love enfolding me;
I feel it make me strong.
I feel it lifting up my soul
Above the doubt and wrong.
And I obey Him as I run
To sing the world His song.

RICHIE TANKERSLEY

A Life in His Hands
by Don Michel

Michael DeBakey, world-famed heart surgeon,
shares a personal ordeal of patience and faith.

The moment I stepped into the surgical waiting room, I
sensed an anxiety. Death is such a personal thing and I
had unknowingly become a part of a family's ordeal. The
small dark-haired woman with the puzzled eyes would be
the dying man's wife, the other two women and the tall
man who looked so much like them, his sisters and
brother. The other man was the priest.

A mutual friend had led me into the small room to
meet them. And yet even in their sorrow they tried to
make me feel comfortable.

I wasn't even visiting a patient here in Houston's
Methodist Hospital. I had come to interview Dr. Michael
DeBakey, one of the world's leading heart surgeons. But
because of an emergency in the operating room, I would
not be able to see the doctor until the next day. I had arrived at one of those moments when the best that medical
science knows is not enough, when even the most skilled
and dedicated doctor must admit defeat. Doctor De-
Bakey's patient was dying and as I looked around the little
room, that fact showed on all the faces.

I could almost hear Mrs. Moses Koury saying to herself as she sat there quietly. "He seemed to be doing so
well. The operation this morning went fine." Doctor De-
Bakey had talked to her afterward and said that the operation had been successfully performed and that hopefully
Moses Koury's heart condition would be improved.

I learned that her husband was only 55 and had come
to Houston from their home in Santa Fe, New Mexico, to

seek Doctor DeBakey's help after a series of heart attacks. The doctor's examination had shown Moses's coronary arteries clogged with fatty deposits. Only a coronary bypass operation offered a chance of survival.

And apparently the delicate surgery had gone without a hitch—about noon Moses had been transferred from surgery into the recovery room.

And there, without warning, his heart had stopped. An hour after he was rushed back to the operating room, Doctor DeBakey had spoken to the family again. He would be able to keep Moses alive on an artificial heart machine one more hour, no longer. That was six hours ago.

There was a chill in the room from the surgical-suite air conditioning. I could sense the family's quiet trust which had so far sustained them in the long day of waiting, while a few yards away a mysterious drama unfolded.

When Moses Koury had been rushed back to the operating room, Doctor DeBakey and his staff attached him to the heart-lung machine to provide at least partial blood circulation to the brain while they reopened his chest. Moses's heart, which had been pulsing so strongly at the close of the operation, lay exposed again and was now all but motionless.

Doctor DeBakey tried electric shock. Taking the long-handled defibrillator paddles from the nurse, he slipped one on either side of the heart.

"Hit it," he said, and the operator pressed a button sending a jolt of electricity between the paddles. The heart convulsed violently, then fell silent. He signaled again and again, calling for stronger jolts each time. No response.

Now they had to move quickly to reconnect the heart-lung machine for full bypass of the heart. This would take blood from the right atrium of the organ, oxygenate it, and pump it back into Moses's system to prevent brain cell damage. Otherwise, even if he lived, he might never regain consciousness.

The pump's reassuring, soft *thud-thud-thud* blended with the other sounds in the room. But it couldn't be depended upon for long. The blood cells will themselves become damaged if pumped too long artificially. In a normal coronary bypass operation the heart is out of action for only about 45 minutes, rarely longer than one and a half to two hours.

Now the skilled operating room team went into action. Sensors were attached from Moses's still form to electronic monitoring equipment enabling them to check his vital body functions on a TV-like screen. In addition, an oscilloscope screen would give a constant picture of Moses's heart activity by tracing with a thin green line of light the faint changes in electrical potential emitted by his heart.

Stimulants were injected into Moses's veins; then into the heart muscle itself. The surgical team watched the screens anxiously. The thin green line refused to reach rhythm.

A hush seemed to fall over the operating room. The hands of the big clock moved relentlessly on. Now it was apparent that Moses Koury was dying. And there was nothing more anyone could do.

Moses's family had gone to the hospital cafeteria where they were located and taken to the surgical waiting room. A nurse gently told them of the emergency. The priest was summoned. Doctor DeBakey shed his gloves and smock to visit them for a moment. Two hours earlier he had had such an optimistic report for them; now he had to prepare the white-faced little group for the likelihood that their loved one was going to die. He would leave Moses on the heart pump for another hour, Doctor DeBakey told the Kourys. If Moses's heart did not respond by then, he would have to abandon his efforts.

Back in the operating room, he and his team continued trying every means of stimulating the heart. But at the end of the critical second hour it had still not responded. The heart pump continued to *thud-thud* in what appeared to be a futile effort. But the team persisted in trying to fan the ever-so-slight spark of life in Moses. Another hour passed as the team worked and watched and waited.

By now Moses was in extremely critical condition. In more than 25,000 cases in his experience, Doctor DeBakey had observed few patients as critically ill recover.

And yet something, some inner, unexplainable feeling beyond the realm of medical science, impelled Doctor DeBakey to keep trying.

Four hours passed. Five hours—five hours in which they had tried everything they knew, not once or twice, but over and over, without results. The eyes above the surgical masks of Doctor DeBakey's associates were searching him curiously, silently asking how much longer they should continue. All medical logic argued that they give up on this case, turn to patients they could help.

And still—that same unexplainable compulsion made him persist.

As the heart pump thudded on through the sixth hour, Doctor DeBakey looked up at the clock. It pointed to seven P.M. The surgical schedule was already hours behind.

Now he knew he must make the decision that his patient had passed the point of no return. It was time to give up.

Just before turning to give the signal that the heart pump be stopped, he noted that the heart had suddenly begun to contract better and upon looking up at the oscilloscope, the thin green line representing Moses's blood pressure had begun to flicker. The team stared at it in fascination. Was it just a momentary impulse? No. The pulse waves rose higher. They turned to Moses's heart. It was pulsing as if it had shaken loose a web that had held it bound.

A silent cheer filled the room as the team watched the fist-sized muscle begin to pump in stronger rhythm. Each surge was surer, more determined. At last the artificial *thud-thud* ceased as they shut off the pump and let the heart take over its God-given work. As they sent Moses Koury back to the intensive care unit for the second time that day, lights were coming on in the city of Houston.

Later, as I questioned Doctor DeBakey about the emergency, I asked if anyone in the operating room itself had been praying. "It's not a matter of getting on your knees and praying at the moment," he said. "We're doing this all the time—communing with God in a continuous sort of way. For without His help in what we're doing, we really don't have much with which to be effective."

Doctor DeBakey took a sip of black coffee and savored it a moment. "I think the most important thing my parents taught us was the meaning of the Christian faith, the need to show love and compassion for one's fellow man." His folks, he said, had run a drugstore in Lake Charles, Louisiana. Whether it was his father getting up in the middle of the night to fill a badly needed prescription, or both parents taking him on regular trips to an orphanage with food, drugs and clothing, his family emphasized the Christian's need to share the pain of those around him.

To share the pain—but that means to share the joy as well. That evening I accompanied the great surgeon to see his patient. Moses Koury was conscious, his handshake firm. Doctor DeBakey gently touched his chest and smiled. And in the surgeon's eyes I could see the compensation for the suffering shared.

Several months later, long after Moses Koury had returned home to Santa Fe and an active life, I visited Doctor DeBakey again in Houston. It was quiet in the hospital lounge where we sat recalling that long vigil. "It is at times like those," he said, "that any doctor who has had much experience cannot help but feel strongly that there is a Supreme Being Who intervenes in these matters. And while you do everything you know how to do, within the limits of your scientific knowledge, those miracles occur. They are just unexplainable in any other way."

Jesus said unto him, if thou canst believe, all things are possible to him that believeth.

MARK 9:23

My First Healing
by Kathryn Kuhlman

A woman with a worldwide ministry of
healing tells the story of how it all began.

I had the most perfect father a girl ever had. In my eyes
papa could do no wrong. He was my ideal.

He never spanked me. He never had to. All he had to
do was get a certain look on his face. Mama wouldn't hesitate to punish me when I needed it. But papa punished by
letting me know I had hurt him—and that hurt worse than
any of my mother's spankings.

When I was a little girl I used to have terrible
earaches. Mama would pour sweet oil in my ear and use
all the home remedies she knew. But the thing that eased
the pain best was for papa to stay home from work, take
me on his lap in the rocking chair and let me lay my
aching ear on his shoulder.

My father, Joe Kuhlman, was mayor of the little
town of Concordia, Missouri. He had been a farmer, but
later moved into town. And that's where I was born, the
third of their four children.

When I was 14 I was born again in the Methodist
church (mama's church) and was baptized in water in the
Baptist church (papa's church). Two years later I was
called to preach.

My first preaching experiences were in Idaho. I went
from community to community, sometimes having to
hitchhike. I would find an empty building, advertise the
services, set up benches, and the people would come—
strictly out of curiosity to see a red-headed, teenage girl
preacher. If I found an abandoned church building, I
would ask around until I found out who owned it, then request permission to hold services.

57

Usually my congregation consisted of a handful of Idaho farmers whose only reason for letting me use the church was that they couldn't pay a regular preacher. I sometimes slept in somebody's guest room or perhaps a small rented room that I had found myself. And once when there was no other place to go, I slept in a turkey house while holding nightly meetings in a deserted church located at the crossroads of a little country community. But I was full of enthusiasm and felt I could lick the world for God.

My only regret was that my father had never heard me preach. I yearned for the day when papa could be in the audience and see his daughter behind the pulpit. That would be a great day.

It was a whole year before I managed a trip home; travel was expensive and I needed every penny to buy handbills and newspaper space. I spent a few wonderful summer days with my parents and my younger sister who was still at home.

Then I was off again. By December I had reached Colorado. It was my second Christmas away from the family, but invitations to speak had started coming and I couldn't stop now. My first services in Denver were in an empty store building on Champa Street and I had arranged with the lumber company to furnish the materials for benches. Mrs. Holmquist, who owned the St. Francis Hotel, rented me room 416 for $4 a week.

It was there at 4:30 P.M. on the Tuesday after Christmas that the phone rang. I recognized the voice on the other end as an old friend from home. "Kathryn, your father has been hurt. He's been in an accident."

"Hurt—bad?"

"Yes," she said.

"Tell papa I'm leaving right now. I'm coming home."

I had bought an old V-8 Ford and I threw a few things into the back and started out. Only God knows how fast I drove on those icy roads, but all I could think about was my father. Papa was waiting for me. Papa knew I was coming.

The weather got worse as I drove out of Colorado into Kansas. The roads were covered with ice and drifting snow, but I didn't stop to eat or rest.

One hundred miles from Kansas City I stopped at a

telephone station beside the deserted highway and called ahead. My Aunt Belle answered.

I said, "This is Kathryn. Tell papa I'm almost home."

"But, Kathryn," Aunt Belle said in a shocked voice, "didn't they tell you?"

"Tell me what?" I said, feeling my heart begin to pound madly in my chest.

"Your father was killed. He was hit by a car driven by a college student who was home for the holidays. He died almost instantly."

I was stunned. I tried to speak but no words came out. My teeth were chattering wildly and my hands shaking as I stood in that forlorn phone booth, surrounded by the swirling snow. I can only remember the biting wind freezing the tears on my cheeks as I stumbled back to my old car and resumed my trip homeward.

I've got to get there, I thought. *Maybe it isn't true.*

The next miles were like a nightmare. The highway was a glare of ice. Mine was the only car on the road. Night fell and my headlights shone back at me from a wall of blinding white. I was crying, trying to hold the car on the glassy road.

Papa can't be dead. It's just a bad dream. If I ignore it, it will go away.

But it didn't go away. When I arrived home, my father's body was in an open casket in the front room of our big white frame house on Main Street. I sat in the bedroom upstairs alone, refusing to go in and look at him. I could hear the soft shuffle of feet on the front porch and the whispered talk around the house.

I was afraid that if I went in there and saw papa's body, I would suddenly have to face the reality of his death. I felt if I awakened from this bad dream and found it was all true, my whole world would come to an end.

And I was struggling with another feeling. Hate. It surged in me like a volcano and to everyone who came into the room I spewed out venom toward the young man who had taken the life of my father. I had always been such a happy person. Papa had made me happy. But now he was gone and in his place were these dark strangers of fear and hate.

Then came the day of the funeral. Sitting there in the front row of the little Baptist church, I still refused to accept my father's death. It couldn't be. My papa, so full of love for his "baby," so tender and gentle, it couldn't be that he was gone.

After the sermon, the townspeople left their pews and solemnly walked down the aisle to gaze one last time into the casket. Then they were gone. The church was empty except for the family and attendants.

One by one my family rose from their seats and filed by the coffin. Mama. My two sisters. My brother. Only I was left in the pew.

The funeral director walked over and said, "Kathryn, would you like to see your father before I close the casket?"

Suddenly I was standing at the front of the church, looking down—my eyes fixed not on papa's face, but on his shoulder, that shoulder on which I had so often leaned. I remembered the last conversation we had had. We were in the backyard, last summer. He was standing beside the clothesline, reaching up with his hand on the wire. "Baby," he said, "when you were a little girl, remember how you used to snuggle your head on my shoulder and say, 'Papa, give me a nickel'?"

I nodded. "And you always did."

"Because it was what you asked for. But, baby, you could have asked for my last dollar and I would have given you that too."

I reached over and gently put my hand on that shoulder in the casket. And as I did, something happened. All that my fingers caressed was a suit of clothes. Not just the black wool coat, but everything that box contained was simply something discarded, loved once, laid aside now. Papa wasn't there.

Even though I had been preaching for a year and a half, that was the very first time the power of the risen, resurrected Christ had come through to me. Suddenly I was no longer afraid of death; and as my fear disappeared, so did my hate. It was my first real healing experience.

Papa wasn't dead. He was alive. There was no longer any need to fear or hate.

Numerous times I've been back to the little cemetery in Concordia where they buried the body of my father. There are no tears. There is no grief. There is no heartache, for that morning in church I knew the Apostle Paul's words to be true: "To be absent from the body is to be present with the Lord." *(II Corinthians 5:8)*

That was many years ago. Since then I have been able to stand at the open grave with countless others and share the hope that lives in me. There have been mountaintops across those years, opportunities for travel and ministry and preaching. But, you know, growth has come not on the mountaintops but in the valleys.

This was the first valley, the deepest, the one that meant most. When I walk offstage today, after hours of confronting sickness and deformity and need in every form, I go back to the dressing room. And often at that moment I have a strange feeling. I feel that papa is there. He never heard me preach, in earthly form, but I know he knows that his girl is trying to do a good job for the Lord. And he knows that now I constantly lay my head on the shoulder of the Heavenly Father, knowing I can claim all the blessings of Heaven through Jesus Christ.

For quiet I like unspeaking trees,
For cares a spirited mountain walk,
For fulfillment someone to please,
For laughter hearing children talk,

For reassurance a hand to hold,
For strength the persevering sea,
For understanding a friendship old,
For hope I turn to Thee.

FRED BAUER

The Healing Beyond Medicine

by Clair B. King, M.D.

"I can remove a cataract," this surgeon writes,
"but God heals the eye."

My nurse read the disappointment in my face. "Harry Rollins?" she asked sympathetically.

"Yes," I sighed, laying his file on my desk. I looked at the medical books lining my office. Not one of them, I knew, contained the answer to Harry Rollins' problem. For his case didn't go by the book, as least not any medical book.

I should have suspected it when Rollins*, a business executive, first strode into my office. My examination indicated he needed a cataract operation. His knuckles whitened. "Ten weeks out of my life?" he snapped. "What rotten luck!"

The operation should have posed no problem. Rollins was healthy, and his prognosis excellent. I wish his mental attitude had been as favorable.

Normally, I have a prayer with my patients in the operating room before surgery. It's a habit I formed when serving on a medical mission in Nepal. Before that I wouldn't have considered asking a patient to pray with me, figuring he'd think I'd lost my nerve or had little hope for his recovery. But I find that prayer not only helps the patient relax, but strengthens my own assurance.

When I suggested this prayer to Rollins, he shrugged it off. It was in line with his get-on-with-it impatience that boiled even more furiously after the operation. More used

---

All patients' names have been changed.

to giving orders than taking them, he shrugged off my recommendations. And then, even though the surgery itself went well, it happened—repeated eye hemorrhages.

Medically, we had done all we could for Harry Rollins. But we could not heal him. No doctor could. After 36 years of medical practice, I have learned that only God heals. An orthopedist sets the bone, yes, but God heals the break. I remove the cataract, but God heals the eye. And the healing, I've found, depends largely on the individual's harmony with himself and God, something which, I suspect, Harry Rollins had not as yet achieved. He finally recovered, but at what cost in time, money and internal damage to his eye.

One doesn't have to see more than a few patients who experience real pain, yet whose suffering on closer examination shows no physical cause, to realize that there's a real connection between the physical and spiritual. For, as many doctors will agree, man is a trinity—body, mind and soul. And though the body and mind be sound, man is not whole if his soul or spirit is sick. As one medical colleague put it: "The cause of almost every illness is the wear and tear of the soul upon the body."

Are there "viruses" which can wound the spirit? I believe there are. Jesus defined them as hate, guilt, resentment, bitterness, unforgiveness, avarice, *any* negative emotion or thought we hold which breaks our harmonious relationship with God.

Most of us would not jump from a ten-story window because of God's physical law of gravity. Yet many of us do not realize that breaking His spiritual laws can be just as deadly. By the same token, I've seen evidence that a strong faith in God is vaccination against the fears and tensions which can damage or destroy a man.

The case of another patient illustrates this. John Miller also faced a cataract operation. Yet never have I seen a man with so much stacked against him. Severely weakened from a series of heart attacks, he was also permanently blind in one eye. His remaining eye, now cataract clouded, was his only hope. He was desperate. But he had a certain something which gave me confidence.

That confidence was confirmed just before the operation. I overheard him ask my son, an eye surgeon who works with me, if someone would pray with him.

"Certainly," my son assured him. "My dad wouldn't

have it any other way." As with Harry Rollins, his operation went well. But again I knew his healing depended upon God.

Three weeks later I stopped at his house with his new glasses. Trembling, he put them on, then grabbed my hand, crying, "I can see!" We knelt there together in his living room, thanking God for His healing touch.

Didn't God want both men healed? I believe He did. But one man wouldn't tune in to His help.

This is the essence of what many call "spiritual healing"—man's reconciliation with God. When we hide from Him within our mortal fears, guilt, frustration and anxieties, our minds and bodies suffer.

Such was the case with a 54-year-old shop foreman. He, too, had only one eye, and its vision was beginning to fail. But I found no cataract or glaucoma. I did spot a defect in the retina due to poor blood circulation.

As we talked, I learned that his job left him filled with anxiety and tension. He was so stress-stricken that I could see he might even develop a coronary or stroke. Fortunately I knew of a minister near his home who offered spiritual-healing services. The foreman began attending, and his vision improved.

In his case, medicine would have been of little help. And because medicine doesn't always work, it's easy for people to say that illness is "God's will," or "sickness is often given to us to strengthen our character."

Nonsense! Jesus never said that. But He did say it is God's will to deliver men from all evil, including physical and mental illness. And so He healed. Moreover, He commanded us to "heal the sick. . . ." *(Luke 10:9)*

Recorded history shows that for the first 300 years after Christ, the early apostolic church *did* heal in His name. But this burning faith began to fade as the church became more institutionalized. As its healing ministry waned, the church concentrated on ministering only to the spirit, and science took over the treatment of the body.

Today there is a resurgence of ministering to the "whole man," and pastors of many denominations are holding regular healing services.

I participate in such services, often assisting the minister. Do I see this as contradictory to my professional role? No, on the contrary, I feel it gives it full dimension. And so I like to begin each office day with prayers with my staff and at times pray with my patients. For I believe I am a better physician when I keep in close communion with the Great Physician, Jesus Christ.

Nor do I feel that there must always be a physical healing for a spiritual healing to be a success. For when an individual has a personal encounter with God, I believe there is always a healing of the spirit which, in the end, is the most important element.

Roderick Allen exemplified this for me. Roddy was on his deathbed with cancer when a minister and I visited him at his request. He knew the end was near. And he writhed not only in pain, but in emotional turmoil. For what lay ahead terrified him. He was frightened not only for himself, but was frantically concerned over his family. There was nothing the minister and I really could say to Roddy, but we could pray for him. We stood by his bed, each holding one of his hands, and prayed for the healing of Jesus Christ.

Two weeks later Roddy passed on. And some may say that prayer did no more for Roderick Allen than medical science did. Yet, I later received a letter from Mrs. Allen:

"It is strange," she wrote, "but our entire family grew tremendously in faith and trust. Roddy's courage and acceptance was magnificent. Until the end, he responded to prayers and called people by name. Roddy had a wonderful homegoing and, though he was not healed physically, he was marvelously healed spiritually. The warmth of his presence seems to encircle us with love and tenderness."

To me, the letter was an echo from heaven, an affirmation of my belief that while medicine seeks healing of the body, *that* part of healing is of only temporary concern. To be *fully* restored, a person needs healing of the spirit which transcends life itself.

When I Learned About Trust

by Anita Bryant

---

*My babies were dying. Could I really believe
God knew best?*

When I was a young girl growing up in Oklahoma, there was a hymn we sang often at Tishomingo Baptist Church. It was titled "Take Your Burden to the Lord and Leave It There."

It's strange as I look back and think of the times I sang that hymn—probably several hundred times. I doubt that I ever thought much about the lyrics. Singing for me then, I suppose, was just an emotional experience, and though I put lots of gusto into every song, I had a very superficial understanding of the words. In the case of this particular hymn, I didn't really get the message until that day nearly two years ago when I made an unexpected trip to the hospital. Actually, I was six and a half months pregnant so I can't say the trip was unexpected—it just came much earlier than I figured.

The day after an appearance at the Orange Bowl Parade on New Year's Day, 1969, I awoke feeling ill. My first thought was about the baby.

My husband, Bob, rushed me to the hospital where a doctor confirmed my fears. The baby was in position for birth two and a half months early.

"What are its chances?" I asked.

"Very good," the doctor assured us. "The infant probably weighs about four and a half pounds. That's not bad."

That was enough reassurance for me, but when I

glanced at Bob, I saw anxiety painted all over his face and I knew what was going through his mind. During the early years of our marriage, we were unable to have a baby, so we decided to adopt one. As soon as we had completed arrangements for Bobby, I became pregnant, and so eight months later we had two children. Gloria Lynn was a full-termer whom I delivered without difficulty. A few years later we decided it was time to have another baby. Again we consulted many doctors and tried all kinds of advice without result. Then about mid-1968 we began talking of adopting again. This time just the thought of it must have worked, because before we could apply I was pregnant again.

"Don't worry, hon," I told my husband. "I don't think God would bring us this far to disappoint us." He nodded agreement as they wheeled me into the delivery room.

"Don't you worry either, Mrs. Green," the doctor said, smiling. "It's going to be all right."

But it wasn't.

Later I was told that the doctor soon appeared before Bob with a paper in his hand. "Sign this," he said urgently. "You have twins. The first one, a boy, has been born. But Anita is having a difficult time. We need this release so we can deliver the second baby by cesarean section. It's our only hope."

Bob signed.

Our son was born January 3, 1969. Then began a series of blood transfusions as the doctors feverishly worked over me. I can remember so little—a few words—that foggy "drifting away" feeling. It was two hours before I rallied enough for them to deliver our daughter. Since she was born after midnight, her birthday was officially a day later.

By dawn the nightmare was over. The twins were alive and though I was more weakened than during my previous childbirth, I was out of danger.

Twins! How miraculous, I thought. But Bob's face still showed strain, the first hint I had that not all was well. We named the boy William Bryant and the girl Barbara Elisabet. Billy weighed just two pounds and 12 ounces. Barbara two pounds and ten ounces. Although they were reported "satisfactory," Bob couldn't bring himself to see them.

"It's still touch and go," he told me frankly. "If they can just hang on awhile, they'll be okay. But I don't want to see them until the doctors are sure. . . ." He couldn't finish.

I felt positive the twins would make it. They were well-formed, strong babies. "God wouldn't let the three of us survive such a rough ordeal, only to take the twins away later," I said, parroting my pre-delivery pep talk.

Four days after the babies were born, the hospital pediatrician brought disturbing news. The twins were losing weight and becoming dehydrated. They also had serious breathing difficulties.

"They're losing ground," he told us bluntly. "Either one might stop breathing at any time."

The doctor had punctured my balloon. I just couldn't believe it. Bob began phoning Christian friends in all sections of the country, asking them to pray for us. He called our minister, Bill Chapman, who came at once to the hospital. Instead of agreeing with me that God would keep the babies alive, our pastor asked me something I wasn't prepared for.

"Can you honestly pray that God's will be done for these babies, no matter what that might be?" Bill asked us. "Can you truly give them over to Him?"

It was too much. "No," I told him through tears. "I can't honestly tell God I'm willing for Him to take my babies." This was the most agonizing moment in my life.

We talked, prayed and I cried. I asked the minister why such a terrible thing had to happen. Was God punishing us for some sin of which we weren't even aware? No, he didn't think God dealt with His children that way.

Then could I ask God to spare our babies' lives?

"Of course you can," Bill said. "Pray that they'll be spared, but tell God that you're willing to accept His perfect will for them, that you're willing to trust Him, that you'll give Him your burden."

It was then that I remembered that hymn, "Take Your Burden to the Lord and Leave It There." For years, I had paid lip service to those words, advised others to heed them, but now it was my turn to test them.

"If your faith means anything at all, Anita," I told myself, "you must be able to trust God in all things—even with the lives of your new children."

The prayer that followed was the hardest I've ever

said, but I prayed it—and meant it. Bob joined me. We surrendered our twins to Jesus and when we had done this, I was amazed at the peace that flooded my heart. The burden was gone. I could accept any verdict.

Late that evening I was struggling with sleep when a nurse ran into my room all excited. "Your doctor phoned," she cried, jubilantly. "The babies are responding. They're going to live!"

What Is a Miracle?

Recently a group of community leaders objected so strongly to a man who claimed to heal people through faith, that they issued this statement: "Miracles ceased with the death of the last Apostle."

I do not claim to be a Bible student, but I do remember many of the verses read to us by the teacher when I was a small boy in school. And I am confident that somewhere in the Book is the unequivocal statement, *Jesus Christ, the same yesterday, and today, and forever.* (Hebrews 13:8)

Now my question to the learned gentlemen is *if* Jesus is the same today and forever, and *if* those divine healings really were made in the days of the Apostles, why can't there be divine healings and other so-called miracles today?

I suppose that it may all depend upon what you call a miracle. Still, I have placed so many thousands of seemingly lifeless eggs in my incubators, and three weeks later taken out husky, healthy, living chicks ready to grow, and later reproduce, that I *have* to believe in miracles of today.

I never took off a hatch of chicks without feeling that I was working in the midst of miracles. To me every life, from the lowest form to the highest, is a miracle.

Just the other day, in the mud under my window, I scattered seeds so small as to be almost invisible. And some day, later this summer, there will be beautiful flowers of brilliant colors with petals that shine like silk, that come from those tiny seeds. If these aren't miracles from God, what are they?

EBEN WOOD

What It Takes to Come Back

by John Hiller

A star pitcher for the Detroit Tigers who recovered from a heart attack talks about his biggest victory.

It was right after I poured myself a second cup of breakfast coffee that I felt the first pain. It started in my lungs and ran down my arms.

"I'm going to lie down," I told my wife Janice, who was sitting across the table with our two young children. I thought perhaps the pain and my sudden dizziness might be from all the snowmobiling I had done the day before in northern Minnesota. Or maybe it had something to do with the pneumonia I had in 1966, five years earlier. Whatever, Janice suggested I call the doctor. He told me to get right to the hospital.

Two days later, while lying in intensive care, I found out what the trouble was. At 27 years of age and as a professional athlete, I found it pretty hard to believe—I'd had a heart attack!

The first thing I did was tell the doctors not to spill the beans. I didn't want the newspapers to know about it because I didn't want my team, the Detroit Tigers, to find out. I figured I'd secretly recuperate and then report to spring training in two months as if nothing had happened.

My plan didn't work. After three weeks in the hospital I went home for complete bed rest. Just one week before spring training I realized I wasn't going to make it and so I called the Tigers. They were mad that I hadn't

70

told them earlier. "Hey," I said, "don't worry. I'll be there in a month."

When a month went by I had to push it back another month, then another after that. The doctors weren't very encouraging. When one asked if I had training in anything besides baseball—I didn't—I began to get scared. Everything pointed to an operation.

Three months after my heart attack I went back in the hospital. Just before surgery I was really frightened. The thought that I probably would never again be able to play baseball was staggering. How would I support my family? We had just bought a new house in Duluth. How could I finish paying for it? I began questioning God, and as I did, my anger grew. Why had He done this to me?

It was just about this time that my dad called me from his home in Canada. "John," he said, "things will be better than ever. You may have to start all over again, but I guarantee you things will be better than ever."

Dad is a man with great faith in God and he's used that faith all his life. He grew up on a poor, remote farm in Saskatchewan, Canada, one of 13 brothers and sisters. He's worked hard to build up a small auto-body shop in Toronto. And, because of his trust in God, he's always remained positive about the future. Just to hear his voice gave me great reassurance.

Soon, though, I'd forgotten it and was home, weak and worn-out. I was like a third child for Janice to care for. When summer came I put myself on baseball's voluntary-retirement list, something that hurt me real bad. Doing it seemed to say that the ball game was over. I found it hard to accept and I felt bitter.

There were many moments when I wanted to spend the rest of my days lying around the house. But we needed money to pay bills so I took a selling job in a furniture store. Even that tired me out. I know I was a pretty hard person for Janice to live with; I guess anybody who's given up on his hopes and dreams is. I was almost getting used to the idea of not playing again when dad's words came back to me, "You might have to start all over. . . ."

Start over? Was it possible? I didn't know, but I've got a lot of my dad in me and I wanted to find out. I knew the first thing I had to do was get in shape physically. It was up to me to build myself up. That July I went to the "Y" and got on the running track. My running was pitiful; I collapsed after 50 yards.

It was discouraging. I wanted to quit a hundred times. I'd take a few jogs and then ask myself, "What am I doing this for—I'll probably never play baseball again anyway. I'm a heart-attack victim—they don't go anywhere."

But something kept me going. In two months I was doing three miles a day. I was also doing calisthenics, playing paddleball and swimming a mile a day. Slowly I got into the best shape of my life and became proud of my new accomplishments. That fall Minnesota doctors gave me a clean bill of health. But the Tigers weren't convinced. They said I could go to spring training in 1972, not as a player but as a minor-league coach. I didn't like the idea but I figured it might be my best chance to make it back as a pitcher.

When training was over that spring, I still hadn't heard anything from the Tigers except, "Wait a bit more, John." I kept working out on my own, throwing every day and making sure my weight was down.

Two months into the season I was still in Florida as a coach when I had a surprise visitor. It was Jim Campbell, general manager of the Tigers. I had been running in the outfield and was sitting on the bench when he came over. As soon as he sat down beside me I knew what he was there for. He was going to let me go.

"Mr. Campbell," I said, beating him to the punch, "I'm as sound as that fence out there. Just let me prove it."

"Look, John," he said, "you're a mighty big risk for us. Nobody who's had a heart attack has ever gone on to play ball again. Suppose you had another one on the field. We can't be responsible."

"I'll sign waivers for myself," I said. "I'll do anything. Won't you take a chance?"

Campbell's final answer was neither no nor yes. He left without releasing me and for that I was thankful, but I still didn't know where I stood. That night back in my lonely little room in Lakeland, Florida, I talked to the One my dad had always relied on.

"Dear God," I prayed, "I know You've been there when I was back picking up my pieces. I know You know I'm okay, but please won't You just show other people?"

Every day after that I was on the telephone with Detroit. My badgering got to them because finally the Tigers set up an appointment for me with a heart specialist.

When I didn't hear anything right away, I went home to Duluth, anxious but with a renewed confidence. Then I got a telephone call from the Tigers that I'll never forget. After a year and a half away from baseball, they were going to take a chance on me!

First it was only some batting-practice pitching. Then on a warm July night in 1972, it was the real thing. We were playing Chicago. In the ninth inning I was sent in for relief duty. My heart was pounding so hard I thought something might be wrong. But it was only nerves.

I was so excited I could hardly concentrate on catcher Bill Freehan's signals. But I was back where I wanted to be—back where I'd worked hard to be. My dad had been right. I had put my trust in the right place. Things were going to be better than ever.

Seek ye first the kingdom of God, and his righteousness; and all these things shall be added unto you.

MATTHEW 6:33

and my dead passed them by. My flowers—I
looked Forest Lawn Cemetery. All day long I saw those
black hearses pass through the gate. It reminded me, again
of Robin and of

When Healing Begins
by Dale Evans Rogers

---

*Her own illness improved, this famous lady
discovered, when she reached out to others in
need.*

I suppose that in a way I had a "right" to feel self-pity.
Within a year's time Roy and I lost our child Robin; then
my own father died; and now I was suffering this miserable disease which made me so blue that I could not even
pray.

Yet it was in the midst of this dry period that God
showed me how He will always help us handle despondency—if we allow Him.

The lesson came through my illness.

Over a period of several days I kept hearing a strange
ringing noise inside my head, like chimes. It was annoying.
Once right in the middle of a dinner party the strangest
thing happened. I began to see two of everything. My
head spun and I wondered if I was about to pass out.

"Roy, I think I'd better lie down for a few minutes.
I'm feeling dizzy."

Roy was alarmed. He took my arm and led me to our
bedroom, covered me with a blanket and only went back
to our guests when I insisted. Later I thought I was feeling
better and made my wobbly way back to the living room.
I sat down on the piano stool and was in the middle of
saying I was all right when I passed out.

In the hospital I learned I had an infection of the inner ear, with complications. But knowing the cause didn't
make the symptoms any easier to take: It was exactly like
being horribly seasick.

For four days I was unable even to hold down a glass
of milk. I couldn't stand up. I had triple vision. I ached

and my head spun constantly. My hospital room overlooked Forest Lawn Cemetery. All day long I saw those black hearses pass through the gate. It reminded me again of Robin and of my father and in my despair I whispered to Roy, "When do you think my turn will come? Quickly I hope."

After the worst of the symptoms subsided I had to struggle like a baby with the art of walking. From the edge of my bed to the bureau, holding onto the back of a chair—that was a victory. Then it was down the hallway. I pushed my straight-backed chair before me as I tried to keep the walls and desks and other patients from swimming.

By the time I got back home my despondency was at its worst. And it was just here that God began to work with me: He asked me to help someone else.

A friend from our church telephoned to say that her two-year-old baby boy had just drowned. Knowing that we had lost a child, she wondered if I would come over to talk.

So, dizzy and miserable, needing still to hold onto anything handy, I made my way outside and over to our friend's house.

She opened the door and I could identify so well with the benumbed look, the red-rimmed eyes. Her husband too had been crying. We sat in their living room as she told me how their baby had found a loose board in the picket fence surrounding their swimming pool and had crawled through. By the time they missed him it was too late.

"Oh, Dale, Dale. God gave you help when you lost Robin. Can we ask His help now?"

And of course we did. As I left their home that day, some of my own physical symptoms seemed lessened. I walked a little bit straighter, carried less of a weight upon my soul.

But the Lord had to work on me some more, for I was far too self-conscious about the way I looked to other people when I weaved around as I tried to walk. The next time that He took my hand, it was with a touch of His marvelous sense of humor.

It was the very next Sunday and I was trying slowly to get ready for church. That Sunday was particularly important to me, for it was the first time I had been able to go to Communion since being taken to the hospital. Four of our children were at home and we were going through the usual bedlam of trying to corral them, comb hair, shine shoes, and insist that the bright orange shirt was not suitable for Sunday school. For the tenth time Roy looked at his watch.

In the midst of all this confusion the front door burst open and an old friend walked right in. Roy looked at John and then at me. Both from the smell and from the looks of him it was obvious that John had been drinking.

John had been a co-worker with us at Republic Studios years ago. "Roy . . . Dale, I need help and I need it now. Please, don't send me away. Help me."

So, over Roy's protests, we worked out a plan. Roy would take the kids to church and shortly I would follow with John.

John agreed. As soon as Roy and the kids pulled out of the driveway John and I stumbled to the kitchen, poured two huge cups of coffee and sat down to talk and to pray. I think I was able to identify with this man in an unusual way because my own faculties and emotions were not obeying me. I was a little out of control just as John was. And being able to pray with him helped me forget myself.

Finally we left the house and got a ride to church. The service had already begun. As we entered, everyone was kneeling. John and I both grabbed hold of the last pew to steady ourselves, waited for the prayer to end.

Then, as the congregation stood for the reading of the Gospel, John and I worked our way down the aisle. We rolled and weaved, leaving behind us John's unmistakable odor of sour mash. A low buzz of whispers went through the congregation. But God was whispering too: "Don't ever worry about what people think; worry about what *I* think."

As we stood outside the church after the service, Father Harley Wright Smith saw us and smiled. "My friend John has a problem," I said softly.

And in his delightful way Father Smith answered. "Well now." He took my arm to steady me. "I'm not sure who needs help the most."

Father Smith was joking, but I was not when I answered, "I know who needs help the most, Father. And God has just given it to me." For again I saw clearly that when I was worrying too much about myself He had brought me John.

That same morning Father Smith took John down to the altar where he heard his confession, prayed with him and offered counseling. Several weeks later, going into church again, I happened to meet both John and the bereaved mother at the same time. How changed they were. John with new color to his face, she no longer with that numbed look about her. And I myself am able now to walk a reasonably straight line. Above all I was completely out of my despondency.

As we met in the vestibule, first John and then the mother offered some comment about how God had sent me to them at just the right moment.

"Oh no," I said. "You've got it backward. He sent *you* to help *me.*"

Each of us smiled, sure that he was the one who understood correctly the ways of the Lord.

WHAT THE HEART HOLDS

> In the breast of a bulb
> Is the promise of spring;
>
> In the little blue egg
> Is a bird that will sing;
>
> In the soul of a seed
> Is the hope of the sod;
>
> In the heart of a child
> Is the Kingdom of God.

WILLIAM L. STIDGER

Healing the Hurt in Your Heart

by Virginia Lively

"Sometimes," this spiritually perceptive woman writes, "our need is a healing of harmful memories."

The woman kneeling at the altar rail was in pain—all of us taking part in the healing service could see that. Her face showed her intense agony.

"Migraine," the minister whispered to me as we moved toward her down the line of kneeling people.

Then I was standing in front of her. "I have migraine headaches," she explained. I laid my hands on her head and asked Jesus Who loved her to take this pain away. Her mouth relaxed, and she opened her eyes like someone waked from a bad dream.

"It's gone!" she whispered.

"Thank You, Lord!" said the minister. "Thank You!" the congregation echoed. "Thank You!" I repeated, most awestruck of all.

Although it was nine years since God had called me to His ministry of healing, I still could never get over the joyous surprise of it. My chief surprise was that He could use me—a middle-aged housewife with a spreading waistline and a kitchen in need of new linoleum—to reach out to people who hurt. But because it happened, over and over again, I'd stopped trying to figure it out and simply and gratefully gone ahead.

Why, then, as this now smiling woman went back to her pew, was I gripped with a strange uneasiness? A person had been in pain. The pain was gone. But all through the minister's closing prayers, I was puzzled.

Then I remembered something which was to shed light for me on the whole mystery of healing. I remembered that I had seen this lady before. It was right here in this same little Episcopal church the last time I'd been here, three years before. She had come forward with a blinding headache that night too. And God had healed her.

Then why was she back tonight? Was God's healing only temporary? Did it wear out and need renewing from time to time—like kitchen linoleum? Or was there something in this lady's life deeper than the migraine that needed healing? Something that lay behind the headaches and made them happen, something that she had never brought to the altar rail?

As people started up the aisle, I got to the woman's side and asked if she could stay behind. And so in a quiet pew we talked. When, I asked, had this last attack begun?

She thought a moment. "I guess it was just after Jeannie was so upset. She's our youngest, and you know how kids are. The older ones wouldn't let her into their clubhouse."

The more we talked, the more we saw a pattern. The headaches seemed to begin when she saw a child mistreated. A story in the paper, a church appeal for hungry orphans, one of her own youngsters up against life's small injustices, any of these could trigger an incapacitating attack that might send her to bed for days. And yet her own childhood, she said, had been unusually happy.

"My stepfather was a wonderful man. You see, mom wasn't married when she had me. But then she married my stepfather, and he raised me just like one of his own. We were a very religious family. Dad was superintendent of the Sunday school, and mom did the flowers, and I sang in the choir, funny as it seems."

"Why funny?"

"Because I—" The woman's eyes grew huge. "Because I can never go to heaven!"

She sat blinking in the dim-lit sanctuary. "I remember my stepfather saying it! He said he loved me and he'd give me everything he could here on earth but little girls like me could never go to heaven."

Not thought of with the conscious mind, perhaps,

but beneath all the other thoughts of her life had lain this monstrous image of an unjust God.

Before we left the church that night, we went to the altar rail, just she and I, and held up to God this ugly, twisted picture of Himself. "Take it away, Father," I asked, "and show her Jesus instead." This is one reason why Jesus came, I told her, so we can know what God is really like. "Read the Gospels," I suggested. "Read them over and over until you have such a firsthand knowledge of Him."

That night, I know from subsequent letters, was the beginning of real healing for this woman. But it also marked a change in my own life. From that evening on, as people described the aches and pains which led them to seek God's divine healing power, I began listening for the deeper aches.

And I made an astonishing discovery. When we got down to the underlying problem, time after time, it was not medical, nor even, at its deepest, psychological. The real trouble was spiritual. And it was precisely the same problem—in a thousand forms—that the woman with the migraines had. These people had trouble loving God.

Some experience, some early training, some false concept, stood between them and true trust.

And there was the businessman who, deep down, did not want to be healed of his alcoholism. The drinking bouts, we began to notice, would start just when he was on the verge of some big sale or about to meet a potential customer. It turned out that he was the son of a pious but unsuccessful shoe salesman who had made a virtue of failure and taught that wealth is contrary to the will of God. My friend couldn't face success. He was afraid of his heavenly Father and didn't want to hurt his earthly father.

The more important a person's faith is to him, the more successfully he has usually hidden from himself this deep distrust of God. People will talk to me almost eagerly about the most agonizing physical condition or the saddest family relationship, but are tongue-tied when it comes to implicating God in these things.

I remember a minister who came to the house relating experiences of strangling attacks of asthma. His story was a familiar one of terror-filled nights and painful days.

When he had finished, I did not immediately begin to pray for healing as I once would have done. Instead I asked him to tell me about his very first asthma attack, and I prayed silently that Jesus would help him expose the real problem.

There was a long, long silence. Then haltingly he began to recall a hunting trip he had missed as a teenager. He was to have left in the morning with a friend and the friend's father, when he had waked in the night struggling for breath. "I wanted to go especially badly because I had no father of my own. You see, when I was nine my own father—my father—" And then this gray-haired man burst into tears. I have discovered that when the root problem is touched at last, there is usually anger or tears or both.

Chokingly the story came out. A well-meaning friend, trying to ease a little boy's grief, had explained to him that God had taken his father because He loved him and wanted him in heaven. And the little boy who loved and wanted his father too had grown up with an unacknowledged fury at a selfish God.

But now that the painful truth was out, we could pray for genuine healing, not just of the asthma but of the far deeper constriction at the very source of the man's life and health.

A portion of the prayer we offered together which brought about the healing of that childhood memory of caprice and cruelty—may help others put to rest the deep hurts, fears and misunderstandings that trouble most of us.

"Jesus, we know that You are perfect love. But we confess that there are blind spots in our souls that hide this love from us. We ask for Your light in these dark places now, although we know that light can be painful. Burn away any false old images we have built and show us Yourself. Amen."

3.

Hope for People Who Need Courage

Wait on the Lord; be of good courage, and he shall strengthen thine heart: wait, I say, on the Lord.

PSALM 27:14

The Hurts I've Had
to Overcome
by Sandy Duncan

A famous TV star tells how a childhood memory helped her through some personal crises.

Last year when I went back to visit my family in the old hometown—Tyler, Texas—I went to a party at which someone came up to me and said, "Sandy, you probably don't remember me, but . . ."

Peggy Boocock. Peggy Boocock from my class in Hogg Junior High. Because I'd been away from Tyler a long time, she figured I had forgotten. But how could I forget, forget Peggy or Josie Caldwell or Alice Lee Swapp or Phyllis Semple or any of those girls who were a more important part of my life than they knew.

I remember Peggy best from the spring when I was 15 years old and life was more packed and more frantic and more normal than probably it will ever be again. I remember the closing weeks of our eighth-grade year when most of my energy and seemingly all of my hopes were centered on one important goal: I wanted to be one of the six girls selected as cheerleader for the next football season.

Of course, now it seems amusing to think that this could have been the most important thing in the world to me, but at the time there was nothing amusing about it. Everybody at school took it seriously. Football was important. What happened to our Razorbacks was of prime importance.

If I won the competition, I would go away to a special summer clinic for cheerleaders where we would be

taught the finer points of whipping a crowd into a frenzy
of enthusiasm, and in the fall I'd go to all the games and
be in on all the parties and pep rallies. Furthermore, being
a cheerleader meant that you'd hit the top. It guaranteed
you popularity in your class, in your crowd.

To tell the truth, I really didn't have a crowd. I think
I was not exactly unpopular, but in the lunch room I always seemed to be sitting with an "un-in" group, often a
group of two.

In those days my "best friend" was probably my
grandfather, Jeff Scott. Jeff—I always called him that—
was my one strong ally, and in anything as important as
becoming a cheerleader, you needed all the encouragement
you could get.

At home my parents watched my feverish pursuits
with varying enthusiasms. Dad, who still operates a gas
station there in Tyler, was a solid man—he's part Chero-
kee Indian—with a great sense of humor, and it made him
smile, I think, to see me twirling about the house shaking
my pompons.

Mom's temperament was different from dad's. She
was the artistic one. I think she was afraid I wouldn't
make the most of any creative talent I might possess, so it
was mom who was behind my debut in a dance recital
when I was five. It was mom who watched me at my ballet lessons in the American Legion hall where we'd use the
edge of a poker table for a practice bar. It was mom, even
though she herself had been a drum majorette in one of
her schools, who had quiet doubts about my being a cheerleader.

"But I can win it," I'd tell her. "I have timing and
rhythm. I can jump higher than the other girls."

"Maybe I'm just a little afraid of that," mom would
say. I knew what she was referring to. My ballet teacher,
Utah Ground, had warned that I might misuse some of
the leg muscles so specifically trained for dancing.

And so it was that more and more I'd seek out Jeff.
He was a lovable man, blond and slender, little like me,
with a pied-piper personality. At that time he had the
night watch at an oil field outside Overton. I'd go out to
see him and we'd sit together in a work shack called the
"doghouse" and he'd whittle on a stick and we'd talk until
he had to go out and do something about one of the
pumps.

Jeff loved politics, and to tell stories, and though he was amazingly well-read, he was always jumbling up his quotes. "As the Bible says," he'd tell me, " 'To thine own self be true.' " Or, "Ralph Waldo Emerson said a mouthful when he declared that 'God is our refuge and strength.' " He may have mixed up the name tags but the product was always solid. "You'll get no junk from Jeff," he used to say to me, and he was right.

Some 40 girls were trying out for cheerleader. On the morning of the competition, the bleachers of the school gym were filled, not just with students, but with parents as well. It was a big event. One by one we were announced, and then each girl had to run out into the center of the gym and give a solo performance.

"Sandra Duncan!" the announcer boomed, and I bounded out, bursting with personality, showing all my dancer's tricks, whirling and swaying and shouting:

"Gimme an 'H'
    Gimme an 'O'
        Gimme a 'G'. . . ."

And then a fantastic jump, coming down to a dazzling split at the end.

I knew I was good, and the applause verified it. Then we had to go back to our home rooms to wait interminably for the decisions. Finally, the public address system crackled and I sat frozen at my desk while the six outgoing cheerleaders began to speak.

"Hi, this is Alva Bloomquist. The girl who is taking my place as cheerleader next year is Peggy Boocock!"

"Hi . . . and the girl who's taking my place is . . . Phyllis Semple." Phyllis was in my home room, and she whooped and jumped up and the kids applauded while she ran out of the room to claim her victory.

Alice Lee Swapp . . . Josie Caldwell . . . Jane Brandt.

They said later I placed seventh. It didn't matter, that didn't make me a cheerleader. I was dazed. Out in the hall between classes, Tom Stokes was waiting for me. Tom and I were going together. We were barely in the hand-holding stage but he was my boyfriend. Tom squeezed my hand. "Sandy, I'm sorry."

It doesn't matter," I said. "It just doesn't matter." Then I hurried off to class. But it did matter. The rest of the day was a torture and when I left school that afternoon I wanted never to go back there again.

At home mom was gentle with me and dad said that the important thing was that I had done my best. But it was Jeff whom I wanted to see. I found him at dusk in the doghouse, the thick smell of petroleum and the churning sound of machinery all around us.

"Oh Jeff," I said, burying my head in his chest and letting the tears flow. "I worked so hard and I wanted it so much. Why didn't I win?"

You would have thought that Jeff himself had been out there in the gym trying to be a cheerleader, that he too had lost out. We were two of a kind and as for why we had failed, there was no answer between us. "But it hurts, doesn't it?" he asked.

I nodded. "The awful thing is it's probably going to hurt for a long time, maybe always."

I was horrifed to think that I might have to endure what I was feeling then for the rest of my life. But Jeff wasn't giving me any junk, and I knew it. "Listen, honey," he said, "I know a proverb you ought to be thinking about. It's just four words, but I've tested these four words in my own life, and I can tell you they're true."

Curious, I lifted my head from his lap and looked into his serious face. Then, as though it were a secret for my ears alone, he told me the four words that sounded too simple and too cute to be profound.

"No pains, no gains."

Hogg Junior High is a good many years in the past now, and though I smile a little, I still hurt a little when I think about not making cheerleader. Yet over the years I've done some testing of my own with Jeff's four words, and he's right, of course—they're true. Easy living doesn't strengthen us, our muscles don't develop without the soreness from stretching them, and pain seems to be part of God's design for our lives from childbirth to growing pains to all the hurts that find us, though we don't know why.

I haven't liked the recent shock of my television show's sudden closing notice, or the misery of a failing first marriage or the unbelievable pain of the tumor that took the sight of my left eye a year ago. But I do not believe that these things have come without reason. I have come to respect the anguish of mind and body. Today I'm more aware of living than I ever was, and more grateful. I think I'm more aware of other people and what they are feeling, and I know that when I'm thinking of them, I worry less about myself.

If Jeff were here today (he's not; he died ten years ago while out in the woods reaching up for some branches to whittle on), I'd tell him about a proverb that *I*, his own little granddaughter, discovered along the way: "There's nothing evil about pain, unless it conquers you."

THE KNEELING HEART

*Lord, not on bended knee—my knees
  are sore.
They're stiff from years and work and
  standing tall.
Yet in my kneeling heart I voice my
  soul.
You listen, knowing well my spirit's call.
Thank You for understanding as You
  ease
The weariness and take my hands.
I cease my explanations, feel Your
  smile:
"It doesn't matter, child—God under-
  stands."*

HAZEL NOWELL AILOR

Unexpected Performance
by Kim Kupper

Suddenly it was time to sing, but my mind filled with fear, and no words came.

No one could have predicted what would happen when our special Thanksgiving offering was given to the Plymouth Congregational Church in Brooklyn, New York. Small, with a Negro congregation, this church had been struggling to pay the rent on its storefront sanctuary.

The reaction was spectacular! The whole congregation of that little church rented a bus one Sunday afternoon and came all the way from Brooklyn to our Stanwich Congregational Church in Greenwich, Connecticut, to present to us an afternoon of "souly" spiritual music! Black and white together, we all sang to the glory of one God. The atmosphere was wonderful. It was God and it was love.

Doctor Adams, our pastor, inquired later if we at Stanwich Church would like to return the visit. Although we felt unable to present to them a musical program with the inspiration that theirs had been, we agreed to join them in fellowship. A bus was chartered, and on a Sunday afternoon Stanwich Church journeyed to Brooklyn.

I brought my guitar, and the whole happy busload of us sang lively songs on the way. When we arrived, I started to put the guitar away and leave it on the bus, but Doctor Adams asked me to bring it inside. As we walked into the church with my best friend, Meg, Doctor Adams asked the two of us and Phil, a boy who had come with us, if we could sing a few songs during the informal service. Meg, Phil and I looked at one another, swallowed, then said, "Yes."

I was terrified, and I'm sure I speak for my two friends as well. We had never sung as a trio, and I didn't want to spoil anything by singing badly in front of the people we had come to visit.

The service began. Reverend Holmes of Plymouth and Doctor Adams of Stanwich spoke with feeling and sincerity. They were both trying to narrow the gap between the two congregations and help them to feel that those around them were their brothers.

Suddenly it was time for us to sing. I had been asked to introduce our songs and say a few words, but my mind was filled with fear, and no words came. The faces, black and white, looked up at me from the pews, expectant. A thousand thoughts occurred to me. How terrible it would be if I said something to offend or hurt their feelings!

Then I remembered a verse from one of our songs. It went: "Till by faith I met Him face to face, and I felt the wonder of His grace, then I knew that He was more than just a God who didn't care. . . . He walks beside me day by day."

If my God really *did* care, shouldn't I put my faith in Him? "God, help me know what to say. Give me the words," I prayed.

I stood and looked at the people. Suddenly I heard a voice, and it took me a minute to recognize it as my own.

"I'm not practiced at this sort of thing," I heard myself say. "I haven't got a good voice, and when I get in front of a group like this, I tremble. And yet I realize that it doesn't matter what my voice sounds like. It isn't important if I'm frightened. Because I'm singing to the glory of God, and it's what's in my heart and in the hearts of you who are listening that's important. My heart is filled with God's love, and He will give me my voice and my music."

I started to sing, and smiles appeared throughout the congregation. Soon the people were clapping in rhythm with the songs, and then they sang along with Meg and Phil and me, loudly and enthusiastically.

When we were finished, everyone turned to his neighbors in the seats and smiled or spoke. The atmosphere was charged with an emotion you could feel. I felt surging waves of love, brother to brother. Everyone stood and radiated this love that was flowing from God through us to those around us. It was beautiful.

I could have tried to handle the situation on my own,

and could easily have ruined this whole gesture of brotherhood. But I put my faith in the Lord, and it was He who made it a beautiful experience.

Editor's Note:

For this story Kim Kupper won a Guideposts Youth Writing Contest scholarship.

SECURITY

I do not know what the future holds.
            Of joy or pain—
            Of loss or gain—
Along life's untrod way;
            But I believe—
            I can receive—
God's promised guidance day by day,
So I securely travel on.

And if, at times, the journey leads
            Through waters deep—
            Or mountains steep—
I know this unseen Friend,
            His love revealing—
            His presence healing—
Walks with me to the journey's end,
So I securely travel on.

                                        MARY SELLECK

My Ten Hours with a Hijacker

by Nancy Davis Hollenbeck

The story of a stewardess who turned to prayer instead of panic.

It was my first flight as a stewardess. As I boarded the Boeing 737 in Anchorage I was so nervous and excited I could almost hear my heart beat. While I checked out the emergency equipment and the galley supplies it never crossed my mind that our Wien-Consolidated Air Line's scheduled flight to Bethel, Alaska, would not land there as scheduled. Unknown to anyone, somewhere in Anchorage the sick mind of an emotionally disturbed young man was making other plans.

I'd wakened at 3 o'clock that October morning a year ago and begun putting on the long underwear that is part of the stewardess' uniform in Alaska. As I dressed I prayed, "Lord, thank You. I'm finally a stewardess. Thank You for what's ahead today, but please keep me from doing anything dumb." It was a hurry-up prayer but it was said with the conviction I'd had since I was a teenager that prayer will make a difference.

When the plane took off at 5:30, we had 31 passengers in the back half and a cargo of supplies for the bush stations in the front. As we leveled off, Margie Hertz, a veteran stewardess gave me directions. "I'll take the coffee forward to the crew," she said, "and you start pouring orange juice for the passengers." As I put the cups on a tray the excitement of my first flight swept over me again. I didn't see the skinny unshaven man in the rough sheepskin vest until he was right beside me.

"Where's your lavatory?" he asked.

"It's right here, sir, across the aisle." He went in, and I started pouring juice.

In a couple of minutes he opened the door, took one step and was right next to me. In his right hand was a pistol and he pointed it between my eyes. "This plane's not going to Bethel. I'm hijacking it. I want you to take me to the cockpit."

He followed me down the aisle, the gun concealed beneath his vest. In the front, between the cargo and the windows, is a small walkway leading to the cockpit. We were turning into the walkway when Margie came toward us.

"What do you think you're doing?" she snapped.

He pointed his gun at her. "This is what I'm doing. Now open the cockpit door."

Margie's eyes were blazing, her voice full of authority. "Just who do you think you are?"

Her aggressiveness upset him. He shook all over and pushed the gun into her face, his finger on the trigger. "Open the cockpit."

"I can't. I'll have to go to the back and call them before they'll open it."

"If it doesn't open in three minutes, I'll shoot." He stood tense and wild-eyed until Margie was out of sight. Then he looked at me.

I didn't know what to do, but something inside me suggested a relaxed friendly approach, so I smiled and said, "My name's Nancy Davis, what's yours?"

He looked at me unbelievingly.

"Del Thomas," he finally said.

I had a chance then to study the man. He was in his late twenties, about medium height, probably about 150 pounds. He had brown hair, a thin mustache and heavy horn-rimmed glasses. His voice was high-toned and nervous.

"This is my first flight," I continued, "and I was nervous enough before you came along."

"Well, I'm scared too," the man said. "If she doesn't hurry up and get back here I'm going to shoot out the window."

"Hey, I wouldn't do that. This cabin's pressurized; we could be sucked right out of the window. I don't know about you but I don't want to go flying without a parachute."

"I don't care if I die or not; there's nothing for me to live for."

"Everyone has something to live for." The thought of my wonderful parents and brothers and all the rich experiences I'd had flashed through my mind.

"No," he said, "I have nothing. I have nowhere to go and not a soul who cares if I live or die."

He told me his age, his hometown, and that he'd been in prison. (What he didn't tell me was that he'd been in prison for killing a man with a shotgun.)

Finally, the cockpit door opened. Del Thomas said to Captain Peterson, the pilot, "I'm hijacking this plane and I want to go south."

The captain said, "Where are we going?"

"I said south."

I pulled at his shirt. "Del, this is a short-range plane and the passengers are making it too heavy. We should take them back and let them off in Anchorage or we won't have enough fuel."

He agreed, reluctantly. The plane returned to Anchorage while the captain explained the situation to the passengers. The hijacker meanwhile kept pistol in hand as he nervously watched this operation.

At Anchorage the passengers deplaned and Del agreed that Margie should leave too. Margie was reluctant to go. We hugged each other, said good-bye and I pulled the door up behind her. As I turned around and faced the empty plane, there was Del at the end of the aisle, his gun pointed toward me. Now what?

I took one big swallow and prayed, "Lord, give me courage, an understanding of this man and the endurance I'll need."

When the plane took off again I was in the stewardess' jump seat behind the cockpit and Del was on the floor next to the cargo, his gun pointed at the pilots. There was nothing to do but talk. We talked and talked and talked some more: politics, families, weather, prison, religion, everything.

I spoke to him about turning back. "Del, why don't you call it off? When we land for fuel in Vancouver, we can get off the plane together and it will be over with."

My dad's an airline pilot and I knew from him that a hijacker usually doesn't change his mind once he's started his crime, but I felt that I had established a bond with Del and I thought I might influence him.

His eyes darkened and his face became cold. His hand trembled on his gun. "No, I've started this and I'm going to finish it. Take me to Cuba."

I said, "Del, they won't welcome you there. They'll put you in jail. And after you get out, you'll have to work in the cane fields for the government. It's hot there, and you'll be sweating and miserable and covered with bugs. You don't want to live like that, do you?"

"Do you really think it would be like that?"

"Sure I do and I'd hate to see it happen to you." And I wasn't pretending. For suddenly he was like one of the pathetic, emotionally disturbed children I had taught while in college. I honestly didn't want to see him go to Cuba and suffer.

One time when I was quiet he said, "Why aren't you talking?"

"I was praying for you."

He looked surprised. "No one's ever done that before."

"Everybody needs prayer."

I saw a strange expression cross his face, but he didn't answer. When I left him and went to make coffee for the crew, I jammed up the coffee machine. I went back to him. "Del, you'll have to help me." He shook his head. He didn't want to leave the front of the plane. "Please help me; I'll get in trouble if the coffee machine breaks."

"You'll get in trouble? Okay, then I'll help." With the gun in one hand, he fixed the coffee machine with the other.

When we landed in Vancouver, I was still hoping that the hijacking would end there. Then Del insisted we take off again and I felt a wave of fright. With nerves on edge

---

A PRAYER FOR FAITH

God grant that I may never be,
A scoffer at eternity
As long as every April brings
The sweet rebirth of growing things.

SARA HENDERSON HAY

and everybody tense, I knew there was a greater possibility that someone could get hurt. I sat on the jump seat, too discouraged to talk.

Del asked, "What's wrong?"

"I'm disappointed in you. I thought you'd call the whole thing off. Now I'm going to have to go to Cuba and I've got this long underwear on and all of us will be hot and miserable." Then I jumped up and went back to the galley.

Immediately he came back with a pained expression on his face.

"What's the matter?"

He sat on the aisle seat and I sat on the arm of the seat across from him. "Del, why don't you give up and have the captain turn the plane around? We'll tell them that you treated us well and it won't be so bad for you. You know it's got to stop somewhere and you're really tired, aren't you?"

"Yes, I'm tired."

"So are we and besides it's time to end the whole thing."

He was silent and tense for a long moment, then his face relaxed. "Yes, I guess so."

"I'll go get Captain Peterson and you can tell him yourself."

I notified the captain and went to the back of the plane. I had the mike in my hand ready to warn the other two crew members if Del started shooting.

The captain approached cautiously, but Del didn't raise the gun. We were now over Oregon and as they talked, Del agreed that we should turn around and land in Vancouver.

When I returned to Del, he was crouched forward in his seat, rocking back and forth, his face buried in his hands, crying in the most pathetic way. I didn't really know what to do, so I patted his back gently and cried too. "It'll be okay. You did the right thing."

When we landed at Vancouver airport, a Canadian officer, Inspector Northrop, came aboard, talked to Del and he surrendered. As the plane, emptied of its lone passenger, taxied across the field I looked at my watch—4 P.M. Had it only been ten and a half hours?

Then I remembered. "Lord, I know You were with me, thank You."

Later everyone I talked to, from pilots to reporters to psychologists, all had the same question: What made Del change his mind? I know the best answer is locked up somewhere in his mixed-up brain. Yet I believe his decision to turn around was linked to the prayer I prayed for him. He knew I cared enough about him to ask God to stand beside him.

And though I'm still not sure how I came to feel so much concern for this desperate, tormented man, I believe that somehow the caring must have reached into his lonely inner self and caused him to relent and give up his dangerous plan.

Editor's Note:
For her heroism in the hijacking, Mrs. Hollenbeck received six awards, including a Presidential commendation.

Forgotten Wings

One winter morning, I put out breakfast for the birds—sunflower seeds, toast crumbs, suet—and then stood by the window watching. Sparrows, chickadees, woodpeckers. But most beautiful of all, the blue-and-silver jays with their crests blowing in the wind.

A jay lighted, picked up the largest chunk of bread and started to carry it away. But the ice-coated platform was so slippery under his claws that he began sliding. He was over the edge, fluttering and falling toward a snowbank, before he remembered that he had wings. Spreading them wide, he took off in a wild flurry for a high branch.

I couldn't help laughing at how silly he looked, skidding and yelling when he needed only to open his wings and *fly* . . . Then I stopped laughing.

Because what else had I been doing? All morning I had been depressed. Everything seemed to go wrong. Yet, I had tried to save myself by my own efforts, when all the time, folded and forgotten, I had strong wings—the wings of prayer which are always ready to bear us up if we don't forget to use them.

FLORENCE B. JACOBS

The Man Who Was Afraid of Water

by John and Elizabeth Sherrill

Explorer Thor Heyerdahl, master of the Ra
and Kon-Tiki, *talks about how he overcame a
crippling fear.*

Thor Heyerdahl was waiting for us outside the hilltop Italian home overlooking the Mediterranean where today he lives between expeditions. Tan and slender, he looks far younger than his 59 years. "What a beautiful setting," we said, "for someone who has always loved the sea."

"Loved it?" He gazed out over the blue-green water. "As a matter of fact, I used to hate the sea—hated and feared it. I had a terror of all water."

A strange statement from someone who crossed the Pacific on the little raft Kon-Tiki, *when for more than three months he and his companions saw no land at all, only giant waves towering over their heads and crashing over the hand-lashed logs, drifting on mid-ocean currents to demonstrate his theory that early South Americans could have reached Polynesia that way.*

He invited us into the cool white-walled house—and this is the story he told.

As a little boy growing up in Norway, I could see ships coming and going in the Oslo fjord from the window of my home. I used to dream of traveling in them to the faraway places in the pictures in my parents' books, especially two huge volumes almost too big for me to lift down from the shelf, called *The Living Races of Mankind.*

As I grew older, my parents, especially my mother,

99

encouraged these interests. Mother was an outstanding natural historian with great respect for whatever could be weighed, measured and researched—and an equal contempt for prudery, superstition, and other "religious nonsense."

My father, on the other hand, was convinced of the existence of a world that could not be seen or touched. In their frequent arguments on the subject, mother seemed to have all the logic on her side, and yet I could not help noticing that father had a special joy. He taught me to say the Lord's Prayer and often, at night, after mother had put me to bed, he would tiptoe into my room to hear me recite it in whispers.

I was still very young when the first water accident happened. In back of our house was a small lake where in winter men used to cut great blocks of ice. One day some bigger boys and I were sliding on this frozen lake when we began daring each other to jump onto one of the blocks.

As the one who weighed least, I was elected to try it first. The great ice block wobbled under me, then capsized with a splash. Suddenly I was in an icy, swirling, utterly confusing world. I thrashed wildly in all directions. Which way was the surface? I was unconscious when at last they hauled me out.

A few years later I had a second near-drowning. I had started school by now and had gone with a group of classmates on a swimming party. I did not go in the water—I could not swim and had refused even to try—but I sat on the bank watching the others.

At last they came out and, to dry off, started a game of tag. We chased each other higher and higher up the steep banks of the fjord. At one point a narrow footbridge led across a deep tidal inlet onto a small island. I started across it with my pursuer at my heels. I scrambled over the edge, leaped—and plunged straight into the churning water far below. I heard the screams of my schoolmates high above me as I rose to the surface, only to be dragged beneath again. The third time the deadly clutch released me—someone had thrown me a life preserver.

We interrupted Mr. Heyerdahl. "These experiences must have made the question of life after death very real and personal."

Heyerdahl agreed. He'd wanted to have his father's

*joyful certainty about God, yet at the same time felt him-
self more and more committed to his mother's concern for
science. But standing in the way of his early dreams of
travel and discovery was his paralyzing fear of water.*

My father tried for years to help me get over my
fear, arguing that it was far more dangerous to avoid
water than to learn to swim. He even tried bribery—a
five-kroner note if I would go into the water up to my
chest, ten kroners if I put my head under—but I couldn't
do it. At last he hired a professional swimming instructor
who buckled me into a harness suspended from a pole by
a rope. But if the rope at my back slackened even a little,
panic swept over me and I clawed wildly at the surface.
At last my father gave up the lessons.

More years went by in which I was developing the
controversial theory of westward migration by raft to the
Polynesian islands. All the experts said no one could sail
the open ocean in a raft. I hoped—if my fear of water did
not stop me—to test my theory by actually floating across
the Pacific on the Humboldt Current, as I was certain
early seafarers had done.

As it turned out, World War II forced me to abandon
my dream for a while. But a wartime incident also made
me face up to my fear.

I was in Canada when the Nazis invaded Norway, so
I joined the Free Norwegian Forces in Ontario, preparing
troops for guerrilla warfare in our occupied country.

In wartime, private fears and phobias are not things
you talk about, and so one day I found myself on a portage
trip with two other Norwegian soldiers from the wild Ox-
tongue River. It was early spring and the river was ram-
paging with melting glacial water; we had to portage our
canoe around innumerable rapids and falls. At last we
reached the foot of High Falls, a vast cataract thundering
over the crest of a precipice far above us. Finally we
wrestled the heavy canoe up the trail and along the portage path above the falls.

There, to our dismay, not 50 yards from the brink of
the cataract, the path, completely covered by the spring
floodwaters, vanished. From this point on, a sheer rock
cliff plunged directly into the river.

Just against the cliff the water seemed calmer, forming little eddies and backwaters against the furious cresting

of the center. Perhaps by sitting in the canoe and clutching roots and cracks in the cliff face we could haul ourselves along the bank far enough upstream to begin paddling.

For 200 yards the stratagem worked. The deafening noise of the falls receded a bit. And then, just ahead, the cliff jutted sharply out into the stream. We were groping our way, hand over hand, around this promontory when a side current caught the bow.

In one awful second I knew we were going over.

Then I was tumbling in the very center of the foaming torrent. When my head finally broke water, I saw the capsized canoe racing toward the falls and one of my companions clinging to the rocky shore. My heavy winter uniform and thick army boots were dragging me beneath the surface.

Incredibly, even as I was swept faster and faster toward the precipice, I had a clear, almost dispassionate thought: *In a moment I will know beyond all doubt which of my parents is right about life after death.* I also remembered my father tiptoeing into my room, and there with the roar from the cataract growing louder each second, I started to pray.

With that prayer came a sudden burst of will. I would fight. I would not yield. As my prayer grew surer, warmth seemed to flood my frozen body. I began to swim with long, strong strokes, while my feet in their waterlogged boots began a rhythmic kicking. As I continued to swim, the warmth turned into a kind of joy, an awareness that something greater than myself was present within me.

There was no doubt about it, the riverbank was slipping away less quickly now; I was almost keeping pace with the water. Each time I thought I must stop, that I could not go on, the strange joy reappeared and I struggled on, helped by nothing I could see or describe.

And then I saw that both my buddies were safe. One of them was holding on to a tree limb and leaning out over the water toward me. Though exhausted, I fought on against the current. My companion was stretching out his hand. I battled the last few inches. Finally I felt his fingertips.

And so years later, after the war, I was able to set out on the *Kon-Tiki* across the Pacific. I had learned for myself what my father had always known, that there is an invisible world of caring all around and inside us—different from ours, unimaginable by us, but as close as a cry from the heart.

TO THOSE WHO HAVE LOST—FOR NOW

The bugles sound retreat, the banners fall,
  The hosts of eager allies melt away.
Many marched bravely with you. Of them all,
  Few will stay.
Now fade the cherished hopes that once were bright,
  Now slowly sinks from sight your dying sun.
Seek you an answer in the gathering night?
  There is one.
Pick up that broken blade with weary hand,
  Shout that this disappearing sun will rise!
Only the hopeless cause, the last stand,
  Wins you the skies!

ARTHUR GORDON

Prairie Fire

by Vera Williams

---

*Mama had done all she could—now we waited
and wondered if it was enough to save us.*

Prairie fires were always a summertime menace in the Ne-
braska sandhills where we lived in the early 1900s. Careful
ranchers protected their families as best they could by
plowing a wide firebreak around the house, barn and corral, leaving nothing for the flames to feed on. But papa
was different. He was on the casual side. Saddles and
bridles were usually flung in the dust of the corral. Haying
machinery was left in the open all year 'round. Papa always meant to get around to things like the firebreak. He
started it in the spring, but the plow was left sticking in
the furrow.

Ours was just a modest ranch, with a sod house to
give us shelter. The house was made of strips of sod cut
out by a plow and placed on top of one another to form
the walls. Over the top arched a roof on which scraggly
weeds and grass grew. Our house was on the fancy side
because we had two windows, a door and a floor. My
mother, a former schoolteacher, had books on shelves; a
Bible lay open on the table. Geraniums bloomed in tomato
cans on the wide window seats and there were rag rugs on
the floor.

Our nearest neighbor came over one hot July day. He
lived only eight miles away and that was practically the
same as if our clotheslines were tangled together.

"We haven't had a fire close to here for a long time,"
he told papa. "But that doesn't mean we won't. You'd better finish that firebreak." But papa still didn't get to it.

Several weeks later the fires broke out. Ranchers

stopped their work—harvesting, haying, rounding up stock—and left their homes to fight the flames.

The men were gone all day. They returned late at night, dog-tired, blistered and seared from the heat. They rolled into bed, slept until dawn and then were on their way.

"I have a cold spot in the pit of my stomach," mama confessed to papa one morning, "and every time you start out again, that cold spot travels all over me." Anxiety made mama's usually gentle voice ragged. "We won't have any protection if a fire heads this way."

Papa wheeled on her. We were frightened by how white his face was under the smoke and grime. His eyes were bloodshot and weary.

"There isn't a fire within twenty miles of this ranch! Men are dropping on the fire line because we don't have enough help! If you want it turned, you'll have to turn it yourself."

He scarcely was gone before mama took up the challenge. We had heard grim stories of families being roasted alive in their sod shacks. If the sod was fresh and new it would not burn as fire roared over it. But if it was several years old and grass and weeds grew on it, there was little chance of escape. Mama read a page in the Bible, closed her eyes and said, "God, please help us. And I'll help You because You don't want these children to burn, either."

She shut my sister and me in the house. She would not let us go into the outdoor heat or take a chance on our meeting a rattlesnake.

We watched through the window as she scraped the rust off the plow and oiled it. She called Lena, the high-spirited Hambletonian mare she had ridden in her school-teaching days. Lena always came when mama called her, no matter how far away she was. Mama hitched her to the plow.

Besides Lena, we had another horse, named Charley. A big gray animal, Charley had served the ranch long and well. When cataracts formed over his eyes and he could no longer see, he was turned loose to graze. We saw him only occasionally, when he came to the big horse trough under the windmill in the corral for a drink. We children usually went out to pet him because we loved him. Little did we know how important a role he would play that day.

Determinedly, mama started to plow a big rectangle that took in the house, the barn, the corral. Never one to do things halfway, mama cut a 50-foot firebreak, the widest in the whole area. The rough, warped plow handle must have hurt her hands. The sun blistered down on her back and we saw her sag with weariness. But grimly she held Lena to the task, stopping only once in a while to wipe her face on the sleeve of her blouse and to drink long and deep from a jug of water.

While mama worked, the wind was shifting. Soon we caught the smell of smoke. The sky was growing darker, the sun scarcely more than an orange ball in the gathering smoke. My sister and I clung to each other. It got so dark the chickens went to bed.

The firebreak finished, mama put the plow in the tool-shed. Then, smelling of smoke and sweat, she came back to the house. "Now you may go with me to the windmill."

We went along with her and tried to help her as she brought back buckets of water and poured them into her galvanized washtubs on the kitchen floor. She ripped blankets off the beds so she could dip them into the water and fight the flames if the fire came too close.

"I have done what You wanted me to do, God," mama said. "It's up to You now."

Mama pushed the geraniums aside and lifted us both up beside her in the window seat. Our eyes searched past the yard for the first glimpse of our livestock. It's a funny thing how stock know about a firebreak. I'd never seen it happen but I'd heard stories about how if there was a fire anywhere near, the stock would run for the firebreak. Somehow they know they'll be reasonably safe inside the break.

And as we watched, the prairie fire came. It came an orange-red sheet of fire on the far horizon, sweeping toward the ranch. Soon we heard that peculiar, ominous roar, a sound like nothing else.

Suddenly mama pointed. "There's Charley!"

Ahead of the flames the ranch horses were running—led by blind, old Charley! Running like the veteran he was, sightless head high, tattered gray mane flying, he was bringing the other horses in to the safety of the fire-break.

The monster that was the prairie fire roared to the firebreak mama had labored over. It gasped, hesitated, then, chagrined that it had been beaten, it slunk around us.

Mama put her arms around us.

"Thank You, God," she said, and that was all.

But we had a can of tomatoes for supper, to celebrate. And Charley got an extra feeding of oats.

A Fragile Moment of Hope

I awoke with a feeling of dread. Although the sun was shining brightly, I hardly noticed. This was my birthday and it depressed me. I remembered how I had looked forward to birthdays when I was little. Now the years were beginning to add up and the day was neither exciting nor welcome. Already I wished it was over.

My family left after breakfast, and the house was too quiet. I switched on the radio to some music, poured a cup of tea and sat down at the kitchen table.

Was I afraid of growing old? No, not afraid, just regretful. The years whisk by so fast—so many years—and so many days and I could remember only a fraction of them.

The music stopped and an announcer began a commercial. "Every day you're a little older," he said, "*if* you're lucky."

I didn't hear any more. I thought about his words a long time. As the reality of its truth sank in, my depression lifted. I realized then that it isn't important whether I'm 20, 40, or even 90. It isn't the year that matters—it is the day. This day, now.

At that moment I resolved to cherish hereafter each day that God grants me. I looked out the window. Why, it was a beautiful day. What a lovely birthday gift!

BILLIE A. BROWN

Lost in the Emerald World

by Gene Savoy

A fever of panic rose as we realized we must find the camp by sundown, or die in that rotting jungle.

Fear gnawed me as evening shadows began to tarnish the spears of sunlight slanted through the jungle. It wasn't the natives' story about men who explored the enchanted Chachapoya ruins being turned into stone that bothered me. It was my revulsion against this South American jungle itself; my fear and hatred of its horrors, its poisonous insects, deadly snakes and diseases.

I had been on the trail of an ancient Peruvian civilization, the Chachapoyas, that predated the Incas. As an archeological explorer, I was convinced that the Chachas had built large cities in these eastern Andes.

Many specialists argued that this thick jungle area would have been too hostile to ancient civilizations. Yet, old Spanish documents led me to believe such cities had existed. It was an argument, I felt, that could never be settled until the vast Peruvian rain forests were thoroughly explored. Already I had found scattered ruins, yet nothing to prove an entire civilization.

We had started our current trek ten days ago. Earlier this day, as we stopped in a small village, a wizened old man spoke to us of ruins somewhere off the main trail.

Taking two men from our group, I headed in the direction he indicated. We picked our way across a vine-wrought suspension bridge leading to a fragment of trail that trickled into a green jungle wall.

With my companions, Segundo and Juan, I plunged into it, machete flailing. Soon we were deep into the steaming, shadowy rain forest. Cedrela trees soared 120 feet above us, their spreading crowns blotting out the sun. Vines clutched at our ankles, and stinging nettles brought red itching welts. Sweat glued our shirts to our skins. Tiny black bees covered our arms; we'd brush them off and they'd return like flies to sticky flypaper.

I remembered to be careful of what I touched. Once before, I had touched a caterpillar—a white crystalline thing that fascinated me. It was like an electric eel covered with nettles; my hand ached for hours.

I shuddered at the memory and again resentment choked me; I hated the jungle. I thought back to my boyhood when my father would take me on trips to the north woods of Oregon. In the still deep beauty of the giant trees I sensed God's spirit. Sitting for hours we would watch deer, pumas and black bears. It was my father's way of teaching me patience and observation.

But that was in the clean pine woods, not this rotting green hell! I winced as we blinked into a smog of mosquitoes. Why, I wondered, did God create such a place? I berated myself for not bringing a snakebite kit, or equipment to survive a night in this jungle infested with deadly bushmaster snakes.

"Let's hurry," I called out. "We don't have much daylight left and I want to see those ruins."

Swinging our machetes, we forged ahead, following the trail which by now was almost indistinct as we neared what we thought must be the area the old man had told us about. By this time my two companions had fanned out, hunting for the ruins. Several hours had passed since we started. I looked up to the tops of the cedrela trees and noticed the patches of sky beginning to darken. My watch confirmed it; we had only enough daylight left to get back to camp. The ruins would have to wait.

"Segundo. Juan," I called. In obvious relief, they turned toward me; and together we started our backward trek. But we hadn't moved more than ten feet when all of us came to the same realization.

We had lost the trail. It was only a fragment at best. And in our search it had slipped away.

My insides turned to water. I knew if we didn't reach camp by sundown, we'd probably never get there. In desperate quietness, we slowly began circling, hunting for the trail. Nothing. We widened our circle, walking faster. Still nothing but untouched jungle; like a deep green nightmare.

We sensed the sun getting lower. And the fever of panic rose. Segundo excitedly pointed to the right. "No," panted Juan. "*This* way!"

"Straight ahead," I shouted, my breath coming short. In frenzied panic I started to run blindly.

And then I remembered the flies.

It had happened a week ago. It was not unusual to step into a swarm of jungle flies. Nor was it unusual for me to swat at them furiously with my hat. The more I swatted the more agitated they became. I ran off through the thicket, trying to get away, but they stuck with me. Finally I thought, *This is ridiculous.* Summoning my willpower, I stood still, not moving. Slowly the flies buzzed off and left me. What was unusual was that this was the first time I had enough sense to stand still.

We were not running from flies now. But something far more dangerous—mind-twisting panic.

I stopped running and stood still. I could hear the heavy breathing of Segundo and Juan beside me. A monkey chattered overhead and a macaw screamed in the distance. As had the flies before, the panic left me. And now a new realization took its place.

This was my Father's house.

My dad who introduced me to the woods had taught me that God was everywhere. I had seen Him in the North American forests. Why had I closed my eyes to Him in the South American jungle? Hadn't He created it, too, as He had all the world?

I relaxed inside . . . and opened my heart to His presence. As I did, a sense of His love welled within and I felt at one with Him. I looked up into a beautiful emerald world of wild orchids and fragrant blossoms where hummingbirds hovered. Yes, He was here, too. My heart quieted.

Somehow in that serenity—and it is difficult to explain—an impulse within me directed: *Walk a few paces to your left.* I obeyed in that state where part of one's mind is under another's control.

Segundo saw it first: dried sprigs of vegetation. "The trail!"

In relief, we laughed. Then, singing with heartfelt release, we started back down our path to safety. I don't know just what Segundo and Juan were thinking, but I was celebrating my revelation.

In the days that followed, I felt as if I were continuing to gain new strength from the insight of this experience. As I moved with a new calm, I began to see things I had never noticed before. Nature seemed to be opening up. My old resentment of the jungle faded as I became one with it and its beautiful and, yes, often dangerous phenomena. But I learned they are phenomena which one could survive by following jungle rules, just as one must follow the rules of big-city traffic.

We went back up that trail another day and this time did find the ruins—an ancient city of white stone hidden away for centuries.

Here was proof that I had been looking for, the first genuine link with the ruins I'd found earlier. And, in time, they proved to be a part of a continuous chain of ruins I discovered strung out along the high forested peaks of Amazonia—the Chachapoya kingdom!

I am proud of my archeological discoveries. But my greatest discovery, I believe, was in recognizing my Father's presence everywhere—a recognition which transformed a green hell into a paradise of revelation for me.

Hope is like a harebell trembling from its birth,
Love is like a rose the joy of all the earth,
Faith is like a lily lifted high and white,
Love is like a lovely rose the world's delight.
Harebells and sweet lilies show a thornless growth,
But the rose with all its thorns excels them both.

CHRISTINA GEORGINA ROSETTI

The Afterglow
by Marjorie Holmes

The author of many best-sellers shares a child-hood experience.

My mother had always savored sunsets until the last lingering glow had faded from our Iowa sky.

"Just look at that sunset now!" Mother was always urging us. "You can peel those potatoes later. Your lessons can wait." We must stop whatever we were doing to follow her pleased gaze. "Isn't that the most beautiful sky you've ever seen?"

Then, after supper when the bright hues had melted into the dusk and there was nothing left of the sunset but a last stubborn band of burning rose, she would return to the porch a minute and stand there, arms wrapped in her apron against the chill, and murmur: "The afterglow means hope."

What could hope possibly mean to this middle-aged married woman whose dreams must surely all be behind her?

I was puzzled. I sensed her hopes but dimly: that the problems of her family would be resolved, wounds healed, frictions cease, worries vanish . . . the doctor's report would be favorable . . . my brother wouldn't have to have an operation, after all . . . that new company would be hiring soon, and Dad would land a better job . . . there would at last be enough money to go around . . . her children's turbulent lives would get straightened out—the boys would find themselves.

Hope? What did it mean to her? It spoke of that marvelous ingredient that keeps men going—something that is almost as vital to man as love—his God-given hope, his belief in tomorrow, his bright expectations that refuse to die.

It was surely what the Lord Himself was talking about when He counseled His followers to be of good cheer, not to despair.

My mother gave her children the gift of sunsets. But an even greater gift was her gift of the afterglow: the message she read in those remaining embers, burning like little fires of faith long after the sunset itself was gone, a lighted bridge across the coming darkness to the stars, "The afterglow means hope."

How to Live Courageously

by *Norman Vincent Peale*

For those trapped by the fear of what might happen . . .

It is a continual surprise to me how many people are made miserable by vague imaginings of sinister events they think might occur. Like this story of one professional man I know, whom I'll call Frank.

During Frank's childhood there was seldom enough money to pay bills, and the family could hardly ever be sure of the next meal. When finances improved other anxieties developed. The mother's uncertain health, for example. She had high blood pressure.

I vividly remember Frank's description of the doctor's visits. The boy watched apprehensively as the physician wrapped the testing apparatus around his mother's arm, pumped it up, studied it, then solemnly folded it away. As a result of her high blood pressure, his mother lived in constant fear of a stroke.

"If something should happen to me," she would say to Frank, "you must help your father take care of the family." For years, especially when away from home, Frank never heard a telephone ring that his heart didn't start to race and his breath come in gasps as he picked up the phone. It might be that long-feared word.

The father, too, projected his fears upon the sensitive boy. He feared the dark and was always testing doors and windows at night. Whenever on a boat the father would say, "There's only a plank between us and the implacable sea." If he was in a plane it was, "You never know when an engine will fail."

Then Frank met and married a vivacious young girl

114

who had no fears at all. She wanted to meet life head-on, to see all the beauty she could and to find adventure in every situation. She had no anxieties, no insecurity, because over all and above all was her total trust and faith in Almighty God.

It took years for Frank to escape from the harsh tyranny of his fears. Aided by the love and inspiration of his wife, Frank did it by a total commitment of mind, body and soul to the proposition that faith in God can cancel out fear.

You can't chase away these irrational fears of what might happen by telling yourself you're being silly. In very serious cases it may take professional therapy and treatment. In less serious situations the following steps will be helpful:

1. Let go and let God. Worry is a spasmodic clutching by the mind of an obsessive fear idea. To counteract it, insert in the mind the thought that you can leave your concerns with God. By a deliberate mental act, take charge of the fear spasm. Order your mind to release its frantic hold on the obsessive anxiety thought. In a word, let go and let God.

2. Remind yourself of one great fact and affirm it constantly by saying, "God loves me and those whom I love. He is taking care of us."

3. Having left your fears with God, having affirmed His watchful care, go about life in confidence.

4. Every day, morning and night, thank God for His loving kindness. Believe and affirm the things for which you are thanking Him.

If you are facing a crisis, or need more help in meeting daily anxiety, repeat each day one or more of the following Scriptural passages:

BIBLE VERSES FOR COURAGE

Be strong and of good courage; be not afraid, neither be thou dismayed: for the Lord thy God is with thee withersoever thou goest.

JOSHUA 1:9

If God be for us, who can be against us?

ROMANS 8:31

For God hath not given us the spirit of fear; but of power, and of love, and of a sound mind.

II TIMOTHY 1:7

I sought the Lord, and He heard me, and delivered me from all my fears.

PSALM 34:4

The Lord is my light and my salvation; whom shall I fear? The Lord is the strength of my life; of whom shall I be afraid?

PSALM 27:1

Peace I leave with you, My peace I give unto you: not as the world giveth, give I unto you. Let not your heart be troubled, neither let it be afraid.

JOHN 14:27

Fear thou not; for I am with thee: be not dismayed; for I am thy God: I will strengthen thee, yea, I will help thee; yea, I will uphold thee with the right hand of My righteousness.

ISAIAH 41:10

Yea, though I walk through the valley of the shadow of death, I will fear no evil: for Thou art with me.

PSALM 23:4

4.

Hope for People Who Want to Change

Therefore if any man be in Christ, he is a new creature: old things are passed away; behold, all things are become new.

II CORINTHIANS 5:17

Mother, I'm Here
by Kris Welland

The story of a love reborn.

My mother's alcoholism became apparent to me when I was about nine years old. For seven years I watched as her illness made a grayish, skeletonlike animal out of the intelligent, charming beauty I loved. Liquor tore her apart and tore us apart too, my brother and sister and father and me, and all the other people who loved her, which included anyone who knew her.

As for me, I changed as much in those seven years as I thought my mother did. I began to hate her because hating hurt less than loving her and watching her destroy herself. Later I felt her drinking was directed purposely at the family, and I steeled myself even more against the sympathy that made me vulnerable to soul-ache. I like to think now that had I known what she was suffering, I would have helped her. But I didn't.

I was 15 when my father carried her limp, gray, emaciated form out to the car and drove her away, and I remember distinctly the overwhelming relief and exhilaration I felt that hot June day. She was going away for good, far away to a rehabilitation center in Minneapolis, Minnesota, and my father was divorcing her. I would never have to see her again. I didn't, either, for almost two years.

During that time, I thought about my mother as little as possible; I was happier than I had ever been before, ignorantly happy. To appease my niggling conscience I read the letters she sent us, full of a love that disgusted me, but I never wondered at her struggle to regain her sobriety, her sanity and her self-respect.

She won that struggle without my help. When I was 16, she wrote to say that she was leaving the rehabilitation center for an apartment and a position as a secretary in an insurance company.

I could not believe she was really well at last. Secretly I resented her licking it without us when she couldn't with us, and cynically, almost hopefully, I expected her to start drinking again within a week. But her letters kept coming; enthusiastically, crisply, she wrote of her activities at work, of decorating her apartment, of skiing weekends.

My mother seemingly ignored the fact that we never answered her letters and she kept writing until we finally did answer them. Courtesy, I told myself. But the truth was, I had to admire her spunk. After a lot of internal struggle I accepted one of her invitations to visit, and two days after my 17th Christmas I boarded a plane for Minneapolis.

I have never felt so frightened as I did when I stepped off the plane that wintry evening. My mother must have been frightened too, but as I glimpsed that unfamiliar, familiar face in the crowded waiting room, she hurried to me and hugged and kissed me and kept her arm around me as we walked away. I wanted to shrug off that arm— one of the principles of my hate had been that I never allowed her to touch me—but she kept it there, and in my confusion I talked furiously.

We picked up my luggage and stepped out into the shocking cold and the cobalt night. As we drove noisily through the dark and snow, fast along the flat highway, my ego and I began to recover from our fright, and my hauteur and hate came back. I answered reticently, even curtly, her eager questions about my sister and brother, about my friends, about school.

Sometimes with deliberate cruelty I spoke of things to remind her of her losses—of my brother's new tallness, the beauty of our Christmas tree, the family jokes around the dinner table at home—a hundred things that could only grieve and sadden her. Never did I speak encouragingly of her amazing return to health; never was I enthusiastic about the details of her new life in Minnesota; not once did I display a particle of affection.

Yet my mother kept her composure and retained in our conversation both untiring interest and, more remarkably, love. By the time we got to her home I was a little ashamed of myself, which only served to make me nastier toward her.

We walked into the warmth of her apartment and I held my breath. My mother adored daintiness and airiness and how beautiful she had made that room! Gauzy white curtains floated at the windows, filtering the light onto the snow outside. The floor was blanketed richly in pale yellow, the light blue furniture was gay with sprays of tiny white flowers and around the room she had scattered great bunches of daisies in crystal bowls.

For Christmas, tables were adorned with graceful candles and delicate silver angels. The little gilt bell that had tinkled *Silent Night* for us so many years at home was now on her desk, and next to the large window stood a dainty little fir tree, bearing bugles and teddy bears and Santas my mother had made by hand. It was all so lovely, so bright and warm and homelike that it caught at my heart.

I stood looking at that room while my mother bustled around putting finishing touches on everything. When she was done she led me to her room, which was as delightful as the other, and exhausted, I got ready for bed. My mother was to sleep on the living-room sofa while I was there, and she too prepared for bed, all the while chattering lightly. I allowed her to kiss me good night before she left the room, and then I climbed into the bed's softness and lay watching the snow swirl against the window. My door was open, and for a long time there was no sound but the *swish, swish* of the icy flakes against the glass. I lay awake for a long time and inside I was as cold and hard and relentless as that snow.

When I finally began to get drowsy, a frighteningly familiar sound started me awake. It was a soft sound, a sound I had heard often in the night, and I got up quietly and padded out into the living room. The fir tree's lights twinkled gently, and in their soft light I saw my mother huddled on the couch, her face in her hands. She was weeping as she had wept many times, alone and in the dark. I stood silently for a moment and watched her, and then my heart couldn't stand it anymore. I went to her and put my arms around her, and from that moment I have never ceased to love her.

Editor's Note:
For this story, Kris Welland won a Guideposts Youth
Writing Contest scholarship.

THE HARD WAY

For every hill I've had to climb,
For every stone that bruised my feet,
For all the blood and sweat and grime,
For blinding storms and burning heat,
My heart sings but a grateful song—
These were the things that made me
strong!

ANONYMOUS

When I Dared to Share Myself

by Paul Tournier

A world-renowned doctor discovers the strength of being merely human.

Because I have written a lot about the need to become "persons" one to another, people have assumed that I am one of those warm, open souls to whom personal relationships come easily. Nothing could be farther from the actual case.

A look at the early, character-molding events of my life provides some explanation of this inability on my part. My father died when I was three months old. He had been pastor of St. Peter's in Geneva, Switzerland—that huge gray landmark where Calvin preached—and sometimes I got the impression that the man who succeeded my father was trying to be a substitute parent to me. He would invite me into his study where he would inquire in his window-rattling voice, "Well, Paul! How are you getting on, son?" I truly yearned to tell him, but neither one of us had the least idea how to communicate such things to each other.

My mother also died when I was very young, and I reached my teens without having formed a real relationship with one person.

When I was 12 years old, I happened into a church that was not St. Peter's. There I heard a passionately evangelical sermon very unlike the staid services I was accustomed to. At the close the minister issued an altar call. Being me, of course, I could not walk forward in front of so many people, but secretly inside my own heart, I gave my life to Jesus.

Immediately I had the most wonderful sensation of being called out of this world—where I had not felt too comfortable anyway—into a place apart. And the astonishing result was that from the safety of my place apart, I became a leader. Throughout my teen years and on into medical school I organized and headed various student Christian groups. The speeches I gave were masterpieces of research, with quotes from a dozen philosophers and theologians. The more abstract it all was, the more I felt I was honoring God. And yet all the while my private self remained as aloof from others as before.

It was not until I had been graduated from medical school and started practice that the first formless doubts about all this began to arise. I was a general practitioner in those days and I saw the things that every family doctor sees: the bright child failing in school, the family torn apart by alcoholism, the lonely and bitter old people.

One night a week I had a respite from these problems when I met for prayer and study with a group of Christian doctors. They were glorious evenings, set apart from workaday worries as I believed religion should be. Why then should the faces from my consulting room keep distracting me? The more I tried to concentrate on theological arguments, the more my mind wandered back to real people with real problems.

I was 34 years old when I heard of a new Christian group holding meetings in Geneva, a group which was attracting world-famous doctors, psychologists, mathematicians. I remember the excitement with which I approached my first meeting with them in a stately old home on *Rue* Calvin. What a feast of learned and intellectual exchange this would be!

Imagine my bewilderment when the first half hour of this assemblage of brilliant minds was passed in total silence! A *listening* silence, they explained, but all I could hear was the ticking of the clock which told me that precious time was slipping by.

At last a distinguished scientist began to speak. He told some inconsequential story of having omitted a detail on his tax return. More silence. Then a world-renowned theologian reported having written a letter to a sister, asking forgiveness for some long-ago offense. A psychiatrist related how he had overcome dislike of a certain patient. And so it went, as I listened in growing disbelief:

tiny trivial personal matters—no great issues even raised, let alone resolved.

Along with the disbelief, I was aware of anger at these people for baring their souls in this way. I remember saying grandly at the close of the evening, "I came seeking bread, and you have given me a stone."

I was, however, a good deal more impressed than I would admit, even to myself. Doubtless the anger stemmed from the fact that these people had been talking about real things, and I knew it.

The next morning, half-grudgingly, in the privacy of my own room, I tried out this business of listening to God. And in the silence I began to realize that I knew nothing about His thoughts in mine. Oh, I could weave erudite speeches about Him in my head, but as for opening my *self* to Him, I knew no more how to achieve that with God than I did with people.

And so I went back to my new friends to learn. And as I gradually began to achieve the first true sharing in my life, I began to discover that religion is not a separate compartment, distinct from our everyday concerns, but that when we let it, it can permeate and transfigure them all. Hardest of all for an individual like me, I began to learn that we draw closest to God not when we step apart, but when we draw closest to each other.

One of the first directives that came to me as I learned to cultivate that listening silence was that I was to visit the minister to whose altar call I had responded at age 12. I fought the idea all the way to his house. What would the man think of a perfect stranger bursting in on his privacy with some personal reminiscence?

What I found when I got there—what only God had seen—was an ill and discouraged man whose life in this low mood seemed to him quite wasted. He was absolutely dumbfounded to learn that his sermons had changed lives and been remembered through the years; it was as though I had given him some priceless gift. Not long afterward I read in the paper of his death.

Through this and dozens of similar experiences, I gradually learned the power that can come through sharing—go against the grain though it might. And as I dared to share myself in my Christian relationships, I realized that this was what was required in my consulting room as well. I must no longer look on my patient as a case, but a person; I must concern myself not just with his symptoms but with his family, his job, his whole complex of past experiences, his hopes and fears for the future.

Most terrifying of all for the withdrawn and private person I remained by instinct, I also would have to become a person to my patient. No longer *monsieur le docteur* in white coat and stethoscope, but a fellow human being facing life problems like his own.

In time the change of thinking led me into psychiatry—where the act of sharing can have startling results. One time God directed me to share with a patient something that to me seemed so trivial—indeed faintly embarrassing—that only years of learning to trust Him made me do it. This particular man had been coming to see me for weeks without ever getting down to what was really bothering him. One morning he asked me, "How do you use the quiet time you speak of in your books?"

Suspecting that he was not really interested but just seeking to avoid some subject that frightened him, I said, "Let's not talk about it. Let's try it."

We closed our eyes, and I prayed earnestly that he might have a real experience with God. How faith-building it would be if He would give us both some inspiring message!

But instead of inspiration all I seemed able to think about was the bills that were due this month. *I've got to sit down tonight,* I thought, *and go over the household accounts with my wife.* This would never do! I should have been setting an example of prayer, not fretting over money!

Then came the unmistakable directive: Confess to this man what you've been thinking about.

Well, I wrestled as I always do, but I finally got it out.

He looked startled. "That is my problem!" he cried. "I must lie to my wife about money every day because I have a secret life. How did you know?"

With the truth at last out in the open, we were able to face his problems together. But it might not have happened if I had tried to hide behind the facade of "spiritual" mentor. If, in fact, I had declined to share my very fallible self.

For I have found that it is not when we are most lofty minded but when we are most human that we come closest to God. It is a truth He must reteach me every day.

Tribute to a Tree

Last night a slight north wind that seemed no more than a gentle puff took the apple tree down. It's lying prone and wilted now, still heavily laden with its last mellow fruit.

For weeks we have known its days were numbered. Its gnarled trunk was infested with a decay that would not be controlled: and yet, again this April, it delighted every passerby with the profusion of its delicate pink-white blooms, followed by apples that soon grew to the "picking stage."

Over the years its spreading branches have been a veritable haven for the small boys and girls of the family, who along with their elders feasted many mornings on apple jelly for breakfast and apple pie for dinner.

Yes, we shall miss our apple tree with a deep and abiding poignancy; and yet, we are grateful indeed for the lessons that its life has taught us—the uncomplaining bearing of one's daily load, the quiet courage of doing one's duty even under physical stress, the necessity for giving to the world all of the beauty and goodness that are ours to share.

FRANCES LOUISE MEDLIN

try an experiment. "Tonight," I said, "if a spoon drops on
the floor, I want you to pick it up, run hot water over it
and put it back on the table."

The Power of Changed Behavior

by William R. Parker

---

*A leading psychologist offers five practical
steps toward healing a wounded spirit.*

When I first started practice as a psychologist 25 years
ago, I belonged to the school of thought which said that
our behavior was an outgrowth of the way we felt. A person misbehaved, let's say, because as a child he had felt
unwanted. To change this behavior, you must first heal
these feelings.

Over the years I found this line of thinking only par-
tially helpful. It tended to work only if you had lots of
time to spend with the patient. More serious, many people
gave up therapy because they ran out of time or money,
or they became discouraged. It was clear to me that something new would have to be tried.

Then one day about ten years ago a woman came to
me seeking help. The most glaring symptom of Margaret's
trouble was a compulsion to sterilize things. Dinner dishes
were first washed, then plunged into disinfectant. If a fork
dropped on the floor, it had to be boiled. Margaret was
making herself and others miserable. Traditional therapy
was not helping.

I began to wonder if this weren't the time to try
something new. Suppose Margaret's behavior itself was
something she hid behind, something that kept her from
looking realistically at what hurt? Instead of facing the
wound inside, was she putting up a smoke screen of behavior so bizarre that all of her attention focused there?

I explained this to Margaret and suggested that we

128

try an experiment. "Tonight," I said, "if a spoon drops on the floor, I want you to pick it up, run hot water over it and put it back on the table."

Horrified, Magraret insisted she would suffer terribly.

"But, Margaret, you *are* suffering already. Try it just for tonight. You can't control your feelings, but you can control what you *do*. I'm not saying 'get hold of yourself,' I only want you to direct your muscles to do one manageable thing. Will you do this for me?"

Well, the next afternoon Margaret came back shaken but radiant. It had not been easy. But when a guest tracked street dirt over her rug, she had simply brushed it off. She had not sent the rug to the cleaner.

It was just the beginning. But by getting the focus off sick *behavior* we were able to see the real problem: Margaret's dread of her own "impure" desires, a dread she had hidden for years. As she faced herself at last, Margaret revolutionized her life. Within six months her compulsion ebbed away, and it did not pop up again in another form.

That and similar experiences marked a change in the direction of my work. Interestingly, other therapists were coming to the same conclusions. Various names were given to the new approach; the one I prefer is Behavior Therapy.

Our emphasis was not new. In fact, it is as old as the Bible. I made a study of Jesus's ministry to see what He did when He met people in need. He concentrated first on symptoms themselves. And He usually did this by calling for pinpoint *behavior* changes.

"Sell your possessions. . . ."

"When you give a feast, invite the poor, the maimed, the blind. . . . "

"Do not sit down in a place of honor. . . ."

He did not ask the woman taken in adultery how she felt; He told her to go and sin no more. He did not say to Zacchaeus, "Let's try to understand why you are cheating."

In the past fcw years, I have spent an increasing amount of time trying to find ways in which the layman can apply some of the Behavior Therapy principles to his own life. The techniques are relatively simple. And they are as safe as the Biblical principles upon which they are in fact founded.

There are five steps to take—steps which can be employed by as few as two people working together, or by as many as 12. It is to this group that you can report your successes and failures. Here, then, are five steps which can help you heal a wound in your spirit.

Step One. Each person in your group should adopt an attitude of noncondemnation. This sets the tone. Your guide is Jesus Himself: "Neither do I condemn you," He told the woman taken in adultery. Note that we are not doing away with judgment, but we are applying value judgment, not moral judgment. We don't ask ourselves, "Is this good or bad;" rather, we ask, "In this situation, is this constructive or destructive?"

Step Two. Be specific about behavior you are going to change. Avoid wistful over-all "self-improvement." Instead localize the particular point at which behavior is messing up your life. With Margaret it was compulsive cleanliness. With another it might be harmful gambling, or inappropriate sex.

Step three. Set a short-term behavior-change goal for yourself. Alcoholics Anonymous, which is applied Behavior Therapy, knows the power of the short-term goal. A too distant goal lacks power. In AA the goal is to stop drinking for just 24 hours at a time. I once had a patient who was cold and rigid toward everyone. When we got to this third step, he committed himself to a simple, realizable goal. For a week he would kiss his wife good-bye as he left for work, and each day in a different way he would tell her, "I love you." It was a tiny start, but my friend eventually became a warm outgoing man.

One point should be made here. Step Three almost always involves suffering. When we drop behavior patterns we have long used as defense mechanisms, we are forcing ourselves to face the very hurts we have been trying to avoid. Anxiety results for a while.

Step Four. Now we are ready to look at the wound you have been trying to avoid by inappropriate behavior. What and who has hurt you? Note that this step comes late in the progression. Only after you are well launched on corrected behavior are you free to begin looking at these wounds.

But even this step can be quite simple. We human beings have but two basic needs: We must have healthy give-and-take love relationships; and we must feel that we are worthwhile. Where these needs are not met, suffering follows. It is when we try to avoid this suffering *outside the realm of reality* that we are acting inappropriately.

Step Five. The final step, then, is to shift your behavior *into the realm of reality.* One of my patients was trying to destroy himself by reckless driving. He was always challenging trucks to a fight on the highway. Just before he came to see me, Dwight tangled with a huge tractor-trailer and barely escaped alive. After we talked, he realized he had to stop this behavior, which he did by driving *exactly* according to the law at all times. Without the dangerous behavior to dissipate in, Dwight's anxiety became more and more focused. At last he begin to recall episodes of terror and shame during a childhood with an alcoholic father. The little boy Dwight could not, and the adolescent Dwight would not, risk a showdown with his father. The fury went inward and eventually expressed itself by attacking vehicles bigger than his own—symbolic of his father.

When Dwight realized this, he made a trip home. He told his father how he'd always been afraid to come into that house. "Your drinking really hurt me, and I must face you with that," he said. "I guess I've . . . hated you. But that's destructive too, so I have come to ask your forgiveness for that hatred, and for the cowardice that kept me from leveling with you." Ultimately a real healing took place between them.

Behavior Therapy is not a way to bypass the hurts in our deep selves. Quite the contrary. It helps us to see them clearly and quickly. For often our behavior conceals what is really the matter; when that behavior is altered by an act of the will, we can see the deeper wounds of the spirit which Christ yearns to reach with His healing.

But my God shall supply all your needs according to his riches in glory by Christ Jesus.

PHILIPPIANS 4:19

To Love the Unlovable
by Marilyn J. Norquist

To accept Eleanor she needed God's help.

The woman across the table from me had brownish hair which was matted with dirt; her clothes were mussed and stained. She was fat and her large clumsy hands were yellowed with tobacco. Hunched over the table, she ate noisily, talking ceaselessly to her unresponsive neighbor.

I looked at my plate. "Dear God, please keep the food in my stomach! Help me to see Your child in this unpleasant creature." I glanced up, hoping that somehow she would be transformed. She was not.

It had all begun when I asked God for work during my final year of graduate school. "Please," I had prayed, "I want to be helpful and I want to grow. I will work wherever You send me."

The position which opened was the managership of Halfway House, a boarding house for 18 recovering mental patients, which helped them to shift from hospital to community life. The opportunity had sounded good. Now, facing these women across the table I wasn't so sure.

The woman was looking at me so I said, "My name is Marilyn."

"I'm Eleanor," she responded, her mouth full. "You going to be the new manager?"

"I haven't decided yet," I said.

"Well, I sure wouldn't take the job," Eleanor declared. "We're awfully messed up, as you can prob'ly see, and not all of them are as brilliant as me."

Suddenly, I did see—Eleanor observed her surroundings; she worried about herself; she was conceited. All

---

NOTE: Names other than the author's have been changed.

132

qualities just like my own! Eleanor was a person! A silent, "Thank You, God" made supper edible. If God could so alter my first impression, He surely would continue to help. With dampened idealism, but new hope in Him, I began work.

Work and struggle were synonymous at Halfway House. Crises came and passed—Joanne ran away. Ned tried unsuccessfully to kill himself, Laura was somehow getting hold of drugs. The emotional drain was incessant, and Eleanor was especially trying. She had been right: She was indeed both "messed up" and intelligent. I liked her sense of humor. But her capacity for gathering dirt on her body and clothes was astounding—and she shared a washroom with me! Furthermore, she whined more often than she spoke, and always about her own troubles.

Still, I liked her. Her aggressive gait, her wisecracks, her arrogance and impulsive eagerness were somehow attractive.

About the third month at Halfway House things seemed to go wrong. Smiling took too much effort. Sharp words were always poised and ready on my tongue. My bones felt brittle, my nerves strung taut. What was the matter with me?

Eleanor was the focus of my growing inner conflict. "Lord, give me patience with her," I prayed as I always did when I became aware of my anger at her.

But how perfunctory it sounded! How lifeless and automatic much of my praying had become! With a shock I realized that these one-sentence cries for help ("Lord, make me kind," "Lord, keep me cheerful") had, in the clamor of demands upon me, taken the place of daily time apart with God. So I spent most of a weekend reestablishing real communion, talking over with Him in detail each of my difficult charges.

And each time Eleanor's name occurred, the most extraordinary thought came along with it: *Tell her you're angry!* "I couldn't do that, Lord! She might fall apart!" I knew how shaky the emotional equilibrium of these people was. My job was to give them acceptance, approval, love—wasn't it?

But so strongly did the thought persist that the following week I talked it over with the supervising psychiatrist. To my surprise, Dr. Martin was all for this showing of my real feelings to Eleanor, while warning me against

abandoning her emotionally. "But anger is not abandonment, Marilyn. Anger is a normal part of the real world in
which Eleanor must now live. Hiding your true feelings
can be the real abandonment."

The following Saturday, the two of us were alone.
With an inward prayer, I began:

"Eleanor, I'm becoming more and more angry with
you and you should know it. You whine at me unendingly
about your troubles. You use *my* washcloth and *my* towel
and leave them filthy. You refuse my friendship except in
terms of your own illness. I'm tired of it." By now, the
pent-up heat in my emotions was raising my voice. "If you
want to be my friend, you'll have to become interested in
something outside yourself."

"Won't you ever listen to me again?" she whined.

"Don't whine. It annoys me." Surprisingly, she
grinned and I couldn't help grinning back. "Of course, I'll
listen to you, but no daily sob stories!"

Over the next few days I was aware of Eleanor
watching me.

And it soon became clear that by being truthful, I
had committed myself to a new honesty in our relationship. No more ducking through a door when I heard her
coming. Honesty meant increased involvement. Was I gen-
uinely willing to let God's love come daily through me to
Eleanor—with all that this meant of personal exposure? I
prayed most urgently to be made willing.

One evening Eleanor asked me to play Parcheesi with
her. I sat down across the board from her. Soon Eleanor
began to whine.

"Oh, Marilyn, the most terrible thing—"

"Eleanor. Be still!" I said, reminding her of our
agreement. Her clumsy hand went to her mouth and she
giggled, embarrassed at her lapse. But then she did not
know what to say. There was an uncomfortable silence.

Finally, Eleanor spoke. "Marilyn, what did you do
yesterday?"

I stared at her, blinking with the newness of it. For
the first time since I had known her, she had reached outside her own jumbled emotions to the world around her.
As I answered her question, I found that without "trying,"
I had seized the large, tobacco-stained hand, and was
squeezing it.

The following weeks demonstrated that her simple

question had been a breakthrough. Eleanor had glimpsed the meaning of mutuality. Before my eyes old patterns began to change. Her interest in others expanded until she even helped another resident hunt for an apartment. She had occasional relapses but the corner to health had been turned.

Eleanor's breakthrough was a turning point for me as well. It was the moment when I realized that love is made up of many emotions—not just smiles and sweetness—and that we have our best example in the unsentimental, all-demanding love of God.

Ask and it shall be given you; seek, and ye shall find; knock and it shall be opened unto you. For everyone that asketh receiveth; and he that seeketh findeth; and to him that knocketh it shall be opened.

LUKE 11:9, 10

were that joyful, and we thought it was a dream when
somebody saw the snow and told Sis and the kids that
Bob got hold of me and shook the snow off his down and
told me

When I Needed Watching
by Mike Douglas

---

*A TV celebrity tells the intimate story of the
big brother who taught him how to live.*

Some boys grow up resenting an outstanding older
brother. That isn't the way it was in my family. My older
brother Bob was a star in everything he did and he was
my hero. He was my special champion and protector. He
still is, though that takes some explaining.

There were three of us: Bob, who was five years
older than I; my sister, Helen, two years older; and I was
the baby. We were all scrappy, healthy Irish kids growing
up on Chicago's west side during the Depression years,
though having no money didn't seem to have much meaning for us then. My father, who worked for the Canadian
Pacific railroad, was away from home a lot, which may be
one reason why early in the game Bob assigned himself
the job of watching over me. I never thought I needed
watching over, but *he* did, and there were times when I
was not sorry.

Bob was big and tough and kind and had a wild temper that could work for my advantage or disadvantage.
One of my favorite memories is of the day an English
bulldog charged at me as I was walking home from school
one afternoon. The dog's owner was sitting on his porch
and I went up and told him he ought to keep his dog on a
chain. The man got so mad that he slapped me. Boy, was
it exciting when I told Bob! He did some charging of his
own. I can still see him standing on the man's porch, that
terrible temper steaming, the man peering out but refusing, wisely, to come out.

There was another time though when some pals and I

136

were out joy-riding and we dropped into a honky-tonk. Somebody saw me there and told Bob and the next day Bob got hold of me and shook me and sat me down and told me exactly why I was not to go into such places. And if I ever went again, and he found out, he said, the shaking I had just survived would seem like child's play. The point was well taken.

Bob was directly responsible for the greatest thrill of my childhood. He was 17 and a basketball star playing with the Question Marks—that's what they called their team—and I was 12 and sitting admiringly on the sidelines during a big tournament. The Question Marks came down to the final minute with a decisive lead when suddenly Bob left the game. He came over to me and shoved me onto the floor in his place. The ball was passed to me, I took aim and scored! Most kids just dream about things like that but Bob had the touch for making them come true.

We were a sports-mad family and athletics were the biggest thing in my life until the afternoon mom took me downtown to a vaudeville show at the Chicago Theater. That's the day the show business bug bit. By the time I was in my middle teens I was picking up money on local singing dates. Before I was out of my teens I was working on an Oklahoma City radio station, WKY, and it was there in Oklahoma that I met Genevieve and we were married. She was a sophomore in high school and I was 19.

The years passed, and though I was only intermittently in Chicago and our life-styles were utterly different, Bob and I remained close. He married, fathered five children, worked as a tile salesman. He came to be an effective and popular member of his community, as I knew he would, and a strong member of his church. I used to look with respect at the way he conducted his life.

On the other hand, like so many other show business people, I spent the years struggling, hoping, angling for the big break. Eventually it came, but not until I was 35. From 19 to 35 is a lot of years waiting; that's a lot of food cooked in hotel rooms and a lot of pants pressed by Gen in cramped backstages. It's a lot of maneuvering to keep our twin daughters and Gen and me together as a real family, the way Bob's family was. When the break came, Gen and I had almost decided to give up show business—we had an infant daughter then, Kelly—and

Gen and I were both taking real-estate courses in a California night school.

Once *The Mike Douglas Show* came into being, however, I worked like a demon. I drove myself like a machine to make sure that what I had achieved for us did not get away. One reason I didn't trust the meaning of the TV ratings and the publicity and the money coming in was that I seemed to be living on a treadmill. It was exhausting. Life as a TV star wasn't that rich, it wasn't that enjoyable or satisfying, even though in subtle, sneaky ways I began to be pleased by the power that TV success can bring. Yet I was to learn that it can be a deceptive power. I was to learn it suddenly.

In September, 1969, we faced one of those crises that most people think happen only to other families. Bob went into MacNeal Memorial Hospital in Berwyn, Illinois, for an operation. The doctors suspected cancer. Mother and dad were on their way to his bedside when their car was struck by a mail truck. Mother was hurt seriously in the crash and an ambulance rushed her to the very same hospital where Bob lay gravely ill.

And so it was that there in MacNeal Memorial Hospital, mother on one floor, Bob on another, the family gathered. It became a time for whispering, for deep thoughts and long silences, a time for looking hard at life and at oneself with fresh curiosity.

The word came for certain that mother would be all right. She was in traction and she was in pain, but she was safe. Bob was not. He was dying.

I paced the halls of the hospital in confusion. I was fully aware that this was my chance, at last, to reverse the roles: This was my opportunity to be Bob's champion and protector. But I was powerless.

During that night I came to terms with some of the subtleties of success and power that I had been grappling with. The very day I had left the show in Philadelphia to fly to Chicago, I honestly had the feeling that I could do something. I could get the best surgeons. I had money and connections. . . .

But I was powerless.

I can't remember how I happened to do it or what made me do it, but somewhere in the middle of those long walks down antiseptic corridors, I began to pray. I knew little about prayer. It had never been like me to rush to churches and light candles; church had always been Bob's department. He had always tried to make me think more seriously about religion, but I had resisted.

My prayer, fumbling thing that it was, was not a begging one. Somehow I just wanted to feel, wanted Bob to feel, the presence of God. I wanted God to know—as if He needed my help—what a fine man Bob was and how grateful I was for him. Strangely, in the midst of approaching death, mine was a prayer of gratitude.

Bob died. As soon as I could after his funeral, I got back to Philadelphia and went to work again. But it wasn't the same kind of work. From the outset I discovered that I had changed. Seeing Bob's wife and kids and feeling once again the texture of his life made me look more closely at my own life. I saw the treadmill clearly this time, and in perspective, and I set out to slow the machinery. I found more time, surprisingly lots of time, to be alone with Gen and with the only daughter still at home, our little Kelly.

In learning to accept and enjoy the blessings at hand, no day since then has passed that I have not said my prayers and thanked God for my family and my health and my job. I am new to it and I do not understand the great ramifications of its power, but today I would not live without prayer.

I find it intriguing that ever since I stopped running so hard, ever since Bob died, people have stopped me repeatedly to say, "Mike, you never looked better." I think I have always seemed fairly calm on camera, but it has only been in the past two years that I have discovered that I *am* calm. Even my golf game has changed. For the better. Are all of these things coincidence? I doubt it.

Before every show there's always a moment or two when I go off into a corner to say a very private prayer. Sometimes then I remember it was Bob, really, who taught me to pray. When this thought comes to me, I smile. You see, he's watching over his little brother still.

The Perfect Victim
by Louis Evans, Jr. *

What happens when a man becomes too ambitious?

When I look back to those early years in Bel Air, I can see now how the migraines began. I had the challenge of starting a new church in this fast-growing suburb of Los Angeles on the rugged, brush-covered Santa Monica Mountains. My wife, Colleen, and I were fresh from five years of student life in seminary and postgraduate work in Scotland. Three small children—"buzz bombs" we called them—filled our house with hilarity and noise.

Days and nights were solidly booked with meetings or calls on prospective members. I suppose I was "programmed" for this kind of hyperactivity, coming as I did from a busy and excitement-filled home with a very effective minister as a father. Dr. Louis Evans, Sr. was once named one of the ten great preachers in America and at one time had the largest Presbyterian congregation in the world.

At any rate, the word that ran constantly through my mind was "production, production, production." Prayer breakfasts, committee luncheons, evening meetings—even days off were planned with more than could be realistically accomplished. I had more home projects going than a hound has fleas; I didn't really work at them—just scratched. It took me eight months to clear the driveway of six truckloads of broken concrete for a terrace walk. Colleen would often say, "Honey, why don't you take one

---

Louis Evans, Jr. is the pastor of the National Presbyterian Church, Washington, D.C.

thing and finish it?" To me, that was an irritating limitation of ambition.

It was not long until an old childhood infirmity set in—hay fever. It came on with a vengeance, but some new experimental shots seemed to help. Then the headaches began, pounding, nauseating migraines. These were followed by massive muscular spasms in my back that often required injections for relief.

One evening, a warm and elderly psychologist whom I had recently baptized (the kind of man whose very shadow was therapeutic), sidled up to me and said, "Louis, how *are* you?" I didn't care for the implication that outwardly things might appear successful but inwardly there were some tensions.

But as the weeks wore on and the symptoms became more intense, his question haunted me. In a reflective moment I took my clinical psychology book from the shelf and read about migraine headaches. "Characteristic of perfectionist, allergic persons, with excessive ambition." There I was in black and white—everything set down except what to do about it.

Then came that Sunday night when people were gathering at our home for evening worship—our church sanctuary was not yet built. I was in no shape to do anything because of one of the increasingly frequent migraines. I was nauseated; any movement, noise or light sent throbs of excruciating pain through my temples. It hurt so bad my eyes watered. I knew I could not fulfill my responsibility that night.

As I lay on the bed, a kind of dialogue began, a dialogue with the Lord, that was to change my life.

"You are very tired, aren't you, Louie?" (Finally some sympathy!)

"Oh, yes, Lord, You know how tired I am."

"Then either you are doing more than I have told you to do, or you are not taking My strength for what I have told you to do."

I didn't like that so much. And then the dialogue took an even stranger twist with the words forming in my mind:

"Why don't you praise Me?"

Praise! With pulses hitting like battering rams and every sound magnified a hundred times? "The situation just doesn't call for it," I replied.

"Do you believe that I can heal you?"

Of course I did. I had seen wonderful healings in our congregation. "Yes," feebly.

"Then why don't you get up and go about your work—and praise Me?"

I suppose it was the years of having learned to trust God; I found myself swinging my legs over the side of the bed and standing up with head pounding. I clicked on the light—horrible! I took a step—worse yet! But as I walked into the living room I felt a strange mixture of faith and experimentation. I chose the three loudest praise hymns in the book with which to start the service. The singing hurt—but something began to happen. As I honestly threw myself into the attitude of praise it seemed to me that the headache receded a bit. By the time the three hymns were over, so was the worst of the pain.

I finished the service and counseled some folks afterward for an hour and a half. A sense of exhilaration swept me—something *had* happened!

A couple of weeks later, I was dashing down the Hollywood Freeway, late for an appointment in downtown Los Angeles. I had had no time for lunch; I had unrealistically scheduled my day and was hopelessly behind. I was angry with traffic and with Colleen—she had asked me to do a few normal things at home. I felt the back of my neck begin to tighten—a headache was on the way. Oh no!

"Praise Me."

That again! I didn't feel like praise. Who would, with the stupid drivers on this road and a wife who timed her requests just when—

"Praise Me."

Once again the battle was on, the struggle inside my own will to shift from a negative, angry mood to thoughts of God and His glory. It was clear I could not indulge both at once.

For the second time in my life I began to praise God from the prison of a foul attitude. I thought of the beauty of my wife, her goodness, our oneness in work and fun, and I praised God for these things. Sure, she needs me at times; it would be awful if she didn't. Praise God for being needed. I guess those in the cars around me thought it a bit strange to see a man in a traffic jam singing at the top of his lungs—but then a lot of strange things happen in California.

I praised God for the shimmer of the sun on the lush ivy covering the slopes of the freeway. I praised Him for the sun itself.

No headache developed that day, and the ones since then I can count on the fingers of one hand. "Praise ye the Lord," the psalmist tells us, "for it is good to sing praises unto our God." *(Psalm 147:1)* When I was very young I used to wonder why God was so eager to have us praise Him all the time—didn't it seem a lot like merely human vanity? Now I know that like all His commandments, He requires it not for His good—but for ours. Praise God!

He Starts My Day Right

On my way to the office in the morning I often see him, a slight, wiry figure, cane in hand, fish pole over his shoulder, bait bucket bobbing from one elbow. He waits patiently for the long line of morning traffic to pass, scoots across the street, and makes off down the hill to the fishing dock at the foot of Main Street. There is always an eager, expectant smile on his lined face.

I don't know his name, or where he lives, but he's my friend. He starts my day off right. Somehow, red figures on the monthly operating statement—a drop in the stock market—news of threats made by unfriendly nations— don't seem so grim. Life is still good and with a hopeful heart we can face the challenge.

You see, the cane my friend carries is a white one. He can't see the autumn flame of red and gold that borders the lake; his eyes can't follow the gull's graceful arc against the vivid blue October sky. But he can smile with faith and hope—and go on fishing.

DOROTHEA ERICKSON

Let Someone Else Be
the Judge

by Jean Stapleton

The star of TV's All in the Family *tells how
she overcame her own Archie Bunker problem.*

When I was growing up in New York City, there was one
thing that I disliked with a passion and that was calf's
liver. My father, an outdoor advertising salesman, loved
calf's liver, and so my mother saw to it that it often appeared on our dinner table. I would rather go hungry—
and often did—than eat it.

The interesting thing is, I never even tasted calf's
liver until I was an adult. I simply disliked the looks of it
and knew, beyond all argument, that I would despise it.
Today I adore calf's liver.

It wouldn't surprise me at all if Archie Bunker hated
calf's liver. If you know Archie from *All in the Family*,
the television comedy series in which I play his dingbat
wife Edith, then you know what I mean. Archie's a bigot,
a super bigot, and we get most of our laughs from his out-
rageous points of view, his rantings against other races and
almost anything new or strange to him. If it's true that the
bravest man who ever lived was the first fellow to eat an
oyster, you have some idea of where Archie would rate for
courage—and how he'd camouflage his fear with a loud
tirade.

By being extreme, and therefore ridiculous and funny
to us, Archie has made millions of people aware of the ab-
surdity of prejudice. I have confessed to my own absurd
dealings with liver because it points up something that I
was aware of long before Archie came along: Prejudice is

144

an assortment of deceptively small personal judgments—deceptive because of their great cost in our daily lives.

No one will ever know, for example, how many families have been racked by stubborn arguments over long hair. Is prejudice involved? Partly, I think, for at its root, prejudice is a matter of judging—of *pre*judging really. We have preconceived opinions that long hair means something about a boy (and therefore about ourselves, since he is our offspring) that may or may not be true.

For myself, I have seen how my own niggling, personal prejudgments often have robbed me of pleasure and peace of mind. There have been times when I have tried to cure these prejudices, and I recall one time in particular when a conscious effort at healing resulted in a crucial breakthrough in my acting career. It happened a long time ago, in the late '40s, after a good many bleak years trying to crack Broadway. Those had been years of constant work, of having a job as a secretary in the shipping department of a railroad company by day; typing manuscripts late at night in exchange for drama lessons; begging time off for summer stock; making precious little progress.

Then one day the chance came to read for one of the Equity Library Theatre productions—shows that our actors' union puts on to give us a chance to work and to be seen. The play was *The Corn Is Green,* and there were two roles in it I felt confident I could handle. One of them was so miniscule, however, that though I knew it meant a job, there was some doubt as to whether it would be a good showcase. Naturally the tiny part was the one I was offered.

I thought about it awhile. "I'll do it," I said finally, irritated that they hadn't given me the larger part.

Ten days before the opening, the actress rehearsing Mrs. Watty fell on some ice and broke her leg. I assumed that I would inherit her role and I wasn't surprised when Ted Post, the director, came to talk to me. He asked me if I would fill in until he could get somebody else.

"*Somebody else!* But what about me?" I protested. "I can play her."

"No," he said, "you're too young."

I didn't believe him. He just was not being fair. He had it in for me.

I got angry. I got so mad that I couldn't even sit at

the same dinner table with my parents that evening. I had to get up and go to my room and try to collect myself. I had to do something about this injustice or I would burst.

In those days—as well as today—I had my own way of finding help when needed. I took out my Bible. After all, I had been going to Sunday school classes in our church since the age of two. And I also took out my concordance, that remarkable compilation of all the key words in the Bible and where they appear. I flipped through the pages of the concordance to the "J's," mumbling theatrically all the while, "Justice is what I need, justice. . . ." But before I could find "justice" my eyes fell on "judge."

"For the Lord is our *j*. Isa. 33:22."

I picked up the Bible and sped to Isaiah. I had explored Scripture in this fashion many times before, sometimes losing myself for hours in random adventure. Now, Chapter 33 . . . there it was: "For the Lord is our judge, the Lord is our lawgiver, the Lord is our king; he will save us."

What was this I was asking about justice? Had I jumped to some emotional conclusion about Ted? Should I pray about this and try leaving justice to the Lord?

I prayed; I relinquished the matter to the Highest Power. My anger disappeared. I was back in the dining room for dessert.

The next day at rehearsal I was no longer driven by an ambition to play Mrs. Watty. I read the part as well as I could and enjoyed doing it, and when Ted found somebody he thought was the right age, I retired with genuine grace.

But that wasn't the end of the story. Three nights later the producer called me at home and said that the new Mrs. Watty hadn't worked out. If Ted should ask me, would I be willing to take over? Very quietly I told her I'd be delighted, and the next day Ted said, "You're too young for it, Jean, but the part's yours."

It's still not the end of the story. Just as all show business sagas ought to unfold, an important agent saw me at the opening. She wasn't fooled by my makeup. She saw me as a young woman, just right, she decided, for the role of the niece in a touring company of *Harvey*. Out of that came my first good job in the theater; I was on my way.

Today, when I get emotional about something I think

somebody has done to me, I try to think back to that experience before I start hurling a few hasty, bigoted thunderbolts. I recall that I never succeeded in changing the director's opinion of me; nor did I change my own opinion. I had simply left the judging to the Lawgiver, and He decided for both of us.

Recently a friend sent me a sermon entitled, "God and Archie Bunker," written by the pastor of the Brentwood Presbyterian Church here in California. In that sermon, Dr. Spencer Marsh, Jr., who enjoys Archie, nonetheless noted his self-centeredness, his cliché-ridden bravado, his imprisonment inside his own narrow opinions. He quoted some dialogue from the show, from the night Archie was talking to "our" son-in-law saying "I've been making my way in the world for a long time, sonny boy, and one thing I know—a man better watch out for number one. It's the survival of the fittest."

Doctor Marsh said that Archie is out of position, that Archie is a mixed-up person "because the number one slot which he claims, is reserved for God." He sees Archie as the elder brother in Christ's prodigal son parable, the one who stands outside the house grumbling about his rights while the welcome-home party is going on inside. The walls that separate him from the party are self-imposed, self-righteous, judgmental ones.

That's one reason I worry about prejudice. It could keep me from the party. It could keep me from enjoying the company of other people and what they have to offer just as surely as it almost kept me from the simple pleasure of calf's liver or, more important, the big break of my career.

And poor Archie, like a lot of us, never listens, never learns. He'll never know that by blindly pushing away the oyster, he might be missing its pearl.

Be still and know that I am God.

PSALM 46:10

How Albert Schweitzer Changed My Life

by Hugh O'Brian

---

*The famed doctor of Lambarene is recalled by
an actor who learned from him a great truth.*

Somewhere across the wide river lay my answer. Anxiously I settled in the dugout as paddles stabbed the Ogowe, each surge drawing me closer to Albert Schweitzer.

Meeting this great humanitarian had become vital to me. For in spite of the success of my acting career, I still searched for that indefinable something.

A magazine article by Schweitzer on world peace had spurred me to ask to visit him. The cable invitation came just as I was finishing a tour for my television role as Wyatt Earp. Grabbing a suitcase, I flew to Africa hop-skipping into the interior by small planes until the battered DC 3 landed on the red dirt strip of Lambarene.

I was met by one of the volunteer doctors serving with Schweitzer, and soon we were heading four miles up the river to the famed hospital.

The jungle loomed higher, and a small knot of people came down to the bank. As we approached, I could make out the white walrus mustache under the white pith helmet. Our dugout ground gravel, and the gentleman stepped forward.

Cobalt-blue eyes looked into my soul. *"Willkommen!"* he said. His compassionate grip helped me realize that this was not a dream. For this meeting had long been a dream ever since I, when a pre-law student, had first read his writings.

Night sinks quickly in Gabon. And with the doctors

and nurses we filed into the dining hall for the evening meal. Before dinner, we listened to the doctor softly play Bach on the zinc-lined harmonium. And then he read from a great Bible, his hands caressing its pages. I can't understand German, but when he gave his interpretation, somehow the message touched me, and I sensed the deep love that flowed here in Lambarene.

Like the time when natives brought a badly injured man to the hospital. An attendant snapped, "This man is a thief. He was here before and stole drugs and sold them. He has no claim on us again." The doctor's eyes flashed. "What would Jesus have answered when someone came to Him in pain? Waste no time; get him to the operating room!"

The next morning I discovered that everyone works at Lambarene. As Schweitzer once said, "Usefulness is the test of value." So I worked in the kitchen, built baby cribs, exercised old plumbing skills, and lugged supplies to the leper colony.

Goats and chickens wandered about the hospital. In the laboratory, I saw an attendant pursue a bee, gently capture it under a glass beaker and release the intruder at the window. It was the doctor's orders. Schweitzer would fight even to save a tree from being cut down, reflecting the philosophy which summed up his spirit—reverence for life.

In explaining, he said, "To live in true humanity means to be inspired by the idea of reverence for all of life. If he finds a creature that needs help (and everyone finds such creatures), he will help. This will bring him happiness because he realizes that it is in his power to act for good. Though freeing a bee may seem insignificant, it should remind man of the mystery of life and the respect he should have for *each* life. It should make him a more human, thinking being."

Love and respect for *all* of life. How far ahead of his time he was! For doesn't his philosophy relate to what our ecologists stress today—that when any form of life is damaged, be it scarlet tanager or tidal marsh, all of nature and mankind suffers?

My opportunity to further explore Schweitzer's thinking came after evening meals when an interpreter and I joined him in his study.

As he expressed his ideas, he'd close his eyes, slowly

forming his words, a gnarled forefinger tapping the air for emphasis. I hung on each syllable, the interpreter's voice just an echo. Again and again he stressed that though we all must work to live, our real purpose in life is to show compassion in helping others. Only then, he emphasized, do we become true human beings.

After our talks, I would lie awake on my cot and think on them. Many reaffirmed old personal beliefs. Others sparked new insight. But my special enlightenment was the full realization of Schweitzer's statement: "So many people come here to Lambarene," he said, "and others wish to but are unable to come. But everyone is capable of his own Lambarene."

This was my truth. I couldn't change the world but I could do something on my own in my own way to put something *back* into life. I thought of the people already hard at work doing just this, from women ringing doorbells collecting for cystic-fibrosis research to men giving time and themselves to underprivileged kids. Instead of only taking from life, they were *giving* to it. Each was demonstrating his reverence for life. Each was creating his own Lambarene.

The mist was rising from the river the morning Doctor Schweitzer and I walked down to the landing to say good-bye. I got into the dugout, and the paddlers picked up a slow chant as we glided away.

I waved at the man in the white pith helmet under which shined those marvelous twinkling eyes. As he receded into the mist, I turned and faced my challenge. Would I just admire a memory, or would I try to create my own Lambarene?

Editor's Note:
After returning from Lambarene, Hugh O'Brian expressed his reverence for life by establishing a foundation to help young men develop leadership. Each year 60 outstanding high school sophomores from every state and ten foreign countries qualify for a special week-long workshop, on subjects ranging from national politics to science.

"I have found my Lambarene," says O'Brian. "And through it I've learned that the true gift is not so much in money but in time given in service to others. It is a gift that anyone can give, the priceless gift."

How to Get Rid of
Resentment

by James A. Stringham, M.D.

---

*A Guideposts Spiritual Workshop for people
who harbor ill will.*

Alice was a middle-aged woman suffering from asthma, skin eruptions and other illnesses severe enough to put her in the hospital about four times a year.

Stella, a young schoolteacher, lived in a succession of boarding houses because landladies "don't like me." She had no friends among her fellow teachers and believed that her second-graders misbehaved in order to persecute her.

Jim had a history of ulcers and business failures.

Those three patients—and dozens of others who have passed through my consulting room—so dissimilar on the surface, revealed in the course of therapy the identical underlying problem. Each had a resentment he had not dismissed.

Resentment comes from two Latin words meaning "to feel again." When we resent, we allow the negative emotions we feel at the time of a hurt—a disappointment, a betrayal—to recur long after the event is over, flooding our systems with their poisons over and over again. Because of its effect on the human mind and body, it does not matter how "justified" the resentment is. In my 27 years as a practicing psychiatrist—and in the 15 years before that when I was a medical doctor—I have come to regard resentment as a cancer of the personality that is as deadly as any physical growth.

I have also seen this cancer healed, through a combined effort of self-understanding and faith in God. The three patients mentioned above have another thing in common. Each got rid of his resentment. They did not rise above it or force it back into its subconscious hiding place, but they were able to deal with it according to the principles outlined here.

Here are techniques that have helped many to find freedom from resentment.

First ask yourself: Am I a resenter? Do I long to get even with anyone? Does the thought of certain past events make me boil inside?

Remember that resentment can be disguised, even from ourselves, especially when it is directed at someone for whom we also feel—or should feel—love. It is safer to get angry at a demanding boss than at the father who expected too much of us. Ask God to help you locate the roots of your feelings.

If you discover more than one resentment, and most of us do, choose one for the purpose of this workshop. Later you can apply these same steps to the others.

1. Make a list of all the good qualities and strong points about the person you resent. Make it a subject of prayer and spend three or four days at it. Carry a notebook with you so that you can jot things down as they occur to you. Even though your feelings have blinded you to the positive factors, surely some exist, and God will show them to you if you ask Him.

2. Try to figure out why the person acted in the way you resent. Often this understanding is the first step toward forgiveness. Ask yourself if he or she was deliberately doing those things to hurt you? If you had been in his shoes, would you have acted differently under the circumstances?

3. Use your imagination. Write a brief biography of this person, using information you already have or can glean from letters, conversations, photographs. Try to reconstruct what his childhood was like.

4. Make a list of all the things you dislike about the person. (Do this only after finishing numbers 1 and 2.) Getting angry feelings on paper brings them outside ourselves where we can look at them (much as talking with a psychiatrist can do). Instead of a turmoil of emotions, we are now dealing with a limited number of specific observations.

5. Memorize Romans 2:1. "Therefore you have no excuse, O man, whoever you are, when you judge another; for in passing judgment upon him you condemn yourself, because you, the judge, are doing the very same things." Reread the list you have just completed, asking God to show you yourself in these things.

6. Make a commitment somewhat like this: "God, I know that my reactions to this person are wrong and sinful because they violate Your law of love. What he has done is not the point. I want to change my feelings but I can't do it on my own steam. I turn myself and all these reactions over to You. Teach me to forgive as You forgive." It helps to make a list of any ways in which you feel you have been wronged and place it in God's keeping.

7. Pray the Lord's Prayer, inserting the name of the person you resent: "*John*'s Father, Who are in heaven, hallowed be Thy name. Thy kingdom come, Thy will be done, in *John*'s life as it is in Heaven. Give *John* this day his daily bread and forgive *John* his trespasses as I forgive those who trespass against me. Lead *John* not into temptation but deliver *John* from evil. For Thine is the kingdom and the power and the glory forever. Amen."

Pray this way slowly and thoughtfully morning, noon and night, thinking of the implication of each phrase. Keep at it faithfully until you know you have forgiven John.

Do not attempt to go to John himself with the good news of your forgiveness until you are absolutely certain that every trace of resentment is purged from your heart. I recall a patient who was struggling to forgive her husband for an infidelity early in their marriage. One day she triumphantly brought me a carbon copy of a letter she had, unfortunately, already delivered to him. "Dear Alex," the note began. "I hereby forgive you for . . ." Then followed a lengthy list of Alex's shortcomings and mistakes. It was obvious, even to her as she reread it, that the letter expressed not so much forgiveness as a desire to hurt.

8. Ask the Holy Spirit to fill you with love for this person. If you do this persistently and sincerely, you will find the hot, angry, vengeful thoughts gradually replaced by concern and caring—and your world will be a far better place.

5.

Hope for People
Who Face
a Crisis

For he shall give his angels charge over thee,
to keep thee in all thy ways.

PSALM 91:11

White Nightmare
by Harold Graydon Simonds

He didn't give up, but used his God-given gifts.

"My dad's missing," I told the Michigan State Police. "He's somewhere north on a camping trip and he's eight days overdue." The officer said that he'd do what he could. Day after day I called, and day after day the report was the same: No sign of him. Sixteen days later we learned the truth. Here is the incredible story.

On November 19, Herman Simonds, 65 years old, sat in the cab of his truck and tugged at his chin in indecision.

"Well, old man," he said to himself, "where now?"

Retired after 40 years as a New York Central engineer, he could wander at leisure. He didn't really hunt anymore; he went forth simply to enjoy nature. He headed for Scott's, a tiny lumber camp now in ruins. Then, passing it, he drove his camper truck deep into the murky swampland of the wild, lonely reaches of Michigan's Upper Peninsula. At a little island clearing, he camped and crawled into his bunk.

It snowed during the night, a deep snow, 12 inches of it, and the morning presented a fantastically lovely sight. Every limb, every briar, every reed, was outlined in pristine white.

"God's good work," he mused to himself, stretching. "A man can build that great bridge at Mackinac, but he can't lay out a blanket of snow—or create that tree under it." These sights, these musings were the joys of camping trips.

"But pretty as it is, old man," he said to himself humorously, "you'd better get out of here!"

157

He started driving, but snow kept tumbling from branches, covering the windshield. He got out and shook the trees ahead with his cane, which he had been using since arthritis in his legs had hobbled him. Then he started up again, only to slide into a deep hole, his wheels spinning futilely in the snow.

Hours were consumed in adjusting chains and working the truck free. Then it was snowing again.

Any progress at all required clearing the path first because he had to be sure of the trail or risk slipping helplessly into the swamp.

Suddenly darkness came, and he realized that after an entire day's labor he had traveled only a few yards. Then for the first time he realized his predicament: He was snowbound, 450 miles from home and nobody knew where he was.

Over his stove that night, he faced the situation squarely. "Don't panic, old man! God gives you eyes so you can enjoy His beautiful world. But He also gives you brains and muscles. So stop fretting and figure your way out of this."

Certain decisions had to be made at the outset. He couldn't return by Scott's, as he had come. That road was too hilly and tricky. No, he would have to push through on the grading until it reached another highway many miles distant. He could not hike out; he had to stay with his truck—his legs could not be lifted through that much snow.

The next day there was more snow, but he rose and methodically started digging. He developed a scheme whereby he would shovel the left wheel track for four hours and then switch over and work his way back on the right for another four. Then he'd move his truck up as far as he had shoveled.

Night came again and again. Some days he worked six hours, some days eight. Now the drifts were knee-high in places, now up to his hip. When the cold became too intense, and his glasses fogged and his hands seemed numb, he warmed himself by his stove. He rationed his food. Gasoline was a problem, too. It might not last. He prayed his back would.

Then suddenly one morning, far in the distance he heard new sounds. "Loggers!" He recognized the noise of their chain saws. First he shouted, then blew his horn, but gradually realized they could not hear him. There was still nothing to do but dig.

The 15th day came and went, and the 16th and 17th. The routine had long since palled from monotony. He was up with the first light, chopping wood, melting snow for water, eating a little, then back to shoveling.

At the end of the third week, a plane flew overhead. He hurried to the box where he kept his flares, but before he could light one, the plane had disappeared.

Now 25 days had passed. A high knoll of the trail suggested to him the chance for a good view of the terrain ahead, and he set about shoveling a footpath to its summit. Once on top, he gazed out below him—and there, there was salvation.

It was a clearing made by the loggers. They were not working now, but they had left behind a truck and, more important, a cleared road.

Now he worked frantically, exultantly. Night closed in, forestalling victory, but Sunday, December 16, dawned brighter than any Sunday he had ever known. About noon, he reached the loggers' road. He wanted to shout, to tell somebody. So he said his thanks to the One Who had sustained him.

His face was heavily bearded, his body 25 pounds lighter from a scanty diet and hoisting 14 miles of snow. Yet he had not panicked, because he used the brains and muscles that God had given him. Now, back on an open road, he praised God for those taken-for-granted gifts as never before.

LET GO AND LET GOD

When you're troubled and worried and sick at heart
And your plans are upset and your world falls apart,
Remember God's ready and waiting to share
The burden you find much too heavy to bear—
So with faith, let go and let God lead the way
Into a brighter and less troubled day.

HELEN STEINER RICE

They're Still Alive!

by Dayle Gruetzmacher

---

*The skidding truck hit their station wagon,
spun it, then fell right on top of the car.*

It happened only 15 minutes away from home. I was sitting in the front seat between my husband, Amber, who was driving, and our daughter, Sue, whom we were taking back to college in Chicago.

From our home in Hobart, Indiana, it is only a 50-mile trip. But the road was slick from rain that morning last September, and there was a lot of traffic on the Kingery Expressway. When Amber pulled to a halt behind a line of vehicles, he looked in the rear-view mirror to see the most terrifying sight in all his years of driving—a huge trailer-truck hurtling toward our car sideways and out of control.

A second later the skidding giant hit our fully loaded station wagon, spun it in a half-circle and then fell with crushing force right on top of us. Crunching metal. Shattering glass. Silence.

With amazement I realized that I was alive and not noticeably in pain. The back of the seat had collapsed, and I was lying flat with the crushed roof of the car a few inches above my face. My knees were wedged against my chest so tightly that I could only manage small gasps for air. With difficulty I could turn my head and I could move my hands, but nothing else.

What about the others? Amber spoke to me. He was lying on his side, and his trapped legs were oddly twisted. One was bent beneath him, and the other stuck out through the windshield of the car and was jammed against the body of the capsized truck. Wedged into a tiny space, he was finding it hard to breathe.

Sue, on the other side of me, was flat on her back, but she could move a little and was apparently unhurt.

None of us was in severe pain, nothing seemed broken, no one was apparently bleeding. But we could do nothing to help ourselves. Worse still, none of us knew how long our battered car could hold off the smothering weight of the truck which covered and surrounded us. At that moment, we simply acknowledged the fact that we were still alive; and we praised God.

I decided to keep my eyes shut. I knew that I had done so consciously to keep calm, that if I let my imagination dwell on what could happen to us, I could kill myself.

I could imagine Sue, with three years of nurse's training, thinking the same thoughts: remembering that what kills a lot of people in accidents is simply shock. Yet as we started to discuss our frightening situation we realized that we weren't panicky. We all had a tremendous sense that God was with us there in the wrecked car which might yet become our coffin, and that He was keeping us calm.

Of course we were afraid. Closing my eyes couldn't shut out the heavy odor of diesel fuel from the capsized truck. The smell of gasoline from our own gas tank mingled with it. A single spark could ignite it all.

Suddenly, amazingly, a friendly face appeared at the shattered window beside Sue. A motorist who had been passing when the crash occurred had squeezed beneath that precariously balanced trailer, risking his life to see if there could be anyone alive whom somehow he could help.

He stayed with us, promising us that help was coming, assuring us that we were in good shape, until the police arrived to relieve him. He was the first of God's shock absorbers.

The ones who followed had names—Mike, Red, Bob, Chuck and John. They were policemen and state troopers and they took turns at the car window, talking, reassuring, holding the hand of Sue, who was nearest the door. We learned that outside on the highway firemen and rescue workers had summoned a crane which would try to lift the truck to release us.

I opened my eyes for a moment and got the impression that the car roof was nearer my face than it had been only minutes before. Surely I was imagining things! I must not panic. I wondered if the others had noticed anything.

"I'm all right," Sue assured me, "but I can't move as much as I could. The space seems to be getting smaller."

Amber was beginning to gasp for breath. The roof above him had advanced several inches, and very little air was getting through to him. We knew then, for sure, that the truck was still moving down on us. Inch by inch, it was pressuring the final resistance out of the crumpled metal of our car. Into how small a space could three people be squeezed and still live?

I had a new surge of reassurance. *God knows how much we can take,* I thought, *and He will hold the space to that.*

A fireman appeared with a tube connected to an oxygen supply, and we managed to maneuver it to a place near Amber's mouth. He began to breathe more easily, and after a while he and Sue started to sing Gospel choruses. (Amber has a terrible singing voice, but it sounded very sweet to me at that moment.)

The young state trooper named Mike was with us when the moment came which all of us knew was our moment of greatest peril. He was ordered out from under the trailer—and no one took his place. Alone for the first time in two and a half hours, we knew that outside a crane must be trying to lift the trailer. If the crane could not hold the giant load, it would fall back again, probably to crush us finally.

Inside the car the three of us held hands. I remember saying, "Don't be afraid. God hasn't brought us through this awful experience to let us die now. It's going to be all right." We began to pray again.

Suddenly the pressure on us seemed to ease. Within a few seconds men were around the car, wedging timbers under the trailer so that it could not fall back on us. Minutes later the car door was being cut open, and we were eased out of our three-hour prison. Sue was lifted out first, and I followed her into the same ambulance. God had given us so much assurance that we were able to joke with the ambulance men as they put their arms around us. When Amber was brought out, he sat up on the stretcher and waved his hat to the crowd!

Police told us that everyone who saw the accident was sure that we had all died in the wreckage. St. Margaret's Hospital, which had been told to prepare for three casualties "dead on arrival," was amazed to find three happy people without a broken bone or sign of shock.

It was God Who took the shock.

Very often in our church I have heard the words from Isaiah: *Thou wilt keep him in perfect peace, whose mind is stayed on Thee.* (Isaiah 26:3) God was very real to us even before that terrible morning—if He hadn't been, I don't believe we could have lasted through such an ordeal. What I know clearly now is what it means to have His peace.

A Fragile Moment of Hope

Three months ago I bought a potted gardenia. I put the plant in the living room. I watered and fertilized it. The leaves remained a healthy green, and buds grew.

For six weeks I lovingly tended that plant, but not one bud developed to maturity. I put it out on the back step, making a mental note not to waste any more money on gardenia plants.

The days that followed were heavy with cares: illness in the family, financial problems, a misunderstanding. The more I tried to struggle with them, the worse they seemed to become. I grew tired. The next step was self-pity. Where was the abundant life Jesus Christ had promised me?

One morning in utter dejection, I gathered up a mountain of dirty laundry and started out the back door to the laundry room. Then I saw it—one lovely, white gardenia. Its face looked to the sun, filling the air with perfume.

All the things I had done for that gardenia inside the house hadn't been enough to make it blossom—it needed the life-giving presence of the sun. I stopped, pondering that. In that moment, as I stood admiring the lovely gardenia, thriving in the sun, I realized I, too, needed a power coming into my life. The things I could do for myself were helpful, even necessary. But I could not know the full life till I turned to face God, depending ultimately on Him.

DOROTHY MEFFORD

The Voice in the Storm
by Van Varner

The dramatic story of one man's risk to protect his neighbors.

The moment Ray Butterfield first heard about the storm it gave him an odd feeling. He couldn't explain why he felt odd—it was just a twinge of uneasiness.

That was Friday afternoon, August 15, 1969. As general manager of WLOX-TV in Biloxi, Ray was only too aware of how vulnerable the coast along the Gulf of Mexico was to the tropical storms that growled up out of the Caribbean every year. Ray himself could never forget the '47 hurricane. He had been a young radio announcer then, and WLOX had been preparing to go on the air for the first time when the storm came and destroyed the whole operation.

Now, 22 years later, Ray was in charge of the TV station that occupied the entire ground floor of the Hotel Buena Vista's west wing. Now this intricate installation, including the costly new color equipment, was Ray's multimillion-dollar responsibility.

Ray was back at his office in Biloxi early that night. The first thing he did was check the storm that the National Hurricane Center had baptized "Camille." At that moment, his chief engineer, Thomas B. Majure, dropped by. Ray and Majure, whom everyone knew as "Blue," were close friends.

"What's the matter?" Blue asked.

Ray shrugged. "This little storm . . ." He didn't finish; he couldn't put his feeling into words. But then, with Blue, words were not always necessary. Blue, though a practical engineer, had come to respect Ray's inner perceptions.

164

Blue leaned over and took a look at the weather report. "Well," he said, playing it as cool as always, "she's not in the Gulf."

It was another way of saying, "Relax; don't borrow trouble." If the storm did enter the Gulf, there would be trouble enough. Out would come WLOX's four-phase Hurricane Plan.

Early Saturday Camille moved into the Gulf. Ray called in his department heads and quietly put the station on a 24-hour alert: Phase Four. "Just routine, of course," he cautioned. There would be a general tightening of studio coordination; a scheduling of emergency duties. There would be storm advisories on the air every half hour.

"Keep in mind that we want only to inform, not to alarm the public," Ray said.

During the day Camille continued in the same northwesterly direction. The weather bureau predicted she would shift north.

Ray and Blue began to track the storm themselves. Its progress was steady and direct. "She can't turn," they kept telling each other. "She's coming straight to us."

Saturday afternoon Ray began Phase Three. All employees were alerted and given specific jobs. As small-craft warnings were out along the coast, the station checked with the Civil Defense and Red Cross, coordinated information about shelters and evacuation procedures, set up a central location in the studio for the filing and cross-filing of messages. Every 15 minutes a storm warning was broadcast.

Sunday morning Camille still had not changed direction. Outside it was oppressively hot and muggy. The wind had a sting to it. Ray and Blue went out together and toured the immediate coastal area. People were boarding up their houses and taping windows; stores were open selling candles and emergency supplies. And yet, Ray felt, it was a time of unreality. Some people they talked to were making arrangements for "hurricane parties."

"I'm worried," Ray said. "They're not taking this seriously."

Ray looked out into the Gulf. Was he silly to persist in thinking that Camille would hit them hard? How bad would she be? The time was dwindling.

Ray had to make up his mind. If he went all out with

warnings, he might be able to frighten the public into proper precautions. But if Camille did not strike—if she did not strike hard—he would have frightened people unnecessarily; crying "wolf" was a risky and dangerous thing to do to a trusting community.

And he himself would look like a fool. This, he admitted to himself, was what he feared most.

The two men drove back to the studio in silence. For Ray it was a time of agonizing appraisal, a prayerful time. The voice within him persisted.

At the station Ray gathered his people together again. "This thing is going to hit us and hit hard," he said. "I want to scare people into believing it!"

Phase Two went into effect. Arrangements were made to bring families of WLOX personnel into the hotel. Sandbags were stacked five-feet-high both inside and outside of the big exposed studio door on the Gulf side of the building. Camera heads were boomed to the highest position on their pedestals. The entire staff of 63 men and women were bustling as Ray himself went before his television audience.

"This is going to be one of the worst storms anywhere, ever. I beg you, if you are south of the railroad tracks, go north. If you are in a low-lying area, get out!"

Outside, the tide rose still higher, the winds came stronger, the atmospheric pressure dropped. "Even if you got through the Forty-seven hurricane safely, don't think you'll be safe in this one," Ray warned over and over.

And then he faced another decision. Should they move their equipment to higher floors? The station had gone deeply in debt to make color TV possible. Should everything be risked now?

Ray's answer was clear and firm. To move the equipment would mean shutting down. They could not do that and continue to warn the people.

Camille did not veer away. In the early evening, dead-on she howled into the Biloxi coast. At WLOX, they moved into Phase One. The staff screened and sorted messages as Ray repeated his last-minute warnings and gave out advice about roads still safe, shelters still available. Outside a monstrous tide surged through the huge motel on the beach, waters roared across the four lanes of Highway 90 and lapped at the hotel. Inside the Buena Vista some 800 people were herded into corridors.

At 9:30, WLOX's power went out. Ray grabbed the telephone and began broadcasting directly to the transmitter 30 miles inland. It was against federal regulations, but Ray did not hesitate. "This is not an emergency. It's a disaster!" The electricity went out. Now they worked with flashlights and candles. For more than 30 minutes they moved about in the darkness. Then even the telephone power went.

The time had come to get out. Ray and Blue were the last to leave. They dashed through the corridors and rooms checking for sure that everyone had gone. Inexplicably Blue was trying to lock a door when atmospheric pressure caused one wall of the studio to blow in, another to blow out. The water and wind poured in just as the two men went upstairs to the hotel lobby.

Ray and Blue sat through the night in a corridor crowded with friends and strangers. Hour in, hour out, the hotel creaked and shuddered as waves washed and foamed at its foundations and debris came slamming against its walls. Matresses were piled up at windows to shield against exploding glass; some interior doors could not be opened because of the air pressure, others suddenly popped open.

Ray was awake through the night, feeling strange that his fears had come true. He knew that WLOX had been destroyed—he could hear and feel the destruction beneath him. But now a new feeling came to him as he sat in the darkness, listening, praying, pondering. It was a feeling of desperate need. The work of the past several days was only the beginning. Storm warnings were one thing; helping the living after the storm was bigger still.

When daylight came and Camille had done her worst and swept on, Ray got up and went out onto a coast where 144 people had died, over 5000 homes had been obliterated, where boats and trees and highways were all a tragic jumble.

And that very morning Ray and his staff went back

Life with Christ is an endless hope, without Him a hopeless end.

—ANONYMOUS

to work. A day and a half later, WLOX, with borrowed equipment, was on the air again. And the "Paul Revere of the Gulf Coast," as Ray Butterfield came to be called, was back at the mike again.

Editor's Note:
For his courage and selflessness in the face of grave personal danger, Guideposts presented its 1970 Good Samaritan Award to Mr. Butterfield.

BECAUSE

*Because somebody cared today
I knew God's love was strong;
I found new hope to bear my cross
And courage for my song.
My neighbor's heart conveyed the love
I needed for my pain;
And happily I felt the faith
To dream and smile again.*

INEZ FRANCK

Miracle at Duval Mine

by Larry Imhoff

By all that's logical, I should have died that day in No. 19 ore shute.

Standing up here on the catwalk at the Duval copper mine, waiting for the swing shift to end at midnight, I can still feel that long moment of terror two years ago as my body hurtled 50 feet down into the steel mouth of No. 19 ore chute. I was on the swing shift because it gave me the chance to work at a second job in the daytime if I wanted to.

Two years ago I certainly wanted to. Sue and I were up to our ears in installment payments on the car, furniture, the nice house we bought when we moved to Arizona from Chicago. My second job at the gas station was helping us to catch up with the bills—and keeping us out of each other's hair.

Our marriage was having a rough time. We didn't seem to have much in common any longer. Sue was always wanting me to take the kids everywhere, even if it was only to the store; but she didn't want to do the things I liked doing—camping and fishing. Our debts were weighing us down. We were talking about a divorce.

Earlier in our marriage we might have talked it over with the pastor, but we weren't going to church any longer. The faith in God that first became real for me at the Youth for Christ meetings at my school in Ohio seemed to have dwindled away.

My job at the mine wasn't very exciting, but it was better than bickering at home. I sat in a comfortable chair next to the control panel, making sure that the great rocks of copper ore kept moving into the chutes and along the

169

belts to a crusher, where they were ground to pebbles. On this particular evening the foreman wanted me to check the piles of ore above No. 3 belt to see if there was enough to keep the crusher working all night. That was something the control panel couldn't tell me.

As I walked up the sloping ramp to the catwalk, 50 feet above No. 3 conveyor belt, I saw Karl Kettelhut and Wes Evans bringing up an oxygen cylinder. I was surprised to see Karl. Our jobs were different and we worked different hours. Most evenings there's no one around during my entire shift. Then I remembered that the maintenance staff was working late, doing some welding on No. 1 belt.

Up on the catwalk I had to lean over the railing to look along the line of chutes beneath me which fed the ore down onto No. 3 belt. Grabbing the handrail for support, I leaned over. Inexplicably the railing turned in my hand. I pitched off the catwalk, went cartwheeling through space, landed hard—then blackness.

It was at that moment that Karl saw my body hit, then disappear behind the mounds of ore. He had only one thought as he dropped the oxygen cylinder and started toward me. In less than two minutes a combination of belts and chutes would feed my helpless body into the crusher; and he—Karl Kettelhut—was the only person around with even a chance of preventing it from happening.

Karl raced to the bottom of the ramp, scrambled across the jagged rock piles to see if I was still lying in the mouth of the ore chute. A ten-foot sheer drop down a rock face confronted him and he went down it like a mountain goat. As he landed, Wes Evans, who had run up the catwalk, shouted down that my body had already disappeared into the chute.

Karl checked for a second, figuring what would happen to me next. My body would be squeezing through a 14-inch space like a big mail slot, onto No. 3 belt, which was moving at nearly 400 feet a minute. Once I was on that belt, tons of ore would be fed on top of me as I sped toward No. 4 belt and the crusher. He must stop No. 3 belt.

He spun around and began bounding across the loose rocks along the outside of the conveyor tunnel, praying that he was keeping pace with the belt inside. Before he could reach the tunnel entrance he had to make a huge leap across a mud puddle. His foot sank deep into the mud but he wrenched it free, pulled the door open and shot down the slope into the tunnel.

The buttons controlling No. 3 belt were 12 feet above him on a railed platform. There were stairs farther on, but for a man full of superhuman energy there was a quicker way. As though he were running upstairs, his feet took him vertically up the slick metal guard-rails and onto the platform. One jab with his thumb killed No. 3 belt. As the belt rumbled to a halt, Karl heaved open the heavy metal inspection door to see if he had been in time.

There was no sign of me. His tremendous effort to stop the belt had been just too late. My body had tumbled through the drop-box and was somewhere on No. 4 belt, rushing toward the crusher. Karl knew he had less than 30 seconds left.

He looked below him at No. 4 belt. My hard hat suddenly appeared. As Karl watched, my body followed it. I was traveling on my back, feet foremost. A huge electromagnet hung 12 inches above the belt, its underside cluttered with jagged pieces of broken machinery sucked from the ore.

Karl leaped down and clawed his way toward me. My left arm was hanging loose over the side of the belt. Once, twice, Karl tried to grab it as he ran alongside, but the belt was moving too fast for him and the slope beneath his feet was too steep. Lungs aching and muscles straining, he grabbed for a handhold to pull him faster up the slope. His fingers found a cord lying below the moving belt, released it as too fragile, then seized it again desperately. It was the emergency stop cord. He hauled on it with all the strength left in him.

But let us, who are of the day, be sober, putting on the breastplate of faith and love; and for an helmet, the hope of salvation.

I THESS. 5:8

For a moment the belt sped on upward. Then it checked, slowed, whirred reluctantly to a halt. My body was just 12 seconds away from the crusher. Karl dragged himself level with me and stared at my sunken chest and battered face, pitted with stones and gashed by the junk on the magnet. He guessed I was dead, but in senseless anguish he yelled, "Start breathing!" My chest heaved, and the breath started to creep back into it. I began to spit blood. "Help," said my mouth faintly.

The next day, Karl went back to the place where he had seen me fall. He figured out then that he had run 700 feet in 45 seconds, over tumbling rock heaps, up and down break-neck slopes. Where he had leaped across the mud puddle his first footprint still showed in the mud—17 feet from his take-off point. He tried to rerun the course he had covered the night before. He couldn't come within minutes of the same time. It struck him forcibly that the night before he had been doing things of which normally he was physically incapable, at a time when normally he should not have been at the mine at all.

At the hospital the doctor was preparing my wife for the inevitability of my death. The nurse said she had never seen a face and head so lacerated. I had a compressed vertebra in my back, and two of my spinal discs had disintegrated. It later took the nurses two hours a day for two days to remove the stitches from my face and head. Yet today I can work again, and the only sign of my accident that you would notice is the scar on my forehead.

By all that's logical I ought to be dead, and I am alive. I have to believe that the good Lord used Karl to save my life that night at the mine, and I keep asking why. I can't give you any good answers, but I can tell you of one or two things that have happened since that night.

Sue and I haven't mentioned divorce, for one thing. When they told her I would die, she knew how much she needed me. And through my long recovery I've learned how much I need her. Today I get a kick just taking my kids to the store with me, and this summer we all went camping together. Sue bought me the camping gear last Christmas.

We've made some good friends since the accident. In the eight years since we moved to Kingman, Sue had never got to like the community. But when the accident happened, she made friends with the wives of several other men at the mine, and she's started doing volunteer work at Kingman Hospital. I've been getting ideas too. When I was in the hospital I thought about those Youth for Christ meetings at my school. I'd like to help get something like that started for the kids in this town. The closest friends we have made are Karl and Jerrine Kettelhut. We found, when we started going to church again, that they go there too.

None of us can quite figure out why I'm alive. But as I stand up here on the catwalk, seeing every day the place where I should have died, I'm beginning to understand what to live for.

Verily I say unto you, If ye have faith as a grain of mustard seed, ye shall say unto this mountain remove hence to yonder place; and it shall remove; and nothing shall be impossible unto you.

MATTHEW 17:20

When I Asked for Help
by Clint Walker

---

*This popular actor tells how his life was changed
by an accident that almost killed him.*

I was skiing last May 24, up at Mammoth Mountain, near
Bishop, California. I am pretty proficient at most sports,
from shark hunting to motorcycling, but skiing is one that
I have only recently tackled, which was why I was
measuring the steep run before me with such a wary eye.

Finally I shoved off down the slope, gathering speed
as I followed the contours of the twisting, irregular terrain.
I still don't know how it happened, but all at once I was
tumbling out of control, and then an abrupt, violent stop.

As I fell, one of my ski poles up-ended in the hard-
packed snow. The momentum and my weight as I fell on
it drove the pointed tip about five inches into my chest,
through the breastbone and into my heart. I rolled over in
the snow. The wind had been knocked out of me, and I
was in terrible pain.

About 400 feet below, my instructor was looking up
at me. I called as loud as I could, "I'm hurt bad—get
help!" Then I fell back.

I remember a sensation of rings of light radiating
from my body, as ripples radiate from a pebble tossed into
the water. At the same time I had a feeling of being pro-
pelled through space; and although the pain was still there,
I became less sensitive to it.

I suddenly knew that I was dying. With the
knowledge came a sense of sharpened awareness. I did not
think of a particular person or event; certainly my life
didn't flash before me. But I knew, with an overwhelming
conviction, that the Power that had given me life could
sustain it—against any odds.

174

My concept of time underwent a change as I lay there; my existence seemed no more than an instant in eternity, and with a clarity I had never known before, I saw life in a new perspective. Things which had seemed so important, simply were not. I had recently gone through a tranquillity that would not have been possible previously.

Although I felt I was slipping away from this earthly experience, I also felt a sense of going on. With it came a sadness that I had not done more with my life, and immediately I had a strong desire to stay, as though there were some unfinished business to take care of.

I said, "God, I'm really in trouble! I can't help myself. I'm not going to make it, unless You will see me through—and I *would* like to stay around for a while." With that, I seemed content to let go.

The next thing I remember is being taken down the hill on a sled-type stretcher used for rescue operations. I supposed I was literally jolted back to consciousness because of the roughness of the terrain. The pain was almost unbearable.

When the doctor examined me in Mammoth, he recognized the necessity of getting me to the hospital in Bishop, some 45 miles away, as quickly as possible.

All in all, close to three hours elapsed from the time I was injured until I went into surgery at Northern Inyo Hospital at Bishop, where the doctors performed open-heart surgery. By then, according to the medical records, I was cyanosed (blue from lack of oxygen) and there was no recordable pulse or blood pressure.

I was operated on, Monday, May 24, and left the hospital walking, eight days later. I spent three days at the UCLA Medical Center in Los Angeles and then went home. The end, you might say, of a remarkable experience.

But actually, it was merely the beginning.

News of the accident had been carried by the wire services, and I had been interviewed by television newsmen. In the course of the interviews I made a statement which was to change my life. I said that I had asked God for help on the mountain, and that I was satisfied that I would not be here now, if it were not for that prayer.

Then the letters began to pour in. Sacks of them arrived at the hospital, and were forwarded to me at home—from Australia, England, New Zealand, Canada, and all over the U.S.

I expected the usual get-well messages, and of course there were those, too. But the majority have one theme: "Thank you, Clint, for saying what you did. What a big outdoor guy like you will tell the world that he prayed for help, and got it, it strengthens my own faith."

"I'm not a member of any church," a Wyoming man wrote, "but what you said up there on the mountain did me more good than all the sermons in the world."

I have prayed at times in my life before, but it took this experience to help me put things in their proper perspective. I was always a loner; even as a kid, I was shy, an introvert. I really didn't know how to get along with people. And worry—I was the world's champion worrier!

But up there on the mountain, I found a new appreciation of life. I realize now that if we are going to accept God's help, we must accept it in His time and in His way. I have found that many of the problems I thought had to be solved at once, can wait. And very often, it is in that time of waiting that the Creator speaks most clearly to us.

The waiting is not always easy, but I understand more fully now the verse from Psalm 62 which has always been a favorite of mine: "My soul, wait thou only upon God; for my expectation is from Him." (Psalm 62:5)

Having made a few records, and sung in several pictures, I know the technical value of the little mark which indicates a pause, or rest, in music. But now it has taken on new meaning. John Ruskin made this point in a letter to his young niece, when he wrote: "There's no music in a 'rest,' Katie, that I know of, but there's the making of music in it. And people are always missing that part of the life melody."

I don't intend to miss it anymore!

A merry heart doeth good like a medicine.

PROVERBS: 17:22

The Wire Cage
by Claude L. Fly

A kidnap victim's story of heroic survival.

On August 7, 1970, five men strode into the laboratory where I was working as an American agricultural scientist in Montevideo, Uruguay. "I'm with the police," one of them said, flashing a badge. "Which one of you is Doctor Fly?"

"I am," I said.

He pocketed the badge and suddenly drew out a revolver. "Come with us!"

In the alley someone tore off my glasses and tied a piece of cloth over my eyes. Hands were stripping off my watch, going through my pockets. I felt rope wrapping around my wrists and ankles, then a scratchy cloth covering me from head to foot, like a sack. I was lifted off my feet and laid on a cold metal surface.

I heard an engine roar, and then the terrible bouncing began. Up and down, side to side I banged, my head striking the hard floor. I tried to raise myself, but hands held me down. Obviously this was the back of a truck; and from the squeal of tires, we were taking the twisting, pitted streets of Montevideo far too fast.

After a while, choking clouds of dust seeped through the sack. We were out of the city then, on an unpaved road. I do not know how long it was before I was carried into a building, where the sack was pulled off, the ropes cut from my feet and hands and the blindfold untied.

I stood blinking at a circle of masked faces. One of the figures stooped and lifted a trapdoor in the floor of the room. On order from behind I was let down three and a half feet to a crawl space under the house. The door thumped shut above me, and I was alone in that chill dark

177

place. I groped along a clammy wall until my hand touched metal. It was a small cot and on it was a blanket. I lay down and covered myself as well as I could, teeth chattering in the cold. Above, I heard the clatter of feet on the floor.

No doubt I was the victim of a kidnapping. But it had happened so fast my brain still refused to take it in. Two hours before, my wife Miriam and I had been sipping coffee in our Montevideo apartment, discussing what we'd have for dinner. And now—now I began to recall stories of Tupamaro terrorism in the newspapers. Kidnappings, murders. But—well, I just shook my head at the idea of myself as a political figure. In none of the 22 countries on all six continents where I had worked as a soils expert, had I had the least interest in local politics. Growing more food, that was my mission. Issues of right and left, class and race I left to those who understood such things.

Inside the dank little cellar, the air was raw and cold, for there in Uruguay, below the equator, it was winter. I'd had pneumonia a few months earlier and now I began coughing helplessly. A guard came and wrapped a thin blanket around me and left. The coughing continued through the night, and the next day I was moved upstairs. Then on the third night I was taken to a new prison—a wire cage.

It was four by six and a half feet, just big enough to permit a narrow cot and an 18-inch walkway. The floor was slick concrete. Heat was provided by a small, fanlike electric heater. Into that cage I was pushed, and the door was locked behind me.

I was totally shut off from daylight, and with no clock or radio or any other contact with the world outside, I soon lost track of time. I could never tell whether it was morning or evening, and so time went endlessly on and on, as if all the hours were part of one day.

There was a small gooseneck lamp to break the darkness, and I could see the passing of time in the rotation of my guards. The guards always wore small cloth sacks over their faces to mask their identity, and it gave me an eerie feeling, living this close to people without knowing them.

I soon discovered, of course, that they were members of the Tupamaro party, named for the Indian chieftain who had tried to drive the Spanish from South America two centuries earlier. I learned that these people were attempting to overthrow a government they considered oppressive, and that taking political hostages was one of their methods. They told me that the condition for my freedom was the release of 150 political prisoners held by the Uruguayan government.

As the days passed, the closeness of those wire walls all around me began to gnaw at my reason. I would catch myself on the brink of violent action. How could I keep my balance?

By work, I decided. By establishing a routine. I begged my guards for books in English. They brought me detective stories, biographies of Lincoln and Woodrow Wilson, histories of South America, also pen and paper. I mapped out a daily program of exercise, reading, writing and prayer.

One day one of the Tupamaro leaders—an English-speaking Uruguayan about 40 years old, agreed to bring me the book I most wanted: the New Testament.

In its pages I rediscovered the bulwark I needed. As I bore into the Bible, passages popped out at me, as if the Lord were speaking directly to me.

"Consider yourselves fortunate," I read from the first chapter of James, "when all kinds of trials come your way, for you know that when your faith succeeds in facing such trials, the result is the ability to endure. . . ."

And in Hebrews: "The Lord is my helper, I will not be afraid. What can man do to me?"

Through the pages of this little book, *Good News for Modern Man,* I was gaining strength and courage to face the ordeal—and possibly death—that still lay ahead.

Twice daily I'd take time to pray, asking that God's will be done and that my wife, my son John and daughter Rita be given the fortitude to withstand this tribulation. And I prayed for the forgiveness of my captors, asking that God bless them.

As my Christian concern grew, a change came over my kidnappers. At first the guards had accused me of being a spy. They read aloud from a soil manual I had written and made angry comments as they claimed it contained secret information that I had gathered for the CIA. They taunted me about Yankee imperialism, calling the U.S. racist and oppressive, bent on dominating South America.

They described to me conditions in Uruguay which they had dedicated their lives to changing: runaway inflation (300 percent in six years), poverty and hunger for the majority, power and property controlled by the few. They showed me books and other information on conditions in South America, and I repeatedly told them that I grieved over them as much as they, that these were precisely the reasons I and other North Americans had come to South America.

And gradually, almost reluctantly it seemed, they began to believe. To believe that I had come out of concern and not greed, to believe that my love and prayers for them were real. The masks never came off, but my guards and I started whiling away the long hours by playing checkers, dominoes, card games. Between us was developing a bond, a trust, simpatico.

One day they brought me a picture, cut from a newspaper, showing my daughter Rita, her husband Dennis and their two children. No! Three children! In Rita's arms was a tiny baby. I knew there must have been an article or something else that had been published with the photo and I pleaded with the guards to let me see it.

One of the guards finally read it to me, translating it into English. It was a letter from Rita to me. She had sent it to every newspaper in Uruguay. I wrote an answer which my guards promised to mail and for long afterward that word from home sang in my heart.

As time passed, however, the elation faded and I came to feel more and more frustrated inside the wire walls of my cage. It seemed an eternity since I had first been brought here. I renewed my prayers for the working out of God's will, for relief from my torment.

Then one day while pacing about fitfully, I suddenly felt as if a gigantic weight had been dropped on my chest. I clutched desperately at the wire of my cell. I opened my mouth for breath but none came. Pain stabbed my arms, my shoulders. The pressure was tightening like a vise.

I knew it must be a heart attack! I slipped down to my knees, then managed to pull myself over to my cot, yelling for the guards to help me. One guard came and helped me onto the cot; another went for a doctor.

For what seemed many days I lay on the little cot unable so much as to lift my head, cared for by doctors and nurses the rebels had summoned. They brought in oxygen tanks and cardiograph equipment and gave me frequent injections. Their records were as painstaking as any hospital's.

Then a tremendous noise startled me from my semi-coma. Brick dust flew about me, stinging my eyes and nose: They were pounding a hole in the basement wall. Hands lifted me onto a stretcher.

"Please!" I begged. "My papers! My book!" My voice was so weak the masked head had to bend closer to hear. As he laid the water-spotted notes beside me, he spoke close to my ear.

"I want you to know, Doctor Fly, that some of us believe in Christ, as you do."

Moments later a woman's hands slipped something around my neck. "Take this—for good luck," she whispered. Weakly I lifted it in my hand: It was a small gold cross. God was surely in that place; I have never felt His presence so strong.

A blindfold covered my eyes, and another jarring, endless ride began. At last the shaking stopped and the stretcher was lifted down. I heard the roar of the motor speeding away, footsteps running toward me. The blindfold was pulled away and for the first time in seven months I looked up into natural light—a million stars twinkling in the sky above—and the outline of a hospital aglow in the night.

The Tupamaros had freed me, had brought me here where I could receive hospital care.

Then the words of Second Corinthians, a passage I'd read again and again in my cage, came back:

". . . the supreme power belongs to God. . . . We are never without a friend and though badly hurt at times, we are not destroyed." (II Corinthians 4:7–9)

The "Sounion" Is Sinking

by J. Philip Griffin

The dramatic account of two people trapped when a cruise ship became a chamber of horrors.

We had looked forward to our trip to the Holy Land for six months, never dreaming it would take us into the most terrifying experience of our lives.

Esther and I were in our 70's. I had just retired from my job as a rural mail carrier and our plans were to sell our small farm to one of the grandchildren and move into a retirement home.

But we had always longed to visit the land where Jesus walked and when our pastor, Joe Timberlake, approached us about joining a tour group going to Israel, we decided it was now or never.

In February, 1973, we joined 250 others, most of whom were about our age, and flew to Cyprus, where we boarded the passenger ship *MTV Sounion*. Esther and I were assigned a tiny cabin on the second deck. It had a double-decked bunk which we didn't like, but we decided to make the best of it. After sailing on the sparkling Mediterranean to Tarsus, St. Paul's hometown, we docked in Beirut, Lebanon.

The fact that we were headed for Israel caused some of our group to wonder if the Palestinian terrorist group, Black September, might try to harm us. However, such thoughts were soon lost in the thrill of seeing places we had read about all our lives.

After a day of sightseeing in Beirut, Esther and I returned to the ship. We ate a quick supper and, because of Esther's bad heart condition, retired early to our cabin.

The ship was to leave the harbor at 1:30 A.M. and, like most of the passengers, we wanted to go to bed early so we could rise at dawn and see the sun coming up over the Holy Land at Haifa.

I was thankful our cabin was next to the dock because the lights of Beirut shone through the thick glass of the small, sealed porthole, giving our cabin a cozy feeling. I reached down, touched Esther's extended hand, breathed a quiet prayer of thankgiving for what tomorrow held, and drifted off to sleep.

Suddenly a tremendous explosion rocked the ship, jolting me awake. Whistles and horns began shrieking. Dazed, I clambered down and turned on the light. Esther had been thrown to the floor. I helped her to her feet.

The lights flickered and went out, leaving us in blackness. The whistles and horns stopped, and we felt the ship begin to lean away from the dock.

"We've been bombed!" Esther screamed. "We're sinking!"

I grabbed the stateroom door. But the twisting effect of the explosion had jammed it tight.

We were trapped. Cold water was surging under the door and rising rapidly in the stateroom.

I released the door and grappled in the dark for Esther. The lights of the city no longer reflected in our cabin as the ship continued to list farther away from the dock.

The water was up to our knees. Esther was almost hysterical; I held her close to calm her.

The floor continued to tilt and the only sound in the inky blackness was the surge of rising water and Esther's sobs. The water chilled our hips, then our waists.

"We're going to die, aren't we?" Esther sobbed.

I knew we were in danger of capsizing. I also knew there could be another explosion as the water reached the ship's boilers. Yet I dared not frighten Esther with such thoughts. Instead, I remembered the scripture I had read the day before we left. "When thou passest through the waters, I will be with thee; and through the rivers, they shall not overflow thee." (Isaiah 43:2)

I began to pray out loud thanking God for His deliverance. Even though Esther had been a Christian for many years, I had never heard her pray audibly. But the moment I finished, she took up the prayer of thanksgiving also. It was strange, but even in that black moment on the sinking ship, sharing our prayers and praising God together drew us closer than we had ever been.

The luminous dial of my watch said 10:45. We had been trapped almost half an hour. There was no sound of help from the outside.

Unable to stand on the slanting floor, we had to brace ourselves against the wall. The cold, oily water rose to my chest and then to my chin. Now I had to lift Esther to keep her head above it.

And then the water seemed to stop rising. But for how long?

Now another danger. Esther and I were rapidly using up the oxygen in the small amount of air left to us. I struggled to the porthole and tried to break the glass. It was much too thick and I knew the steel hull was at least an inch thick. I slipped back down, urging Esther to relax while I held her head out of the water. I knew that with her bad heart she could not stand much more.

We prayed. Waited. Listened. And prayed some more.

Our clothes, the expensive camera we bought for the trip, the souvenirs were all lost somewhere under the dark water. But they were of no concern. Only our lives counted now. An hour and a half passed. We could not last much longer.

Unbeknownst to Esther and me, everyone else on the ship had safely escaped. The ship's captain was making plans to get the passengers into hotels.

Only our pastor, Joe Timberlake, objected. He had been frantically searching for us and was now convinced we were trapped in our cabin. The captain, irritated over Joe's demands to check the ship, suggested that we had not returned to it.

In desperation Joe angrily charged the captain with being more concerned with his own comfort than two lost elderly passengers. Finally the captain agreed to send a crew member onto the hull to shine a light into our porthole to prove the stateroom was empty.

Down in our water-filled cabin I knew our oxygen was almost gone. We prayed aloud once more. When we slipped below the surface, I wanted our last words to be ones of praise to our Heavenly Father.

Suddenly a light flashed through the porthole. Releasing Esther to cling to that top bunk, I crawled to it and waved my hand under the glass. "Air," I croaked, knowing I could not be heard.

But God heard, and moments later a sledgehammer smashed the porthole. Slivers of glass showered us, but with them came a wonderful rush of fresh air.

Moments later Joe Timberlake's anxious face appeared in the tiny window. The captain had asked him to comfort us while they prepared an acetylene torch to cut through the ship.

Then another face appeared. It was Russell Bennett, a young garage mechanic. He had come on the tour because he felt God had a special purpose for his life. He had seen that the Lebanese dockworker could not operate the torch. An expert welder, Russ leaped onto the side of the ship and grabbed the torch. Moments later the intense flame was eating into the steel plates.

But as the flame broke through, white-hot molten steel peppered us. Esther screamed in pain and I cried out, "We're being roasted!"

Instantly the torch was withdrawn.

"Get down in the water as low as you can," Russell shouted. "We'll spray you with a hose and I'll try to deflect the flame."

They sprayed cold water on my head and back. A shaking chill convulsed me as I hung to the top bunk, holding Esther. My grip weakened as nausea flooded me and I feared I might lose Esther, who was now semiconscious, into the dark water. I prayed once more and the convulsion stopped.

It took 20 minutes to cut an 18-inch hole in the side of the ship. I pushed Esther's nearly lifeless body up and minutes later I was also lifted out. An ambulance rushed us to the hospital. Esther's heart had almost stopped beating and she was placed in intensive care.

Thank God Esther recovered. Our Holy Land tour was cut short but we had already found the revelation that no sight-seeing trip could have ever given us. Esther and I are now able to praise God for our difficulties that night. That top bunk, for instance, saved our lives. And the jammed door. If we had gone into the dark passageway, we would have surely become lost in the bowels of that sinking ship.

Our lives have been much different since we've returned home. For one thing, material possessions no longer occupy first place in our lives. We learned how meaningless they really are.

Neither am I looking at tomorrow for our blessings. That night in Beirut we thought our greatest blessing would come when we set foot on the Holy Land the next day. Now I understand the full truth of Jesus' statement, "Don't be anxious about tomorrow. . . . Live one day at a time." (Matthew 6:34, The Living Bible)

If we let Him, He will bless us *today,* even in our times of darkest despair.

Treasures of Darkness

In the famous lace shops of Bruges, Belgium, I am told certain rooms are used for spinning the finest and most delicate designs. Each room is completely dark except for a tiny window which admits light directly on the pattern of lace. There is only one spinner in the room and he sits where the narrow stream of light falls on the threads of his handiwork. The choicest lace is wrought when the worker himself is in the dark and only his pattern is in the light.

When troubled or confused about life's tragedies, I see myself as a lace spinner working in darkness. Little do I know how the events of today fit into God's plan for tomorrow. He weaves the master pattern. And God is the Stream of Light. When we let ourselves be the instruments of His handiwork, the trouble of today becomes the triumph of tomorrow.

DORIS H. JARRETT

The Accident
by Anne Shelly

---

*An unusual set of circumstances saves a young
girl from tragedy.*

Lying on the asphalt of the runway at the Van Nuys Airport, I clutched my bleeding left side with my right hand.
I was in great pain. My boyfriend stood beside me,
screaming. I turned to comfort him and saw my left arm.
It was lying a foot from my body.

My arm had been completely severed by the propeller
of a small Cessna airplane. I reached out to touch it. I
wanted a whole and complete body. Then I grew angry.
The idea of having only one arm repulsed me. I was 15. I
loved to swim, to dance. Silently I shouted, "No!" Death,
so very close, was a welcome thought.

The sound of my boyfriend's voice swept me away
from the thought of death. Remembering my faith, I asked
God for my arm back.

I have had faith in God since I was very young.
When I was 11, my family finally settled into a church.
We felt welcomed and comfortable for the first time. Love
and support surrounded us. We attended classes which
reaffirmed our trust in God.

As I learned and grew, I began to use my faith. I had
my prayers answered with little things—good grades on
tests in school, harmony instead of meaningless spats with
my brothers. With each passing manifestation of belief, I
became more aware of the importance of faith; I trusted
God.

There on the airport runway, my arm separated from
my body, I turned to God. Pain left. Calmness soothed my
body. God was with me. Not as a prayer, or some hopeful

wish, but through His presence, holding me in protective
arms.

The fire rescue squad arrived minutes later. While
one man clamped my arteries and veins, another packed
my arm in an ice-filled plastic sack. I was then rushed to
Van Nuys Receiving Hospital.

The hospital called my father. (My mother was vacationing in the mountains with my youngest brother.)
When he came to see me in the emergency room, I asked
him to call my Sunday school teacher and have her start a
circle of prayer for me and my family.

At first the doctors were going to keep me at the
emergency hospital and merely sew up my armless shoulder. But one of the doctors remembered that Orthopedic
Hospital in downtown Los Angeles had reimplanted a fireman's severed arm several years before. They decided to
send me there. I was loaded into another ambulance and
driven 20 miles over the freeways.

I felt very sleepy in the ambulance. Wanting to stay
awake, I asked the attendant to whistle. The continuous
rolling movement of the ambulance and the soft whistle of
the attendant comforted me. I quietly began to sing "Let
There Be Peace on Earth," a song we often sing at my
church that has always given me a sense of God's peace.

Although it was now about 10 o'clock on a summer
night, the exact team of surgeons who had performed the
other rare operation was available when I arrived. Three
and a half hours after I had lost my arm, I went into surgery to get it back. By now the circle of prayer for me
was spreading throughout the city.

After six hours of surgery, I was told that the operation might not work. The doctors explained that my body
might reject the arm and that there was a danger of infection since my arm had been carried in an unsterilized plastic sack.

I did not feel concerned about the outcome. My faith
told me that "all things work together for good to them
that love God" (Romans 8:28) and I did love God. His
presence stayed with me and I had no doubt.

Ten days after the accident, I celebrated my sixteenth
birthday. The party was held in the recreation room at the
hospital. My most beloved friends were there. The newspapers and television reported on the girl who got her arm
back as a birthday present and I received thousands of

birthday wishes from all over the world. The light of God touched us all.

Five weeks later, with no rejection or infection, I was ready to go home. But now I was told that I would not be able to use my arm for two years. Again I trusted God to help.

On Thanksgiving Day, only four months later, I could move my fingers. Now, a year later, I can swim 40 laps, knit, sew, throw a ball, skip rope, drive, dance, participate in gym activities and hug my family and friends.

That night at the airport I trusted God with my life and my arm. Today I have both. My faith was not only reinforced that wonderful night, but the fact of God's presence became my greatest joy.

Editor's Note:
For this story, Anne Shelly won a Guideposts Youth Writing Contest scholarship.

6.

Hope for People with Unfulfilled Dreams

But seek ye first the kingdom of God, and his righteousness; and all these things shall be added unto you.

MATTHEW 6:33

Miracle at the Pier

by Angie Brooks

The onetime president of the United Nations General Assembly tells how a wondrous spirit of help and sharing made her dream come true.

How well I remember the day my father asked me if I'd like to live with a foster family. This was not an unusual idea in Liberia where we lived.

My father was a clergyman, and though his income had been enough to support his nine children in our home in the interior, when we moved to the capital city of Monrovia, we found there was not enough to meet the needs. So when a lady named Adelaide Anderson asked me to come live with her, it was agreed that I should go. "You'd be a playmate for Mrs. Anderson's little girl," father said to me.

Until I was 14, then, I lived with Aunt Tootoo, as I called her. Aunt Tootoo was relaxed in most things, but she was adamant about two rules: one, you never told a lie; and two, you always went to church on Sunday. I'll never forget how she emphasized those.

Her influence on me continued right up until the minute of her death. She became ill and was confined to the hospital. One day on my regular visit I was astonished to see how feeble she had become. "Come close, Angie, so you can hear," Aunt Tootoo whispered. I stood next to her. "Angie, will you promise that you will go to the United States to study and then work with your people?"

"You know I can't do that," I said. I wanted to study law but had no money. The government helped pay college costs, but only for medical students.

193

"You can if you will to, Angie," Aunt Tootoo said. "You're a headstrong girl. Put your stubbornness to work." Aunt Tootoo gripped my hand. Then her grip relaxed, and she was silent. A nurse came in and felt Aunt Tootoo's pulse. "Mrs. Anderson is dead," the nurse said.

I was left very conscious of the fact that her last wish was for me to go to the United States.

The next Sunday in church, after the rest of the congregation had left, I sat alone in my seat and made a pledge to myself that I would at least try to live up to Aunt Tootoo's dream. No sooner had I whispered this pledge than I felt crushed, for the goal seemed far too big for me. Our minister came by and sat in the chair next to mine. "What's the trouble, Angie?" he asked.

When I explained, he told me that he knew some people at Shaw University in North Carolina. He offered to send a letter of recommendation along with my own letter requesting a scholarship.

Weeks later I got a letter back and could hardly believe it when I saw that I was really being offered a scholarship! But then my heart fell. For there was an "if." I could have the scholarship *if* I could pay my transportation.

In Liberia in those days it was possible to see the president of our country about such a problem. I did so. I explained my needs, and the president replied, "The government allows grants to medical students. Are you studying medicine?"

I suddenly remembered Aunt Tootoo and knew she would never want me to go to the United States because of a lie. "No, Mr. President. I want to study law."

The president was silent for a long time. "Perhaps we could make an exception," he said. "Would it help if we gave you five hundred dollars?"

My spirit singing, I left the president's office. The $500 was to allow me to settle my affairs and buy my ticket. When I paid my debts and settled some medical bills my parents had incurred, I had $200 left, the price of my ticket, plus five dollars for spending money. With this in my hand I went to the dock.

There I learned the fare had gone up $100! I stood on the pier crying. Around me moved my countrymen who had come to the docks to sell their raw rubber. One young man came up to me, his brow wrinkled.

"Sister, why are you crying?"

I told him my story.

"Maybe I can help," he said. "Do you want me to try to sell that chain?" A little hesitantly I gave him the gold chain from around my neck, and he disappeared.

By then a small crowd had gathered. One man—better dressed than the rest—was especially interested. His name, he said, was Charles Escaron. "Here, take this money," he said, reaching into his pockets. The total came to $37.50.

The boy who had taken my chain ran up. He held a bill in the air—ten dollars. So now I had $47.50, nearly half the money I needed.

Together the crowd of my new friends nudged me into the ticket office. Outside I could see stevedores casting ropes from dockside to the ship railing. Now another man walked up and shoved money into my hand. He said his name was William Sherman. "I was going to send this money to my daughter. I'll find money for her, somehow."

A cheer rose. We spread the money out and counted it. There was a moan—three dollars short.

Then a very tall man tapped my shoulder. "Here, let me have that money," he said. "I want to show my friends how close you are to going to America. Maybe we can get the rest."

I hesitated for a moment, then handed the tall man my bills and coins and watched him run off into the trees at the edge of the pier. He stayed there until the ship's crew—now part of the drama—reluctantly began to raise the gangplank.

At the last minute, just as the ship's engines were beginning to shudder, the man came back. "I have it!" he shouted. We all counted the money together. It came to just over the amount of the ticket. Several hands pushed the bills and coins under the bars of the ticket window, and the agent hurriedly issued my precious passage. Just as the boat was pulling away from the pier I jumped into the arms of welcoming crewmen and turned to look at my friends.

They waved and shouted and cried, sensing that they were a part of my adventure.

And, of course, they were. My parents, Aunt Tootoo, the pastor from our church, our president, the boy who sold my chain, Mr. Escaron, Mr. Sherman, the unknown tall man—those and many others helped me at every step, just when I needed help. They all are responsible for my being in the United Nations today, and a little of each of them works with me here, continuing to share their wonderful African spirit of concern with the people of our world. _____

What Do You Plan for Tuesday?

One Monday night, several years ago, when my two oldest were five and three, they were pretending to play house, as children do. I heard the five-year-old say: "Now it is time to go to bed, but first we must say our prayers." The sister and little brother knelt down, folded their hands and bowed their heads while she prayed: "We've had a lovely day today, God. What do You plan for Tuesday?"

To me, these simple words express a perfect faith and trust in God's loving care and providence for us—His children. A sort of "Thy will be done" in the words of a child.

Many times in the years since this incident occurred, I have tumbled into bed too weary to form a prayer. As I drifted off to sleep I would whisper those simple, but to me, beautiful, faith-filled words of my young daughter: "We've had a lovely day today, God. What do You plan for Tuesday?"

MIRIAM B. RANDLES

The Lithuanian Assessment of Near

till stare—these and many others Police me at every turn
between I grades-men. They all are hospitable everyone

Neil Armstrong's Boyhood Crisis

by Mrs. Stephen Armstrong as told to Lorraine Wetzel

The astronaut's mother recalls another important step her son took—this one as a boy in Ohio.

Most people think Neil Armstrong took the most important step in his life when he set foot on the moon. But as his mother, I remember an even greater step taken in our old home on Pearl Street in Wapakoneta, Ohio, on another July day—twenty-three years earlier.

The story begins when Neil was two and his father and I lived in Cleveland, not far from the airport. Like many families during the Depression days of the early 30s, one of our inexpensive Sunday-afternoon pastimes was airplane watching. Neil stood between us, his little face pressed so intently against the fence that it often left red marks. We were always ready to leave long before he was, and his plea was always the same: "Can't we see just *one* more airplane?"

I was often uneasy about Neil's obvious fascination with planes. And I had to admit to myself that this child, our firstborn, was very special to me. After Stephen and I married, I was haunted by the fear that maybe I couldn't conceive. I had been an only child and often thought, *What if I can't have even one baby?*

Then finally the day came when our doctor assured me I was pregnant. The minute I got home I went down on my knees and thanked God for His blessing to us and, in the fullness of my heart, I dedicated this child-to-be to Him. In the months that followed, I prayed steadily that

197

this child would be given a thirst for knowledge and the capacity for learning which someday would accomplish noble deeds—hopefully to serve the work of the Lord.

One Sunday morning, when Neil was five or six, he and my husband left for Sunday school. When they returned, both had peculiar expressions on their faces. Stephen was a bit white-faced, but Neil was beaming from ear to ear.

"What is wrong with you two?" I asked. There was utter silence.

Suddenly a thought came to me. "Did you go up in that airplane I read about in the paper!"

Now they looked relieved. Yes, that is exactly what they had done. A pilot was barnstorming in town, and Stephen said rates were cheaper in the morning. He had not really enjoyed the flight, but little Neil had loved every minute of it.

One morning Neil and I were walking down the cluttered aisles of a dime store looking for cereal bowls. My husband and I now had a wonderful family of three active children who consumed vast quantities of cereal. Somehow the bowls were always getting chipped or broken. I was selecting five shiny new ones when I felt a tug at my arm. "Mom, will you buy this for me?" Neil held up a gaily colored box.

"What is it?" I asked cautiously.

"It's a model-airplane kit." The eagerness in his voice betrayed his excitement. "Mom, this way I could learn how to make airplanes. It's twenty cents."

Quickly I thought how twenty cents would buy two cereal bowls, but how could I resist the urgency and enthusiasm in my son's voice?

"Honey," I said gently, "could you find a kit for ten cents?"

"Sure, Mom!" His face radiant, he raced back to the toy counter.

Although Neil was then only eight years old, that was the beginning of two important occupations in his life. The first was his meticulous assembly line for making model airplanes. We put a table in one corner of the living room, and it was never moved—even when company came.

The second occupation made the first one possible. Beginning with his first model plane, Neil was never without a job, no matter how small. First he cut grass in a cemetery for ten cents an hour. Later he cleaned out the bread mixer at Neumeister's Bakery every night. After we moved to Wapakoneta, Neil delivered orders for the neighborhood grocery, swept out the hardware store and opened cartons at Rhine and Brading's Pharmacy.

When Neil wasn't working or studying, he rode his bicycle three miles north on a gravel road to the Wapak Flying Service Airport. Today this field isn't used, but in 1944 it bustled with activity. A young instructor, Charles Finkenbine, kept three light airplanes busy as trainers. Budding pilots came from surrounding counties to learn to fly, and Neil at fourteen was a familiar figure sitting on the sidelines, his eyes glued to every takeoff and landing. One afternoon I was making grape jelly when the screen door banged as he rushed into the kitchen.

"Mom," he shouted, "Mr. Finkenbine let me *touch* one of the airplanes!"

"That's fine, son," I said.

"He says from now on I can be a grease monkey and one of these days he'll teach me to fly!"

"Are you sure you're old enough, Neil?" I tried to hide the anxiety in my voice.

He flashed his wide, confident grin. "Don't worry, I'll be careful."

The screen door banged again, and he was gone. I'm afraid his assurance did little to comfort me. By now I was beginning to wonder how the Lord could be served by a youngster so completely captivated by airplanes.

From then on every penny Neil earned went for flying lessons. At forty cents an hour at the pharmacy it took him between twenty-two and twenty-three hours of work to pay for one nine-dollar lesson. But both Dick Brading and Charles Finkenbine were generous men: The first often let Neil off early to go to the airport, the latter managed free flying time for our son in exchange for odd jobs around the hangar. Neil's goal was to get his flying license as soon as he reached his sixteenth birthday in August.

In July our two boys, Neil and Dean, with their father as scoutmaster, attended Boy Scout camp in Defiance, Ohio. The evening they were due back I planned a special homecoming supper. They thought they'd be home at five o'clock, so I peeled potatoes and put them on to boil at 4:30, then started to set the table.

At 5:15 I picked up my darning basket and started to

mend some of Dean's socks. An hour dragged by. I finished the socks and walked to the window. They were more than an hour overdue, and I knew something was wrong.

Then looking through the grape arbor, I saw our car drive into the garage. My husband appeared in the doorway, his face pale and drawn. Fear clutched my throat.

"What's wrong, Stephen? Has something happened to the boys?"

"No, they're all right. Dean is here with me, and Neil will be along soon. But there has been an accident."

"What do you mean?"

"Viola, come into the living room, and I'll tell you all about it." He put his arm around me, and together we walked to the sofa.

"We were on our way home this afternoon," he continued, "when we noticed an airplane flying parallel to us. Neil recognized it immediately as one of the trainers from the Wapak Flying Service. Some student was practicing takeoffs and landings in a field near the road. Then he must have dipped too low over the telephone wires, because suddenly the airplane was in trouble."

"Oh, no!" I whispered.

"It nose-dived into the field, and at the same time Neil yelled, 'Stop the car!' and before I knew it, he had climbed over the fence and was running toward the plane. Then we all got out and ran over to help too. Neil was lifting a young fellow out of the cockpit, and just as we got there he died in Neil's arms."

"Oh Stephen, how awful! That poor boy and his family." Then a terrifying new thought seared my brain. "It might have been Neil."

"Yes, Viola, it could have been." My husband's voice roughened with emotion. "Instead it was a young man from Lima whom Neil knew. Neil is staying with him until the ambulance comes.

A car door slammed, and I heard slow footsteps coming up the front-porch steps. Then suddenly Neil and I were in each other's arms, tears streaming down our faces.

"He was my friend, Mom. And he was *only* twenty!" I could hardly bear the anguish in his voice.

"I know, honey." I released him, with a mother's sudden awareness that her son was no longer a boy. I forced my voice to sound cheerful. "Do you want some supper?"

"No, thanks. I'm going up to my room." He stopped on the landing and tried to smile. "Don't worry, Mom. I'll be all right."

"I know you will, Neil." I watched him walk up the stairs and quietly close the door as dry sobs tore through me.

Stephen and I both thought it best to let him alone for a while. But we could not help wondering if Neil would want to keep on flying. Both of us agreed he must fight this battle himself.

The next two days were the hardest of my life. As all mothers know, whatever hurts your children hurts you twice as much. And yet I knew he had to make this decision himself. Had our closeness with the Creator and the nightly prayers through the years prepared him to find the help he needed so desperately now? At this stage, it was out of my hands. All I could do was wait.

I tried to carry on a normal life, but my heart and mind were always in that back bedroom with the iron bed, yellow wallpaper, the single overhead light fixture and the bureau covered with model airplanes. What was he thinking? What would he decide?

Finally, near dusk on the second day, I couldn't stand the silence and separation any longer. I baked oatmeal and raisin cookies and took a plate of them and a glass of cold milk upstairs.

"Neil, may I come in, please? Here are some cookies still warm from the oven."

He opened the door, and I walked into the stuffy little room and put the cookies on the bureau. What I saw made my heart leap. Next to a model airplane was an old Sunday school notebook with a picture of Jesus on the cover. It was now turned to the page where years before Neil had written in his large childish hand, "The Character of Jesus," and had listed ten qualities of His. Among those that caught my eye were: He was sinless, He was humble, He championed the poor, He was unselfish. But the one which struck me the most was number eight—He was close to God.

Suddenly I felt like singing hosanna. "Honey, what have you decided about flying?" I asked him.

Neil's eyes held mine in a steady gaze, then he said firmly, "Mom, I hope you and Dad will understand, but with God's help, I *must* go on flying."

For a minute I was jolted as I thought of that other mother only a few miles away in Lima, brokenhearted and perhaps standing in her son's empty room at this very minute. I asked God for strength and the right words, and He gave them to me.

"All right, son. Dad and I will go along with your decision." My heart was pounding. "And, Neil," I said, "when you get your license in a few weeks, may I be your first passenger?"

> *Behind the cloud the starlight lurks,*
> *   Through showers the sunbeams fall;*
> *For God, who loveth all His works,*
> *   Has left His hope for all.*
>
>   —JOHN GREENLEAF WHITTIER

A Place for Me
by Louis DeJesus

At the circus I dreamed of being somebody special, a lion tamer, a soaring aerialist or, best of all, one of the clowns—not the pint-sized boy the other kids taunted.

"Shrimp! Midget! *Chiquito!*"—the laughing taunts flung at me hurt worse than stones as I scurried to the stairs of our apartment building. They were a struggle to climb because I was the smallest 12-year-old in New York's East Harlem, maybe in the whole world.

"Mama," I cried, "why did God make me so small?" She knelt down to hug me. "Luis," she answered, "we should trust God in all He does."

I wasn't so sure. Life was hard enough. My parents had come to New York from Puerto Rico. And though Papa worked hard, he made just enough to keep our family going.

When it became obvious I wasn't growing like my brothers, my folks took me to the doctors. They shook their heads. "Glandular problems," they said. "Luis will probably always be small."

But to be so little I had to ask a younger kid to lift me up to a playground swing?

One day I went to our priest, Father Orafano. In his quiet study, I climbed onto a chair and poured out my anguish.

"Luis," he said, his gentle eyes full of compassion, "there's not a person alive who doesn't wish he were bigger in some way—smarter, richer, handsomer. We can either make ourselves miserable over what we aren't, or we can believe God made us what we are for a reason and has plans even for the things about us we wish were different."

In the evenings, sitting alone on the roof of our building as the setting sun softened the ragged skyline, I'd ask, "What *is* Your plan, God?"

There was a time each year when I really forgot my troubles. When the circus came to New York, Papa would scrape together enough money to get tickets for all the family. When we sat high up in Madison Square Garden, I was no longer tiny Luis but the aerialist soaring through the spotlights, the lion tamer or, best of all, a clown.

But in the cold, gray morning I was shrunk once again—like the morning of my freshman gym class at DeWitt Clinton High School. The other boys were learning to tumble. Mr. Traetta, the gym teacher, came over to me, "Hey, how about you, Luis?"

"Naw," I said, shrinking against the wall.

"Come on, we'll teach you. You have to try, Luis. *Try.*"

I tried. Surprisingly, I found an agility I never dreamed I had. By the time I was a sophomore, I was on our school's tumbling team. We won first place in the city championship, and I won fifth prize in the singles—me, the size of a baseball bat!

But the summer I went to Camp Pioneer was my real turning point. Run by New York's Fresh Air Fund, it's a mountain camp that gives underprivileged kids a chance to learn about the outdoors.

But when I got off the bus with all those strange kids, the years suddenly slipped backward. Again the cries: "Peanut! Pipsqueak!" Camp director Bill Hubner found me standing behind a tree. He sat down so he could look into my eyes and said the strangest thing—strange because it seemed I was back in Father Orafano's study, hearing him say again, "Luis, you must face up to what you are. Perhaps God wants you to be this way for a reason."

I felt better. I straightened up to my full four feet, two inches and had a good two weeks.

Next year I applied for a job at Camp Pioneer as a counselor's aid and was accepted. Strangely enough, I felt I really helped the kids that came. These kids suffered their own blows from life in the slums and many arrived with a pretty low opinion of themselves. Seeing that my small size didn't make me feel inferior gave them a new look at their shortcomings.

In 1968, when I was 17, I returned as a junior counselor. That was the year that God revealed something to me.

Each time a new group of kids would come up from the city, we counselors would put on a show for them—stunts, gags—to make them feel welcome. I'd do my tumbling act, trying to make them laugh, because a lot of them looked a little scared and uneasy when they got off that bus.

Pretty soon they'd all be smiling, then laughing. I, little Luis, was making them forget their troubles. And suddenly I knew God was telling me something.

Larry Mickolic, the Fresh Air Fund's associate director, put it into words when he said, "Luis, you're the star of the show!"

It was only natural that I thought of my first love—the circus! Could it be possible? And I remembered what my gym teacher had said: "Try, Luis, try!"

I sent a letter to Ringling Brothers and Barnum & Bailey Circus, saying I'd like to become a clown. Back came an application form.

My brothers laughed good-naturedly. "Luis, you'll never make it," they said. "That's big-time stuff!"

But I was accepted. In the fall of 1968 Mama helped me pack my suitcase, and they all saw me off to the circus' winter headquarters in Florida to attend clown school.

I found out clown school was serious business. Two months of intensive hard work taught me that what looks like a moment of buffoonery in the ring takes weeks to perfect. Split-second timing and agility are essential.

After earning my clown-school diploma—and a contract—I spent weeks in rehearsal. Then the "greatest show on earth" hit the road.

Just about any dream
Grows stronger
If you hold on
A little longer.

MARGO GINA HART

I'll never forget the day my mother, father and brothers Angel, Carmello, Victor and Edwin, came to see me when the show opened at Madison Square Garden.

In the highlight of an act, I played the part of a little boy who dreamed of becoming an astronaut. In my space-suit costume, I "flew" to the top of the arena where I perched on a crescent moon to watch the "space extravaganza" unfold below.

I looked down, waved at my family, then saw the bright faces of thousands of people who had come to forget their troubles for a while.

"Thank you, God," I whispered, "for showing me Your plan."

I was glad, very glad, to be small.

They that wait upon the Lord shall renew their strength; they shall mount up with wings as eagles; they shall run, and not be weary; and they shall walk, and not faint.

ISAIAH 40:31

Faith and Four Tables

by Fanny Lazzar

---

*Her little restaurant seemed doomed from the
start.*

I slowly lifted the shade at the front door of my little
restaurant, looked at its four tables, then sank onto a
counter stool, burying my head in my arms. It was six
A.M. on a special day in 1944—my first day in business.

"Dear God," I prayed, "I don't know what to do or
how to do it. Please lead. I will follow."

With two sons to support, I had borrowed capital and
opened this restaurant. Yet, any businessman would
predict failure. It was in an across-the-tracks area of small
homes in Evanston, a Chicago suburb.

More than anything else that morning, I needed reassurance that He had put me on the right path.

I remembered when I first really learned about His
help. Years of tragedy had left me convinced I was completely alone. One night in my apartment I sobbed bitterly.
There was a rap at the door. It was my landlady.
"Fanny," she said gently, "don't you ever pray?"

"Of course," I answered. "Always."

She put her arms around me. "But maybe not correctly," she said. "Remember that God's love has always
met, and always will meet, every human need. When you
pray, remember *that,* and He will never fail you."

At the time I was working in an office. However, I
wasn't able to save anything for my sons' college educa-
tion. And I knew I must find some other kind of work. Finally, one evening I dropped to my knees and asked God
to show me the way.

The direction came some weeks later. On my lunch

hour, I stepped into a restaurant advertising "Good Old-Fashioned Irish Stew." My mouth watered. But I could hardly swallow the first spoonful. It was terrible. I asked the waiter, "How can you serve this?" He glanced about, then leaned down. "Lady, I agree. It is terrible. You know why? Because the owner is greedy. He buys cheap and serves cheap."

I looked around aghast and thought, *If a person with this kind of soul can fill up a restaurant, then it seems to me someone with higher principles could do even better.* At that moment I *knew* this was His answer to my prayer. I would open a restaurant.

I didn't know a thing about the business. And I had no money.

"Lord, You have given me the will; please show me the way."

I borrowed money from friends. Twenty-five dollars here, $50 there, till I had $2,000. Still not enough. Finally, a Chicago bank lent me $2,000 with two friends co-signing the note.

I rented a corner store in the poorest part of town because the rent was only $50 per month. Now what would I serve? I prayed, "Dear God, I need Your guidance; *You* lead and I will follow."

Thoughts began to flow. This being the age of specialization, I felt it wise to concentrate on one or two dishes, such as spaghetti. They'd be my best.

So my adventure began. By closing time that first day, a few working people had wandered in, and there was $12 in the register. I scrubbed the floor, then went into the kitchen to make sauces. As I worked, I smiled to myself; here I was, chef and owner, and yet I couldn't eat Italian spaghetti sauce! I couldn't digest it.

The thought came: Why not develop a new kind of sauce, one that would not only be digestible but unique in flavor? For the next 50 weeks, I spent almost every night working on it, cooking, tasting.

Finally one night I evolved a sauce made with chicken, beef, butter, tomatoes, herbs and spices. Rosa, a friend from across the street, tasted it, and looked up with shining eyes, "Ah, *fantastico!*"

Then I penciled on my menu, "Fanny's Famous Spaghetti Sauce."

But after little over a year, I was still taking in only

$12 to $14 a day serving daytime customers and had sunk $1800 more into debt. However, I felt in even closer communion with God and constantly turned to Him for guidance. I was given an inspiration which led to a bold decision. Instead of daytime hours, I rescheduled my restaurant to serve the evening dinner trade from 5 P.M. to 10 P.M.

Most anyone would have laughed at me. I sold no liquor. In fact, I offered no inducement except good food and reasonable prices. But I could expand my menu. Again the guidance: Why not some real Southern fried chicken?

It seemed right. Only I didn't know how to fry chicken. I advertised for a chef. Four or five men answered the ad. But they knew little more about chicken than I.

I was sitting alone in my restaurant's kitchen, praying for an answer, when an elderly man shuffled in, his white hair reflecting his years. He said his name was Bob Jordan. Love radiated from his face, but he looked too old for the job. However, to be polite, I gave him an application.

He handed it back, shaking his head. "Ma'am, I can't read or write."

"Then how did you read my ad?"

Looking me in the eye, he answered, "I didn't see any ad. I was coming down the street looking for a job and the Lord said, 'Man, open that door and enter. Your job is waiting for you there!'"

Bob Jordan got the job. And he fried the best chicken in the world!

But even with an expanded menu, I had to acquaint more people with our out-of-the-way location. Again, His help came.

I had always enjoyed writing and I began to wonder about writing a weekly column and running it as an advertisement in our local paper. I called a friend on the paper and broached the idea.

"Fanny," he chided, "no one would read it. Besides, display space is very expensive."

"What about back in the classified ads?"

"Then you'd be sure no one would read it."

"Well," I said, "I've prayed about this and I think He knows more about it than you or I."

My first column reminisced about my childhood in Italy when, visiting my uncle's farm, I'd find escape in fields of fragrant violets. "All of us need 'escape channels,'" I wrote, "and one good escape is to have a good quiet meal alone with your husband or a friend who is dear to you." Naturally, I mentioned my restaurant.

People did read it, including a Northwestern University professor who sent a clipping to the *New Yorker* magazine, which published it as a curiosity. Soon diners were thronging to our restaurant.

Along with this success came an ever deepening awareness that all of this was possible through Him. And I learned that the only way one could really thank Him was to pass on love and appreciation to others.

Today my restaurant, which has expanded several times, is as I visualized it 26 years ago—checkered tablecloths, oil paintings and books, thousands of books lining the walls. My sons are raised and happy in their own careers. And each night, when the last guest has left and I sit alone in the dining room, I give thanks for God's blessings.

I realize that this is not my restaurant, but His. For by myself I could do nothing. But when I in complete faith turned to Him, He led me each step of the way.

Many people wishing to start their own restaurant ask me the secret. I tell them what He taught me, "Be more concerned with love and appreciation for others than with your margin of profit."

Or, as Bob Jordan would say, "It's the giving not the getting that makes the difference."

You cannot put a great hope into a small soul.

JENKIN LLOYD-JONES

How to Aim Yourself
by Marilyn Helleberg

---

*Having trouble reaching your goals? Here's a
practical way to accomplish more.*

It was my 35th birthday and all day I had been struggling
against the gnawing awareness that my life was half over
and what did I have to show for a life half-spent? I realized that what I really needed more than anything else was
a feeling of achievement. I guess we all need that—almost
as much as we need food and water.

As I cleared the table, I thought of how often I had
heard myself say, "Gee, I really intended to do that," or
"I'd do it if I just had more time," but I never seemed to
get anywhere. Maybe my aim was wrong.

That one word, *aim,* hovered strangely in my
thoughts for a minute before it connected unexpectedly
with the memory of my first bowling lesson, given me by
my father. Strange that something as unprofound as a
bowling technique could rescue me from the quicksand of
unproductivity, but as soon as I started applying a bowling
formula to my life goals, things began to happen. I earned
my master's degree, gained a pilot's license and launched a
career in writing, in addition to reaching some other less
ambitious goals. But more important, it helped me exchange my vague feeling of unworthiness for the bold
hope that maybe my life could really count for something
after all.

I'd like to share the ways in which the "aim yourself"
technique has worked for me, in the hope that it might
help you, too.

The first step in my father's bowling formula is: Pick
a spot just in front of you that's in line with the center
pin. When I applied that advice to my life, I realized I had

to aim toward one goal at a time and that each goal had to be exact. My vague desire to be a better housekeeper was not good enough. I had to really pin it down and resolve to "clean out the linen closet and the coat closet *today*."

I also learned to choose goals that I could start on right now and accomplish within a limited time. I had always thought that someday I'd like to go back to college and get a master's degree, but the prospect was so overwhelming that I kept putting it off. So instead of aiming for my degree, I signed up for just one class. Aiming for a spot "just in front of me" made it easier to begin. We need long-term goals, too, but I have found that we reach broader, distant goals by the route of today's well-aimed single steps.

Since the "spot" must be "in line with the center pin," I try to test each goal with these questions: Will it make me more nearly the kind of person I want to be? Will its accomplishment further my long-term goals? Is it important?

After I have selected a goal that is exact, short-term and in line with my long-term goals, I am ready for step two:

Aim your whole self toward the goal. In bowling, golf, archery or any other sport where aim is important, the whole body has to get into the act. Single-mindedness is just as important in aiming for short-term goals in life. Here are some tricks that have helped me keep my attention focused on my current goals.

As soon as I have chosen a goal, I do something *right then* toward its accomplishment. When I resolved to paint the bedroom, I ordered the green paint; when I decided to take flying lessons, I made an appointment for my first lesson.

I tell someone about my goal. This makes it harder for me to talk myself out of it later.

I make three copies of the goal, including time limit, placing these reminders by things I use every day—in my silverware drawer, on the refrigerator door, in the coat pocket that holds my keys. Every time I run across one of these reminders during the day, I try to stop what I'm doing and make some further effort toward my goal. If I can't stop, I can at least plan what my next step will be and exactly when I will do it.

As I sit down to each meal or snack during the day, I try to remember to picture my goal as already accomplished and say a short prayer of thanksgiving.

After I have done everything I can toward the accomplishment of a particular goal, I take the third and final step: Let go of the ball. I turn the outcome over to God, knowing that, just as there are physical laws that make a bowling ball keep rolling once it's started, there are also spiritual laws that take over for us after we have chosen an exact goal and aimed our whole self toward it. Sometimes it's hard for me to let go and let God, but I have learned that if I can do just that, the ball I started rolling will continue on its way with the help of God and by His sure laws.

I still give up on goals sometimes. My housekeeping never did improve all that much, and my thumb is not getting any greener; but I find that I'm succeeding far more often than I used to, because the formula keeps my aim short, direct and concentrated. And it's the very best remedy in the world for that I-never-seem-to-get-anywhere feeling.

If any man be in Christ, he is a new creature: old things are passed away; behold, all things are become new.

II CORINTHIANS 5:17

The Lift I Needed

by Janet Lynn

This four-time U.S. figure skating champion won more than a bronze medal in the 1972 Olympics.

I never expected what happened in Sapporo, Japan.

When I went there for the 1972 Winter Olympics a lot of people were counting on me to bring back a gold medal.

You can imagine the pressure this builds. Everyone you know talks about it; you read it in the newspapers. I didn't let myself think much about it, but deep inside I sort of hoped to win one, too.

Before any competitive meet, the pressure really intensifies. But it's the day you skate that you can really get in trouble. You can sit there going over and over your routine until you get so uptight your head swims.

My competition at the Olympics was to take three days. The first two for school figures, and the last for free skating. There are 64 different school figures—such as the eights, counters, rockers and paragraph threes. And you must know each one perfect, because in competition you are assigned only six. Only at the last minute do you know which six they are.

The first day I did fairly well. And I vowed to do better the next day. But I had put myself under such tension that I didn't do as well at all. Sure I had prayed—prayed to win. And the Lord showed me after each figure that day how far off the track I was. In the middle of the second day of figures I was almost in hysterics, ready to quit.

We had a little room where we rested. Mom and my

214

coach, Miss Slavka Kohout, came in to calm me. But it didn't help.

That evening at the Olympic Village, I lay on my bed crying and praying, wondering where I'd gone wrong. As I prayed I seemed to hear a soft voice: "Cast your burden upon Me, Janet. I still love you."

I drew a deep breath, remembering that moment when I first met Him. It was at a church camp in Lake Geneva, Wisconsin, where I had asked the Lord Jesus to come into my heart.

"Remember, Janet," said my counselor then, "Jesus is always with you, wanting to help you. When you suffer from fears or feelings of inferiority, just give them to Him. He promised to take them and give us peace.

"Don't forget," she emphasized, "He can handle *anything*. He doesn't want you crippled by inhibitions, worries or cares."

Now I knew what was wrong. As I had done so many times before, I'd forgotten His help and ended up hugging all my fears and inadequacies to me.

Right there in my room I relaxed and let my negative feelings float up to Him. It was like being loosened from a vise. It all came so clear. The Lord seemed to say: "Janet, it doesn't matter whether you get a gold medal or not; I just want you to skate for Me."

On the next day—my most important day—I felt good. My free-skating program was scheduled for the evening. So I had almost a whole day in which to get uptight. Instead, I just relaxed, didn't do much except talk with teammates, and sit quietly in my room and have fellowship with Him.

Whenever those fear-thoughts would start creeping in, I'd pray: "Lord, I know I needn't worry now about how I'll do tonight. I *know* You will give me the right feelings at the right time."

When I stepped out on the ice in front of those 8000 people, God did give me those feelings—a sense of freedom and love. Then, as I skated little circles to get the feel of the ice, I could hardly believe it. For suddenly I could feel His Spirit descending on me like a warm blanket of love. I felt free.

All I wanted to do was tell a story. That's what my coach always says as I step onto the ice: "Go out and tell a story!" And that's what I try to do in free-skating.

Miss Kohout and I choreograph my program. We choose various selections of classical music, put them together, on tape, and I interpret it in skating. The judges decide on composition, style and technical merit. It's a four-minute combination of ballet and skating gymnastics.

As I launched into my program, whirling and leaping, I felt wonderful. I didn't care about material things. I just wanted to skate my best for Him, for joy and love.

And then a strange thing happened. I fell.

In front of the whole world watching on television, I fell.

It happened in a flying sit spin, right in the middle of my program.

But an even stranger thing happened.

I hardly noticed it. In fact, I lifted right into my most difficult jump and finished the program well enough so that it helped me earn the Olympic bronze medal.

Afterward Miss Kohout and I watched my program on videotape to analyze what had happened; I had never fallen before in a sit spin in competition and hardly ever in practice. We figured it happened because I had launched my previous jump in the wrong place on the ice and thus started my preparation for the sit spin at a wrong angle.

More important, I thought of what would have happened if I'd reacted to the fall in my old way. Shame and embarrassment would have flung themselves at me with an accusatory, "You fell!" and I would have blown my program.

I went to the window of my room and looked up to the beautiful snow-covered mountains around Sapporo. And I thought of how He is always there to lift us.

For in completely giving ourselves to Him, He gives us back the best part of ourselves so we can face whatever life brings us.

Each morning brings its promise,
Of good things yet to be.
And nightfall will affirm again,
That God is good to me.

GORDON THOMAS

New Words for the Old, Old Story

by Kenneth Taylor

The paraphraser of The Living Bible *tells
how the book came into being.*

The puzzled little faces surrounding our dinner table worried me. I had just finished reading from Paul's Letter to Timothy in our evening Bible session and had asked my eight staircase children to explain what Paul had said.

Silence.

"Well," I explained, "Paul tells us that as a soldier of Christ, we should do whatever He wants us to, and not just the things we like or want for ourselves. We should follow the Lord's rules just as an athlete must follow the rules."

"Why didn't you say that in the first place, daddy?" asked eight-year-old Janet.

Yes, why? I wondered as I looked at the King James Bible in my hand. The answer to the world's problems lay between its covers. Yet, so many people had difficulty understanding it. Not just children, but adults.

Next morning on the train heading for the Moody Press offices in downtown Chicago where I worked, I stared out the window pondering this problem. As a writer, I was especially aware of the importance of communicating ideas quickly and clearly. And then the idea came—*Why not write tonight's Bible reading in words the children will understand?*

It was an attractive thought. The older children were twelve, eleven and ten. We were just graduating from reading Bible storybooks to the Bible itself. Taking out my

Bible, I opened its pages to Timothy and began scribbling on an old note pad.

In the King James version, the book of Second Timothy chapter 2, verse 13 reads: "If we believe not, yet He abideth faithful: He cannot deny Himself." *The children would have a difficult time with that one,* I thought.

I opened my mind to His inspiration, and then began paraphrasing the verse in simple, conversational style: "Even when we are too weak to have any faith left, He remains faithful to us and will help us, for He cannot disown us who are part of Himself, and He will always carry out His promises to us."

I struggled to say as exactly as possible what the scripture writers meant, and to say it simply, expanding where necessary for a clear understanding. The Bible writers often used idioms and thought patterns that are hard for us to follow today. Sometimes their thought sequences leave us far behind. And often they compressed enormous thoughts into single words full of meaning, as with this passage from Timothy.

Even so, I found it enjoyable work. And when my train pulled in, I had finished the chapter.

That night I read it to the children. This time the older children could answer the questions.

The next morning on the train I tackled another chapter. Through the drumming of the coach wheels, a thought welled in my consciousness: *Paraphrase all the Epistles.*

Today I'm convinced the thought was put there by God.

Every morning, every evening I scribbled on the commuter train.

Even with a master's degree in theology and extensive Bible background, I found it a challenge to transmit the exact meaning of the original so that not a jot of meaning would be changed or lost.

Summer, fall and winter passed, and finally I finished the Epistles. Then I settled back and read the copy. It was disappointing. It was rough in spots, and the great doctrinal thoughts were still not as clear as I had hoped for. It took a year to make the necessary corrections. Once more as I reread it, I was dissatisfied and penciled in many changes. This happened seven times and required seven years.

Finally I sent copies to Greek scholars for scrutiny. More changes.

At last in 1961, I felt the time had come to submit for publication what I called *Living Letters*. For by now I was sure they were part of God's plan. However, publishers didn't know this. One by one they turned them down.

One morning I shocked my wife Margaret at breakfast when I said, "Honey, I guess we'll have to publish them ourselves."

She looked at me quizzically. Our family had grown to ten children. And we had little money. Still, she agreed.

I found a printer, a Christian brother, who was enthusiastic about the idea. "Pay me when you can," he said. So I ordered 2000.

Then, how to sell them? I took half a booth at the Christian Booksellers convention in 1962 and sold 800 copies. Encouraged, I sent out letters and samples to book agents.

Nothing happened.

This continued for four months. Now our family devotions included prayers for those remaining 1200 copies. And then, four orders arrived in one week. They began to trickle in, in twos and threes. God seemed to be reassuring us.

Then God opened the floodgates. Someone sent a copy to Billy Graham. He happened to be in the hospital at the time and had time to read. He liked *Living Letters* and offered copies on his telecasts.

The demand was tremendous.

Accustomed now to the discipline of working on this in my spare time, I kept on. I tackled the so-called minor prophets. I knew they should be speaking to us today, but who was reading them?

Soon we published the second book, *Living Prophecies*.

Then I left Moody Press, after 18 years, to administer our own small publishing company. It was called Tyndale House after William Tyndale, the translator of the first New Testament printed in English.

Quickly we outgrew our dining-room office and garage shipping room. We moved to rented quarters in the basement of a commercial building and two years later moved to our own modern building in Wheaton. Now I could give more time to writing. *Living Gospels* in 1966 was followed by *Living Psalms and Proverbs* in 1967.

With a dedicated staff we were able to have *The Living Bible* ready by the summer of 1971. Within seven months, 1.5 million copies were sold.

If someone asks me if the work was worth it, I only have to think about a 23-year-old boy in prison who wrote me about how a preacher came into his cell and handed him *The Living Gospels.*

"In courtesy I took it," he wrote, "then threw it into the corner of my cell. Several times in the past I had tried to read the Bible but just couldn't understand it. However, one day I idly picked up *The Living Gospels* and became fascinated because I could understand what they were saying. It was through them I met the living Jesus Christ Whom I have invited into my heart."

I thank God for the inspiration to begin and continue this work for I find myself constantly revising to make it even more understandable. So I will continue to spend my life in helping others find the universal solution for all troubled hearts—the Lord Jesus Christ. And I shall weep for those who cannot find Him.

SEND ME

Dear Father, to the hopeless ones,
That are in such deep need
And have no one to turn to,
They need one friend to heed.
Oh comfort and uphold them
And draw them close to Thee.
And if there is no one to guide,
Dear Lord, send me, send me.

ROSINA STALLMAN

The Day the Band Left Me

by Lawrence Welk

"I felt sick, numb, almost paralyzed with shock. . ."

The first sign that something was wrong was the way the boys acted in the poolroom.

We were playing an engagement in Dallas, South Dakota, back during the Depression, and I was on my way to check out the auditorium. When I walked by the local pool hall, I looked through the window and could see all the boys grouped around one end of a pool table, talking very earnestly about something.

I started to go in, but then stopped. There was something odd about the way they were talking with such intensity. And just as I peered in, Rollie Chestney, my piano player, looked up and caught my eye. Immediately, he reached behind him and grabbed a pool cue out of the racks, and the rest of the boys did the same thing, waving casually as they did so. I waved too, but there was something about that little scene that left me uneasy.

That night, however, I put the whole incident out of my mind because we played to an unexpectedly large crowd and made a good deal of money. When I divided the receipts with the boys, it was the most we had made in some time.

"Well, fellows," I said happily, as I handed each of them his share, "it looks as if things are really going to change for us now!"

"Yeah," said Rollie. "I guess maybe they are."

The next morning I was up early and walked over to

a restaurant for breakfast. I was astonished to see one of my boys already there, drinking coffee. "What in the world got you up so early?" I asked, sliding into the booth across from him. "Couldn't you sleep last night?"

He laughed a little self-consciously. "Well, as a matter of fact, I didn't sleep too well. Funny you should come in here, Lawrence; I was just on my way up to see you."

"Oh?" I gave my order to the waitress. "What's on your mind?"

He looked a little embarrassed, unhappy even, and finally said, "Well, Lawrence, the other boys have asked me to be their spokesman and come and tell you that—well, we've been talking things over and we think the best thing to do is to, well, to leave."

For just a minute I didn't understand him. "Leave? Where do you want to go?"

"No, no. I don't mean like that. I mean we want to leave *you*. We want to leave the band." He paused. "We're quitting!"

"Oh, no," I said instantly. "Don't tell me that."

"Yeah, well, we've been talking it over, as I said, and we just think it's the best thing for all of us. And for you too, Lawrence. You won't have any trouble getting another band together."

I hardly heard him because I was still hearing him say, "We're quitting." "But, where are you going?" I asked.

"We'll probably go to Chicago."

"But we couldn't get anything in Chicago."

"You mean *you* couldn't get anything in Chicago! Maybe we can. I'm sorry, Lawrence, but"—he shrugged and spread his hands wide—"that's the way it is. So thanks and best of luck."

"Wait a minute!" I caught at his arm. "Just a minute. I know things haven't been going too well, but we're doing better now and we have the whole summer booked up! So why leave me now?"

He looked very uncomfortable. "We just feel we can do better on our own, that's all."

I persisted. "But why?"

Suddenly his face got red, and he leaned across the table and said tensely, "I'll tell you why. Because of you, that's why! We don't want to spend the rest of our life out here in these sticks and, Lawrence, that's where you're gonna be for the rest of your life! You're never gonna make it in the big time! Let me tell you something." He gestured angrily. "You still bounce around like you're playing at a barn dance somewhere and you can't even speak English! So if you want to know the real reason we're leaving, it's *you*. You're the one who is holding us all back."

I was so bewildered, so dumbfounded at his sudden attack, that I just sat there staring at him, and after a moment he said awkwardly, "Lawrence, I'm sorry, but you asked for it. You wanted to know."

I paid the waitress and got up out of the booth and was surprised to feel how unsteady my legs were. I realized I was shivering a little, and I walked out into the early morning sunshine and then went back to the hotel and did something I had never done in my life before—I went back to bed in the daytime.

I felt sick, numb, almost paralyzed with shock, and I couldn't get those blunt words out of my mind: *You're never gonna make it in the big time; you can't even speak English. You're the one who's holding us all back!* Suddenly I swallowed hard and rolled over in bed and buried my face deep, deep into the pillow. I think it was the lowest moment of my lifetime.

The next few days were a blur to me. The word got around very fast, and I had several telephone calls from other small bands offering me a chance to join their groups. But something kept me from accepting their offers. A very strong conviction began to gnaw at me: Music was my life and no matter what had happened, I should get my own group together. In the light of what had just occurred, that seemed almost idiotic, but I felt strongly about it. I would try to start all over again with a brand-new band.

A day or so later I did something I recommend for anyone who has had a life-shattering experience. I dropped into an open church during the day for some quiet reflection. It was a small church, plain, but comfortable. In front of me was a crucifix. As I stared at the form on the cross, I had a flash of insight which ever since has helped me anytime I feel low.

All men are vulnerable—even Jesus was as a man— and whenever we put our love and faith into other human beings, we open ourselves to hurts and disappointments.

It's a part of life—we hurt each other—often unintentionally. The only one we can trust completely is God.

I came out of church that day able to function again and soon had another orchestra together. The bitterness drained away. And when there were insults or rebuffs or defeats, I didn't take them so personally. For how could any of our wounds compare with those He suffered for us?

7.

Hope for People Who Need Forgiveness

Judge not, and ye shall not be judged: condemn not, and ye shall not be condemned: forgive, and ye shall be forgiven.

LUKE 6:37

I'm Still Learning to Forgive

by Corrie Ten Boom

The author of The Hiding Place *remembers the day she learned the full meaning of "love your enemies."*

It was in a church in Munich that I saw him, a balding heavyset man in a gray overcoat, a brown felt hat clutched between his hands. People were filing out of the basement room where I had just spoken, moving along the rows of wooden chairs to the door at the rear. It was 1947 and I had come from Holland to defeated Germany with the message that God forgives.

It was the truth they needed most to hear in that bitter, bombed-out land, and I gave them my favorite mental picture. Maybe because the sea is never far from a Hollander's mind, I liked to think that that's where forgiven sins were thrown. "When we confess our sins," I said, "God casts them into the deepest ocean, gone forever."

The solemn faces stared back at me, not quite daring to believe. There were never questions after a talk in Germany in 1947. People stood up in silence, in silence collected their wraps, in silence left the room.

And that's when I saw him, working his way forward against the others. One moment I saw the overcoat and the brown hat; the next, a blue uniform and a visored cap with its skull and crossbones. It came back with a rush: the huge room with its harsh overhead lights, the pathetic pile of dresses and shoes in the center of the floor, the shame of walking naked past this man. I could see my sister's frail form ahead of me, ribs sharp beneath the parchment skin. Betsie, how thin you were!

Betsie and I had been arrested for concealing Jews in our home during the Nazi occupation of Holland; this man had been a guard at Ravensbrück concentration camp where we were sent.

Now he was in front of me, hand thrust out: "A fine message, *Fräulein!* How good it is to know that, as you say, all our sins are at the bottom of the sea!"

And I, who had spoken so glibly of forgiveness, fumbled in my pocketbook rather than take that hand. He would not remember me, of course—how could he remember one prisoner among those thousands of women?

But I remembered him and the leather crop swinging from his belt. It was the first time since my release that I had been face to face with one of my captors and my blood seemed to freeze.

"You mentioned Ravensbrück in your talk," he was saying. "I was a guard in there." No, he did not remember me.

"But since that time," he went on, "I have become a Christian. I know that God has forgiven me for the cruel things I did there, but I would like to hear it from your lips as well. *Fräulein*—" again the hand came out—"will you forgive me?"

And I stood there—I whose sins had every day to be forgiven—and could not. Betsie had died in that place— could he erase her slow terrible death simply for the asking?

It could not have been many seconds that he stood there, hand held out, but to me it seemed hours as I wrestled with the most difficult thing I had ever had to do.

For I had to do it—I knew that. The message that God forgives has a prior condition: that we forgive those who have injured us. "If you do not forgive men their trespasses," Jesus says, "neither will your Father in heaven forgive your trespasses."

I knew it not only as a commandment of God, but as a daily experience. Since the end of the war I had had a home in Holland for victims of Nazi brutality. Those who were able to forgive their former enemies were able also to return to the outside world and rebuild their lives, no matter what the physical scars. Those who nursed their bitterness remained invalids. It was as simple and as horrible as that.

And still I stood there with the coldness clutching my

heart. But forgiveness is not an emotion—I knew that too. Forgiveness is an act of the will, and the will can function regardless of the temperature of the heart. "Jesus, help me!" I prayed silently. "I can lift my hand. I can do that much. You supply the feeling."

And so woodenly, mechanically, I thrust my hand into the one stretched out to me. And as I did, an incredible thing took place. The current started in my shoulder, raced down my arm, sprang into our joined hands. And then this healing warmth seemed to flood my whole being, bringing tears to my eyes.

"I forgive you, brother!" I cried. "With all my heart!"

For a long moment we grasped each other's hands, the former guard and the former prisoner. I had never known God's love so intensely as I did then.

And having thus learned to forgive in this hardest of situations, I never again had difficulty in forgiving: I wish I could say it! I wish I could say that merciful and charitable thoughts just naturally flowed from me from then on. But they didn't. If there's one thing I've learned at 80 years of age, it's that I can't store up good feelings and behavior—but only draw them fresh from God each day.

Maybe I'm glad it's that way. For every time I go to Him, He teaches me something else. I recall the time, some 15 years ago, when some Christian friends whom I loved and trusted did something which hurt me. You would have thought that, having forgiven the Nazi guard, this would have been child's play. It wasn't. For weeks I seethed inside. But at last I asked God again to work His miracle in me. And again it happened: first the cold-blooded decision, then the flood of joy and peace. I had forgiven my friends; I was restored to my Father.

Then, why was I suddenly awake in the middle of the night, hashing over the whole affair again? *My friends!* I thought. *People I loved!* If it had been strangers, I wouldn't have minded so.

I sat up and switched on the light. "Father, I thought it was all forgiven! Please help me do it!"

But the next night I woke up again. They'd talked so sweetly too! Never a hint of what they were planning. "Father!" I cried in alarm. "Help me!"

His help came in the form of a kindly Lutheran pastor to whom I confessed my failure after two sleepless weeks. "Up in that church tower," he said, nodding out the window, "is a bell which is rung by pulling on a rope. But you know what? After the sexton lets go of the rope, the bell keeps on swinging. First *ding* then *dong*. Slower and slower until there's a final *dong* and it stops.

"I believe the same thing is true of forgiveness. When we forgive someone, we take our hand off the rope. But if we've been tugging at our grievances for a long time, we mustn't be surprised if the old angry thoughts keep coming for a while. They're just the ding-dongs of the old bell slowing down."

And so it proved to be. There were a few more midnight reverberations, a couple of dings when the subject came up in my conversation. But the force—which was my willingess in the matter—had gone out of them. They came less and less often and at last stopped altogether. And so I discovered another secret of forgiveness: that we can trust God not only above our emotions, but also above our thoughts.

And still He had more to teach me, even in this single episode. Because many years later, in 1970, an American with whom I had shared the ding-dong principle came to visit me in Holland and met the people involved. "Aren't those the friends who let you down?" he asked as they left my apartment.

"Yes," I said a little smugly. "You can see it's all forgiven."

"By you, yes," he said. "But what about them? Have they accepted your forgiveness?"

"They say there's nothing to forgive! They deny it ever happened. But I can prove it!" I went eagerly to my desk. "I have it in black and white! I saved all their letters and I can show you where—"

"Corrie!" My friend slipped his arm through mine and gently closed the drawer. "Aren't you the one whose sins are at the bottom of the sea? And are the sins of your friends etched in black and white?"

For an anguishing moment I could not find my voice. "Lord Jesus," I whispered at last, "who takes all my sins away, forgive me for preserving all these years the evidence against others! Give me grace to burn all the blacks and whites as a sweet-smelling sacrifice to Your glory."

I did not go to sleep that night until I had gone through my desk and pulled out those letters—curling now with age—and fed them all into my little coal-burning grate. As the flames leaped and glowed, so did my heart. "Forgive us our trespasses," Jesus taught us to pray, "as we forgive those who trespass against us." In the ashes of those letters I was seeing yet another facet of His mercy. What more He would teach me about forgiveness in the days ahead I didn't know, but tonight's was good news enough.

When we bring our sins to Jesus, He not only forgives them, He makes them as if they had never been.

REQUISITES FOR CONTENTED LIVING

Health enough to make work a pleasure.
Wealth enough to support your needs.
Patience enough to toil until some good is accomplished.
Strength enough to battle with difficulties and
   overcome them.
Grace enough to confess your sins and forsake them.
Charity enough to see some good in your neighbor.
Love enough to make you useful and helpful to others.
Faith enough to make real the things of God.
Hope enough to remove all anxious fears concerning
   the future.

JOHANN WOLFGANG VON GOETHE

How Could I Take Him Back?

by Eunice Thomas*

Bill had left me for another woman, and hate was about to destroy me.

I realized my relationship to my husband had changed some time before he moved from our room to the guest room. Later, after weeks of tension, tears and unanswered questions about late hours, Bill admitted the truth. He was in love with Ellen, his secretary, and asked me to file suit for divorce. He wanted to marry her.

When I could speak over the suffocation of shock and pain, I said, "Bill, our marriage was for keeps." Then in anger, "I'll see you dead first."

As the battle intensified, with Bill unmoved, I crumpled to the floor pleading for the children and me. He left.

The pattern of our lives changed. Sundays passed unheeded, with Sunday school and worship unattended. Soon my friend and neighbor, Sally, began taking my children to church with her family.

I simply couldn't face people. Sally was my only contact. I shopped at a distant market, evading friends, and refused to answer my door even when my pastor called.

If tears could have healed, I would have been healed. And intermittently I prayed to God to bring Bill to his senses, begging Him to punish Bill, to hurt him, anything to bring him back.

The only contact I had with Bill was by mail when he sent support money with notes begging me to proceed with

---

*Names in this story have been changed.

232

the divorce. Each note hardened the fact that I would hold him. If he couldn't belong to me and the children, he'd never belong to Ellen.

As the months passed, I ceased my efforts to maneuver God. The breast-beating and tears had frozen into utter hate. It soon affected my relationship to the children. Often I corrected them harshly and served them grudgingly.

Even when I noticed that they were lean, nervous and unhappy, I couldn't stir from my muteness.

Bill came by in March. I was stone. He asked my forgiveness and told me he'd sent Ellen away two months ago. Now he wanted to come home to me and the children.

Calling him a fool, I explained I had refused to divorce him to spite him and now for the same reason, I would file suit for divorce.

The color drained from Bill's face. When I showed him the door, slamming it, I laughed all the way to the kitchen. I laughed till the tears flooded.

Sally came over a few moments later. Taking in the situation, she spread her sweater over my shoulders, then poured coffee for the two of us.

When the chill subsided, she said, "I knew Bill was coming. The pastor and my husband have been with him lots lately—praying it out with Bill, I mean. Bill didn't feel he could ask you to forgive him."

"He has killed me, that's what he has done! Now it's too late!"

Sally said, "Maybe. But, Eunice, you're making the mistake of your life. Now you are more guilty of sin than Bill. You're withholding love from the children."

"Don't come here with your self-righteousness and accuse me of sin," I said angrily. "What do you know about this? Nathan has been true to you!"

Tears surfaced in Sally's eyes. "Right, I can't come in with self-righteousness, Eunice. You see, I once had an affair with another man and left Nathan and my babies." Her voice trembled. "Nathan loved enough to forgive me and ask me to come home."

It was hard to believe. The Cummingses were such a happy family. Sally was crying quietly now. I felt the steel give in me and I said, "I'm listening, Sally."

Finally she said, "I know what Bill is going through.

He's been so mixed up and he asked the pastor for help. You need help, too; admit it. You are not the same person. You are as sick as Bill was."

Angrily I threw her sweater at her and asked her to go. She started to leave, then stopped at the door with tears on her cheeks and said, "Before I go, I have to tell you that your sins can't be forgiven until you forgive Bill. It's in the Lord's Prayer. I also suggest you read First Corinthians, Chapter 13, to see what you are not."

Sally had penetrated my shell. I couldn't stand it. I wanted to die. I couldn't forgive.

When evening came, I sent the children to Sally with a note asking if they could spend the night with her. Alone with myself, I faced the idea of death. But now an alarm surged through me. Something inside me rejected the death wish and I knew I wanted to live. *Dear God, I do want to live.*

A great sleepiness overcame me. Sleep might ease me, but as I lay in bed, suddenly I was wide awake and felt impelled to open my Bible to the chapter in First Corinthians. It disclosed the truth of all my guilt and lack of love. I said aloud, "Lord, please help me."

On my knees I started the Lord's Prayer, struggling to a stop when I came to, "Forgive us our trespasses." I couldn't go on. Then I asked God to take over for me, to pray the words for me.

Now I was weeping new kinds of tears, repentance tears, the great healing tears for the human heart. It was as though God spoke the words for me the way a teacher coaches a child. I felt His presence about me like a glowing radiance and at the same time His unspeakable dearness filled my heart. I tried to ask forgiveness as I forgave Bill, but the words were extinguished from my mind. The act of forgiveness had become a condition.

I wept in joy. Christ in my heart for the first time was intensely beautiful. It was as though Christ revealed to me the sorrows of the crucifixion and the absorption of human sorrows in the divine act of dying. He revealed to me the glory of the resurrection and the unspeakable happiness in this completion of His love.

Later I called Bill. His voice was dear. I said, "Bill, I love you, darling. God has dealt with me. Please come home."

Bill came. Neither of us had to plead forgiveness. The

restoration was a sacrament that no one can know without experiencing it. Our children experienced it too. They too have been restored in the sacrament of our love which is God's love in us.

―――――――――――

A Fragile Moment of Hope

For many years we planned and talked about our home. We drew the blueprints and did most of the construction ourselves. Finally, one June day, we moved in.

Several nights later I sat by the fireplace sewing, warm and dry, though it rained wildly outside. Suddenly a bolt of lightning shot down the fireplace, splitting it asunder, and hung suspended before me. Then it jumped to the steel beam and traveled out, taking the cellar blocks with it. Through the darkness that followed that earsplitting crash, I corraled the family, and hastened them out into the rain just as flames lit the windows and roared themselves into an inferno.

Morning came and we stood beside a steaming hole of fire, water and debris. The home we had dreamed about and worked on for over 13 years, had been swept away in 30 minutes. Dick's face seemed to mirror my heart; why try to rebuild? This slap of fate hurt too much.

Unable to bear the charred pieces, I turned and walked away.

"Marjorie!" Dick called. "Come here!" There was excitement, almost joy in his voice. Puzzled, I hurried over to where he stood.

There, amid scorched shrubbery, six feet to the right of where the cellar door had been, stood our rambler rose bush. Where yesterday it had boasted only green leaves, now it stood out in full flower—the heat of the fire had caused it to bloom overnight.

Its heavenly message of beauty and hope lifted our heavy hearts, so that we turned and faced again the smoking ruin. . . .

With the help of friends, neighbors, and even strangers, we did build again, and have lived now in our second dream home for 13 years.

MARJORIE ARRIS MEEHAN

The Forever Decision

by Barbara Jones Melendez

My parents told me I must give up my baby—and give up Frank too.

Frank and I had been dating for a year. During this time I had been forbidden to see him. His nationality was Spanish and his religion was Catholic—a far cry from my own strict Anglo-Protestant background.

My father said, "There's no use asking for problems by dating someone you could not possibly marry." I thought this was so unfair that I sneaked off to be with Frank anyway, and soon we were very much in love.

One night our feelings got too much for us. I felt so guilty afterward, and so did Frank. We both swore it would never happen again, but it didn't have to. That one time had been enough. I was pregnant.

God, God, God! What shall I do? What shall I do? Suicide? My mother helps answer the phones at the Suicide and Crisis Prevention Center. I have heard her tell about the terrible feelings of guilt that families have when a member commits suicide. "Search me, oh God, and know my heart; try me and know my thoughts: And see if there be any wicked way in me, and lead me in the way everlasting." (Psalm 139: 23–24) That was the first Bible verse my mother ever taught me, and now it came to mind. That was the day I put my faith to work.

I remember that day so clearly. I had told my parents a huge lie about where I was going. As I left, my sweet mother stood in our front yard waving. Oh, how I loved her. If she only knew what I was doing! I cried all the way to Mexico. Frank and I got married there by lying about our ages.

Then the next day we drove back to Frank's home and told his parents. They were surprised, but understanding. They had a small apartment in back of their house and said we were welcome to it. Frank's whole family took me into their home so warmly.

The following day I wrote a long letter to my family. I let Frank's little brother stick it inside their screen door. I could not face them myself. They contacted the pastor of our church, and he came to talk with Frank and me. He told me how hurt my parents were and asked me to go home right away as they wanted to see me.

When my mother saw me, she kissed me and burst into tears. I never felt so bad in my life. They told me that my marriage would have to be annulled. They put me in a local home for unwed mothers.

All the girls there were so different. Most of them were in love with men who would not marry them. After a few hours of hearing their stories, I knew this was not the answer to my problem. I phoned my parents to come and get me and take me home.

They came right away and took me home. They said I could stay at home and have the baby, and we would put it out for adoption. I could then go back to school and finish my senior year and go on to college as we had planned. In college I could meet someone from my own background, marry and forget my past.

The next day my parents took me to the lawyer's office to sign the papers to have my marriage annulled. The papers were already prepared, and my parents signed first. Then it was my turn.

I took the pen in my hand and just stood there. All of a sudden I thought of all those girls in the unwed mothers' home. The boys they loved didn't care enough for them to accept responsibility for what had happened. But my Frank did. He loved me and wanted our baby. It was I who was letting my parents solve my problem.

"Oh my God, lead me in the way everlasting!"

I laid the pen down and asked my parents if I could talk to Frank once more before I signed.

When we saw each other, we knew what we must do. We could not be children any longer. Frank and I prayed together and asked God to give us the wisdom, strength and courage to continue our marriage and make it a good one, and to give our coming baby a happy life.

Frank and Michelle, our little girl, and I live now with Frank's parents. He has a job, and I am finishing my senior year of high school at night. We plan on working hard and putting ourselves through college. We know we have many strikes against us, but we love each other and are determined that with God's help we will make our young marriage work.

My parents, now that the shock is over, have come to accept Frank and they love their first grandchild. I'll never forgive myself for the hurt I have given them, and I only pray that Frank and I can be as good parents to our children as our own parents have been to us.

Forgive us our trespasses as we forgive those who trespass against us. Amen.

Editor's Note:
For this story, Barbara Jones Melendez received a Guideposts Youth Writing Contest scholarship.

Lord dismiss us with thy blessing,
Hope, and comfort from above;
Let us each, thy peace possessing,
Triumph in redeeming love.

—ROBERT HAWKER

I'm a Free Man Now

by Johnny Cash

This famous singer reveals the intimate story of his struggle with drugs.

The old man asked, "Are you feeling better now, Johnny?" I'd been lying there a long time, staring at the ceiling and fighting off the sickness. Now I looked at the old man. He looked like he was behind bars. But I knew that I was the one behind the bars, only I didn't know where the jail was or how I got there.

The old man said, "Let me know when you're ready."

I forced myself to sit up. "I'm ready now."

Ready for what? I wasn't sure why I'd been arrested. I figured it had something to do with the pills. Once before the pills had put me behind bars, but that time I was lucky.

That was in 1965. I had gone into Mexico to get a supply of the pills I felt I needed to stay alive. As I was reentering at El Paso, the customs inspector found the pills. That time I spent a day in jail. Because it was my first arrest, the judge let me off with a year's suspended sentence. There was a newspaper reporter in the courtroom; his story went out on the wires, and that's how people found out I was an addict.

A lot of people already knew. By then, I had been on pills five years. I took pep pills to turn me on enough to do a show. Then I took depressants to calm down enough to get some sleep. That, at least, was what my friends said. They said I was working too hard and traveling too much and trying to squeeze too much out of every day. They said maybe I should take some time off.

I knew better. I tried pep pills the first time because

239

they happened to be available one day when I was in the mood for a new kick. The high they gave me was beautiful. I felt I owned the world, and the world was perfect during those lofty moments. I couldn't believe that a couple of little pills could contain so much beauty and joy. I stayed on pills because they made me feel great. If people wanted to give excuses for my habit, I let them.

Then I began to realize that the highs were getting lower. The few pills I was on every day weren't enough anymore. I had to go from a few to several, then to dozens. Still that old feeling wasn't there. I was always nervous and tense and irritable. I didn't want to eat. I couldn't sleep. I started losing weight.

So I went on depressants, looking for lows, looking for peace. When I found peace, I couldn't trust it because I knew it was a fleeting peace. Soon I would crave to get high, and the highs would not come to me.

After the El Paso mess, I took an apartment with a friend who was also on pills. One day when my supply ran out, I remembered that he had some in his car. He was asleep and I couldn't find his keys, so I went out and broke into the car. When he later accused me of this, I denied it violently and we almost fought. He knew I was lying, and I knew he did. Next day, I admitted it, and he said he understood. We were like two cowardly kids forgiving each other for being afraid of the dark.

In time, I became afraid of everything. I would be a nervous wreck before a show; I was never sure of myself during a performance; I didn't believe people when they said things had gone all right. Sometimes I was too sick to work. Sometimes I didn't even show up. It didn't take booking agents long to stop risking their money on me. Even though I knew this meant a loss of income to others in the show, people who were good friends, I didn't care. I didn't care about anything.

I knew I was killing myself. I had seen drugs kill others. Whatever drug an addict is hooked on, he has to keep increasing his daily dosage to feel anywhere near normal.

---

*The word which God has written on the brow
of every man is Hope.*

—VICTOR HUGO

This is the nature of addiction. The day comes when he takes the overdose that kills him. Knowing this, I accepted early death as the inescapable fate of addicts: There was just no other way out. Even when I thought of all the things I had to be thankful for, I could find no hope for myself, no chance for change.

I was 12, I remembered, when electricity came to the small Arkansas farm where I was raised. Dad bought a radio, and I'll never forget the first Sunday night I heard the exciting country music from the Grand Ole Opry, in Nashville. That moment, I discovered my future. Right away, I started writing my own country songs, and I told everybody I was going to become an entertainer. I guess only my mother believed me. We were poor, and so she took in laundry to pay for a few voice lessons. At 17, I earned my first money at performing: the $15 first prize in an amateur contest. Then I learned to play the guitar.

In 1954, I attended a radio-announcing school, hoping that becoming a disc jockey might open doors to performing. To earn a living, I sold houseware door-to-door. I got to know guitarist Luther Perkins and bassist Marshall Grant. We put together an act; we rehearsed a lot; we worked whenever we could, whether or not we got paid. After a year, we agreed that the only way we could find out if we were ready for the Big Time was to audition for somebody big.

We auditioned for Sun Records, which led to our first recording. This led to a two-year contract at the Grand Ole Opry.

We made more recordings. We went on the road. We became known. By 1960 we had advanced enough to put together a show of our own. Then I moved on to the high of pills.

By 1967, I was on the verge of a nervous breakdown, and I knew it. I was usually on a hundred pills a day, but I got no pleasure from them, no peace. I couldn't stand my life, but I couldn't find my way out of it. One day my friends talked to me about entering a mental institution, and the thought of that completely shattered me. I got into my car, well supplied with pills, and headed south. I remember crossing the Georgia border. Next thing I knew, I was staring at a ceiling and an elderly jailer was asking me if I felt better.

I got up. He unlocked the door. I asked, "How did I get here?"

He said, "One of the night men found you stumbling around the streets. He brought you in so you wouldn't hurt yourself."

I followed him down a corridor and into his office, and I asked, "How much time do you think I'll get for this?"

He shook his head. "You're doing time right now, Johnny, the worst kind." He handed me an envelope. "Here are your things." As I was putting things into my pockets, he said, "I'm a fan of yours, Johnny. I've always admired you. It's a shame to see you ruining yourself. I didn't know you were this bad off."

I'd heard that sad song before, from concerned friends. I said, "Yeah. Sure."

He said, "I don't know where you think you got your talent from, Johnny, but if you think it came from God, then you're sure wrecking the body He put it in."

I said, "Yeah. Sure. Thanks. Can I go now?" He nodded.

That morning, as I stepped into the warm sunshine, I took a quick but deep look at my life over the past seven years, and I knew that I was a better man than that.

Maybe it was the reference to God that suddenly cleared my mind. I had been raised by religious parents; faith had always meant a lot to me; I have tried to express it in some of my songs. But until that morning it hadn't occurred to me to turn to God for help in kicking my habit.

I remembered this: "Know ye not that your body is the temple of the Holy Spirit which is in you, which ye have of God, and ye are not your own?" (I Corinthians 6:19) This helped convince me that I must try to break my habit. But how?

And I remembered this: God had given me a free will, and I had freely used it in deciding to experiment with the drugs which had now robbed me of it. I realized that to be free again I would need all the will power I could acquire and I knew this power could come only from God, Who had created me free. I asked Him to go to work on me, to forgive me then and there.

Back in Nashville, I went to June Carter and Marshall Grant, and I told them, "I'm kicking pills, as of now. I don't expect it to be easy, so I'll need your help. See to it that I eat regular meals. See to it that I keep regular hours. If I can't sleep, sit and talk to me. If we run out of talk, then let's pray."

We prayed a lot. I am a free man now, as I have been since that morning when I discovered that I could be once again.

Because of the kind of work I do, it is difficult to sweep past mistakes under the rug. Every once in a while, I meet some youngster who knows I used to be an addict, as he is now, and he asks me what he can do to kick his habit. I tell him what I learned, "Give God's temple back to Him. The alternative is death."

The Lord is my light and my salvation; whom shall I fear? The Lord is the strength of my life; of whom shall I be afraid?

PSALM 27:1

The Old Bureau
by Hazel F. Zieman

It's hard to believe that an old piece of furniture could kill a friendship.

I would never have believed an old bureau could have caused such bitterness between Barbara and me. Next-door neighbors for six years, we were close friends, one or the other always on hand if needed.

But then came the sale. Distant cousins of mine were moving out of state. They had to get rid of much of their furniture.

"She's letting several of her lovely pieces go," I told Barbara. "One of them is a bureau of solid walnut, over a hundred years old. You must go with me to the sale."

"Always trying to get me interested in antiques," Barbara laughed. "All right, I'll go," she agreed.

"And be prepared to buy something this time," I urged her.

My grandmother had told me how great-great Uncle Ned had built the bureau, had carved the oak-leaf handles himself, had taken it across the country in a covered wagon. I'd admired the bureau many times, not dreaming I'd have the chance to own it.

At my cousin's suggestion, we went over very early the day of the sale, so we could choose any of the things we wished. My cousin was on the phone when we got there, but her husband began to show us around. I was looking at some old pieces of silver, waiting to tell my cousin I'd take the bureau, when Barbara walked up and said, "Well, I did it. I bought something."

"Good! Show me what you got," I said. She took me over and pointed to the bureau. "Not my bureau!" I must

244

have shouted, for Barbara backed off, looking shocked and hurt.

"*Your* bureau! I thought that's what you wanted me to buy," she said.

I must have gone temporarily insane. I said some awful things to Barbara: how she *knew* I wanted that bureau more than anything in the world. How I thought she was my friend. How I hated her for this. Barbara ran out of the house. I never did find out how she got home.

I felt sick inside. Several times in the next few days, I started to go over to apologize. When I finally did get up my nerve, Barbara saw me coming and ran from her yard into the house. I didn't know what to do, so I went back home. Weeks passed without our talking with each other.

One day, we unexpectedly came face to face in the supermarket. Both of us stammered "hello," but that was all. Gradually the whole thing began to look pretty ridiculous to me. I'd got us into this mess and I'd get us out.

So I went over and rang Barbara's door bell. "This whole thing is silly," I said.

"I've known that for a long time," she answered. But her voice was icy, and she didn't smile.

I choked up and turned away. How could she make it so hard for me?

The next month, at PTA meeting, Barbara and I were both assigned to the planning committee for our annual spring festival. I thanked God for another chance. Maybe Barbara would have changed her mind by now and be willing to meet me halfway. But when the committee met, she didn't show up. "Isn't Barbara coming?" I asked the chairman.

"Said she couldn't possibly serve. Personal reasons."

Well! I thought. *That's certainly a slap in the face!*

A strange ugliness settled inside me. It squeezed my throat muscles, slithered into my head, until the pressure gave me a headache.

When my cousin had phoned to say Barbara didn't want the bureau and when would I like to pick it up, I had told her to take one of the other offers she had on it, that I never wanted to see it again. And now I hated it more than ever.

One day I was reading my Bible for a few minutes after the children left for school. I'd got into the book of

Ephesians and was starting the fourth chapter. A couple of
lines pricked at me.

"Accept life with humility and patience, making al-
lowances for one another." (J.B. Phillips translation)

I read that passage over and over. "Making al-
lowances . . . because you love one another." Hadn't I
tried to love Barbara with Christian love? Then I put the
Bible down and kneeled beside my bed in desperation.

"God," I prayed, "this is such a little thing, but it's
got so terribly big inside of me. All I can feel for Barbara
is resentment. I've tried to love her, but it just doesn't
seem to work. I know You have enough love. If I could
just borrow from You for a while, I'm sure the feeling will
come to me."

A great sense of relief filled me. I moved happily
through my household routine and felt a joyous antici-
pation for my husband and children's homecoming and
our family dinner, for the countless little things of the next
few days.

But God wasn't through with me. A couple of days
later, as I was reading on in Ephesians, I came across
these words: "If you are angry, be sure that it is not out
of wounded pride or bad temper." (Ephesians 4:26, J.B.
Phillips translation)

No wonder I hadn't been able to feel Christian love.
All this time I'd been blaming Barbara for refusing to do
her part. It began to be clear that God expected something
more of me. If His love was going to show through me, it
needed some sort of action on *my* part!

I was going to have to demonstrate my feelings.
Several times that week, I called "hello" to Barbara across
the backyard fence. By the end of the week, she answered
my greeting.

Open house at school was coming up the next Tuesday, so I went over to her house that morning.

"Barbara, I'm going down to open house tonight.
Won't you ride with me?"

She hesitated, giving me a long puzzled look. Silently
I prayed, *God bless you, Barbara,* and I tried to beam a
feeling of love toward her. Aloud I said, "I'd really like to
have you."

I'm sure she felt something, for she smiled suddenly.
"All right," she said.

Every time I was with Barbara, I beamed love toward her. It wasn't long until our old relationship had returned.

I know those verses from Ephesians by heart now. They taught me that what I can do is pretty limited. But what God can do through me, if I let Him, is something else again.

A Fragile Moment of Hope

The sun had not yet risen as I walked alone along the beach. The night's high tide had left the beach strewn with debris. An egret, which once had glided in the blue, lay lifeless on the sand. Matted seaweed, once a living part of the deep, now was discarded by the waves. Driftwood, too, once green and growing, lay in silver-gray desolation.

Tears welled in my eyes. Those tragic bits and pieces, broken and still, were reminders of something in my life which had once been vibrant and alive, but now, too, was dead.

I slumped on the sand and closed my eyes. How long I sat there I do not know. Then a child's shout rang across the beach.

Two children were running down the beach. As I looked up, they stopped. They had found the egret. For a moment they stood silently around it. Then they dug a grave with a piece of driftwood, buried the bird, and placed shells in an elaborate pattern on the mound.

With a whoop, they then dashed to the seaweed. Draping it around their waists, they wiggled their hips and, in their imagination, were in Hawaii. A long tendril became a jump rope. In each newfound object there was fresh discovery.

Everything they looked at, I had looked at. Yet while I saw only death, they saw wonder and excitement.

I rose and started home. A fragment of Scripture, half-forgotten, came to mind: *Forgetting those things which are behind, and reaching forth unto those things which are before . . .* (Philippians 3:13)

The rays of the rising sun flooded the hills. The sand became thousands of diamonds, and I walked on them. It *was* the beginning of a new day.

JOSEPHINE JENSEN

By that summer of 1964 I had come up the circuit
somewhat and had already been in some races against the

My Race Against Hate
by Mario Andretti

One of auto racing's great drivers tells how a
personal rivalry almost ruined his life.

The green flag drops and my foot flicks the 700 horses
throbbing behind me into a roaring snarl. The pavement
of the famed Indy 500 slips past, and snugged within my
Lotus Ford's cockpit I swing into the warm-up laps.

One has time to think in the warm-up . . . and to
pray the little prayer my mother taught me as a child in
Italy. Somehow it encompasses all the important things—
to return safe, to do well in the eyes of God. It does not
ask to win. I figure that's something I must earn. It will be
the same with the other drivers. Each will be fighting to
win, as it should be.

Honest competition is healthy. But there is one element that must not develop within it, on the track or in any
other phase of life—personal animosity. I know how
deadly this can be, for it happened to me.

I don't exactly remember when the vendetta between
racing driver A. J. Foyt and myself started. But I remember when it came close to killing one of us, or both.

You might say it began to develop in 1964. A. J.
Foyt had already won four national championships and
two of his three Indianapolis 500 victories. I was a brash
24-year-old kid just cutting his teeth on dirt-track racing.
Only nine years earlier I had come over from Italy with
my parents, sister and twin brother, Aldo. Aldo and I already had the racing bug and not long after the family
settled in Nazareth, Pennsylvania, we were bouncing
around in local dirt-track races in an old home-built
jalopy.

By that summer of 1964 I had come up the circuit somewhat and had already been in some races against the famed A.J. He was the next thing to unbeatable. By summer he had racked up six straight championships and in most of them he finished so far in front he had time for lunch before the other drivers even saw the checkered flag.

Being a young upstart, I began to fester about it. It didn't help any when Clint Brawner, our head mechanic, said, "Let me give you some advice, Mario. Don't worry about Foyt. Let him run his race and you run yours. There is no way you can beat him. So there's no sense skinning your back trying."

Then, when Al Dean, owner of the cars we were driving, tried to offer me some fatherly advice on the same subject, I blew off in his face. "Al," I yelled, "I just want you to put it on paper that you will give me a thousand dollars every time I beat Foyt." Al just laughed and walked away.

Well! I muttered to myself. If the other drivers wanted to believe they couldn't beat Foyt, it was their business. But for me, it wadded up in my stomach like a soggy batch of pancakes.

It came to a head August 15 when I entered the 30-lap sprint race at Allentown Fair in Pennsylvania. Sprint racing, by the way, is with small fast racers on a bumpy dirt track. You're usually bunched together and every move is a reflex.

Until then I still hadn't won a major race, but I'd been close finisher in many. At the Allentown event I qualified for the pole position. Foyt started fifth. When the green flag dropped, he charged for the lead and accidentally bumped my left front wheel while we roared into the first turn. I swung out high, out of control, looping into the second turn and skidded sideways to a screeching stop. Maybe it was seeing a good chance for victory fly out the window, but I was hotter than my smoking tires. I went berserk. By the time we restarted my car I was a lap behind. But I jammed that accelerator to the floor and roared off like I was possessed.

There was no way I could win the race this far behind, or even finish in the top ten. But my mind had shrunk to a size that could only carry one thought—*get Foyt.*

It took me several laps to catch the tail-end cars. But

once I got them in view I charged past them all over the track. The crowd sensed something was up and began screaming like spectators at a Roman circus. The track was slick and I still don't know how I stayed on it. I nipped the outside wall several times and broke my right rear wheel late in the race. But I was blind mad, passing cars in unbelievable places, running some of them off the track.

Rufus, my mechanic and car owner, was going nuts, jumping up and down and waving his arms, trying to get me off the track.

Near the end, Foyt was running third with veteran driver Branson fourth. As I snarled up to Branson's tail, he must have thought I was out of my mind. Here was a nut in last place fighting him as if it was for the world championship. We dueled for several laps before I slipped past him on the final one. As I roared out of the last turn, Foyt was in my sights—but he was crossing the finish line. Thank God. If I had caught him, I would have bumped him, which would have been indefensible and could have wiped us both out.

When it was over, I was ashamed of myself. However, it seemed inevitable that Foyt and I had got on a collision course.

Once I began winning races, the ingredients were there for the people who like to start feuds. Foyt was the champion. I was the new boy in town, a challenger to the throne.

Next thing you know, so-called friends were sidling up to each of us with all sorts of "confidential intelligence."

A fellow would mutter to me: "Foyt says you are too brave for your own good and somebody should tell you that you should use your brains."

Somebody would tell Foyt: "Andretti says your reputation is much bigger than you are and he will smoke you off the next time."

Most of this was pure bunk, if not a gross exaggeration of casual remarks. But it did the devil's work, stirring the fires of our personal enmity.

I remember when we were racing at the Minnesota Fair. Usually all the drivers stay at the same hotel. There's a lot of camaraderie and kibitzing around. But Foyt and I couldn't enter into it. We were both letting our grudges eat into us. When we'd meet in the hall, it was like two icebergs passing.

Worse, our animosity spilled over onto the track; we were cutting each other off, bumping wheels. At 150 miles an hour a wheel bump can be as deadly as a cannon shot.

Our friends were becoming quite concerned about us. For one has enough worries at the wheel without this element. One way or another, we had to have a showdown. It happened, in a very unusual way.

It was just before the DuQuoin Fair race in Illinois in 1966. We were all at the drivers' meeting about an hour before the race. There was the usual hubbub, men talking, asking questions, straightening out details.

I was by myself. I happened to look up across the room, and there was A.J. standing there alone. Suddenly from somewhere deep within myself came the conviction that it was wrong to let rivalry turn into bitterness. We should not be enemies. Somebody had to put an end to the bad feelings. So I walked over to him. "Maybe we should talk," I said.

"Sure," he said, with a light in his eye.

We walked out to the parking lot behind the building, just the two of us. A hot Midwestern sun beat down on the asphalt and somewhere a racer rumbled in warm-up. We stood there and talked, openly and frankly.

Foyt and I viewed the whole picture together. We didn't say much, just covered the important things, talking objectively, without anger, two people discussing a situation to which they were witnesses instead of participants.

We admitted to a mutual love—racing. And we knew if we kept going the same way, we would divide our world into two camps. We decided that it did nobody any good for us to nurse a grudge.

That was it. The air was cleared and we walked out of the lot together, each minus a ton of weight from his shoulders.

Sure, we still go at it every time we get a chance. Foyt believes there is only one position in which to finish—first. So do I. But that little undercurrent of viciousness is no longer there. He's a great driver, some say the best. All I'll say is that the big dude will keep you busy on the track. If you are leading and he's in the field, you know that sooner or later he will be nipping at you. However, today we race wheel to wheel and do not worry.

There's something in the Bible that says if two men have a bone to pick with each other, one should go to the other and talk it over with him in private: "Moreover if thy brother shall trespass against thee, go and tell him his fault between thee and him alone: if he shall hear thee thou hast gained thy brother." (Matthew 18:15)

Well, I can tell you it works. It did for A.J. and me in the parking lot at DuQuoin.

My grace is sufficient for thee; for my strength is made perfect in weakness.

II Corinthians 12:9

And Then One Day
Nancy Became Beautiful

by Waulea Renegar

The story of a young woman who found a friend.

I first saw Nancy when she strode through the foyer doors of our church. Black mesh stockings stretched between white leather boots and a matching leather skirt. Her hair flamed crimson above blue eyes, and I was hypnotized as she moved toward me, for I knew Nancy to be, at 22, a drug addict and a prostitute.

My protected, church-oriented life flashed neon for her. Even the dullness in her eyes could not veil the contempt she had for me. I suddenly felt I had wronged her, even though I had never seen her before. She walked past me without a word, down the aisle and directly into my husband's study.

Behind the closed door Nancy voiced her hatred for people like those straights in the foyer.

"Look, I'm a junkie. I'm a prostitute. I'm wanted by the police for hot checks. A pimp's out to get me for a bad debt." She opened her handbag and cradled a revolver in the palm of her hand. Her eyes were like flint as she spoke more to inform than to convince: "He'll never lay a hand on me." She shot a defiant look across the desk. "I'm in trouble. What are *you* going to do about it?"

For months my husband had been working with the local vice and narcotics squads and had seen women like Nancy. The Holy Spirit let him hear her cry for help. "Is that all?" he asked calmly.

Her eyes narrowed. She apparently had expected

253

shock, disgust. His calm acceptance threw her momentarily.

"Well?" she snapped.

"Well?" he countered.

She whirled around and stalked across the study to the outside exit. She paused, her hand on the knob. "I can't talk tonight. I'm high. Can I see you tomorrow?" Without looking around, she added, with effort, "Please."

"Two o'clock." He gave her our home address.

That evening my husband suggested that Nancy could be serious about wanting help. I nodded, casually accepting his advice to keep cool if she should call. Aware of my naiveté, he stressed that I should not show shock, contempt or rejection, regardless of her crude revelations. Those reactions would make her feel justified in returning to drugs with me as the culprit.

The next day Nancy was on my doorstep, her liquid eyes checking me sullenly. I invited her in; she scuffed past me, flopping into a chair.

"Wanting drugs is hard to get rid of," she began. Nancy was not one for small talk. She not only hit the nail, but she sent it crashing through the wood on impact. "When I want a fix, like now, the hardest thing to do is tell somebody. I know people want to help me. I know in my heart drugs are wrong. But when I need them, I don't want help—I want a fix." Her eyes rolled back in her head and I noticed how damp her face was becoming.

My eyes began to sting. I wanted to speak. I could not think of a thing to say. She opened her eyes and read me again. "Not this time," she said with genuine regret. She rose and left, handing a paper to me as she passed. On it was written:

DIRTY SUNDAY

I'll more than likely sit completely still in my easy
*   chair with my two bare feet*
And watch the reckless rats rush off to worship and
*   reek in their role of the meek*
Where there they will learn how to make one more
*   false face to wear in their new moneymaking*
*   week.*

That was Nancy. She walked up and asked for my

hand, whacked it good, then became offended if I did not appreciate the slap. I was irritated, but kept in mind what my husband had said.

It has always fascinated me how people like Nancy eat the scum of life, experience the ultimate in rejection and humiliation, then hold on to the myth that they have a lease on honesty. Straight people, like myself, somehow could not know or be as honest as the degraded sufferer. Our motives and actions were suspect. Our words must be scrutinized for truth. Yet she expected me to accept every word she spoke as perceptive, knowledgeable gospel. She was batting me around like a ball.

I prayed much over my attitude. A change gradually came in my thinking. As her visits continued, I began to share with her what Christ meant to me. Sometimes she laughed. Other times I knew He was speaking His love to her. It was a startling revelation the first day I realized that Nancy was worth knowing even if she never changed. When Nancy realized I felt this way she no longer had the upper hand.

Then came the afternoon when she had been unusually critical of people in general and she made a crack about "my sort of people."

"Look, friend," I snapped, "quit walking on my feelings. You don't like people cutting you down. I don't either. Being straight doesn't mean I don't have feelings. Friends don't walk *on* each other, they walk *with* each other." I extended my hand. "Friends?"

"You think of us as friends?" she asked in half-belief.

"You're drinking my coffee, aren't you?"

Something new began for Nancy. It had begun for me earlier. It was no more than a month later that she accepted Jesus Christ and ceremonially surrendered her needle with an announcement, "I'm kicking it, cold turkey."

I accepted the news in innocent, unabandoned joy. I was soon to learn the sentence she had passed upon herself. I listened to her labored breathing and heard her swallow air like a tiring swimmer. By degrees her voice deepened, slowed and drew out into nauseated groans. The groans extended, rising in pitch and weakening. I shall never forget her pain.

She began to attend church services three times weekly. "Boy, if my friends could see me," she hooted one evening after services. "Talking and shaking hands with all those *church* people." From habit, she made "church" come out sounding dirty. She flinched. "That's another habit I've got to break."

"That makes ninety," I parried without smiling. Her face exploded into a kaleidoscope of gaiety. She was beautiful.

From the first, the people of our congregation knew about Nancy. They accepted her conversion as payment in full to join the family. They had her in their homes for meals and they prayed for her as the mounting crises developed.

"I just don't get them. They know what I've been and yet they treat me like I'm one of them."

"Nancy, when will you quit enjoying self-pity?" I allowed my irritation to show. "Christ has done no greater favor for you than He has for them. He forgave us all, and not a one of us deserved it—you included. We can no more reject you than you can reject us. We're stuck with each other. You put up with us. We'll put up with you. And, thank God, Christ will put up with us all."

She looked stricken. I forced a smile and extended my hand. "Friends?"

Her blue eyes melted before me. Those were the first tears I had seen her shed. "Oh, yes," she choked, grasping my hand tightly. "Thank God, yes!"

Now abideth faith, hope, love, these three; but the greatest of these is love.

I CORINTHIANS 13:13

those church people? From habit, she made "church"
sound out and and

A Sponsor for My Life
by Abbot Mills

---

*A former combat news cameraman recounts
his roughest assignment—defeating alcoholism.*

It was nearly three in the afternoon but I was still in bed
at home in Connecticut, alone, sick—mentally and physically sick from a month of hard drinking while on assignment in the hot Texas sun.

My wife Jody and our three youngest children were
off at a summer camp and tomorrow I was supposed to fly
to California on another assignment as cameraman for a
TV documentary. But as I lay on the bed, it became more
and more evident that I just wasn't going to be able to
make that California assignment.

I fumbled for the phone and called Liz, the secretary
for the firm I was working for.

"Are you okay?" she asked.

I admitted being tired and having an upset stomach
and said I'd call back. Liz was an alcoholic, but she was
one who had hit bottom and come up with the right answer—an organization of alcoholics who were helping
each other overcome their problem. I'm sure she was the
only one who knew I was an alcoholic. My wife and children didn't know. And neither—at that point—did I.

I had been this sick before and had thought about
slowing down on the drinking. I even worried about being
an alcoholic but knew that with a few drinks and a little
rest I would be as good as the next drinker.

Being in a creative field, I felt that I needed liquor
for stimulation.

I lay on the bed, becoming sicker. For a moment it
seemed I was back in Vietnam where I had been a TV

257

news cameraman, hanging out the side port of a helicopter gun ship with my camera as we swooped in low for a rocket attack.

Suddenly the phone rang. It was Liz: "How would you like me and two fine gentlemen to drive out there and pick you up? We'll get you a room in New York. You should get out of that house."

"Why not," I said, too weak to argue. I hung up the phone and collapsed, weeping with self-pity. So it had come to this at last. People were coming to get me.

As we drove into New York, I remember liking the men because they didn't talk very much.

I spent a long, miserable night in that New York hotel, realizing that I was finally going to turn down a good work assignment because of alcohol.

I was helpless and lonely. Long ago I had stopped thinking about God. He was for those few who were able to believe. Why should He care about someone in my rotten shape?

Church? You could have it. Everyone sat there looking so sanctimonious and then out in the parking lot they honked at you to let them by.

Morning came, and I called Liz and gave up the assignment. Then I went to my folks' home in Washington, D.C., where I tried to recuperate. My parents were kind and didn't lecture me, but the doctor I visited said that I might die in six months if I kept drinking. He said my liver was damaged, but with the proper care it might heal in several months. I assured him and everyone else that I was never going to touch the stuff again!

For three months I drank a lot of iced coffee and chewed great quantities of gum. Then another doctor pronounced my liver well.

Well, I had proved I could handle it. So it wasn't long before I started planning a course in "safe" drinking. However, my "controlled" drinking became less and less controlled and so did my life. The 1970 business recession didn't help either as photo assignments became scarce. When I did get jobs, the 20-pound movie camera on my shoulder seemed more like 100 pounds. Every aspect of my life started coming apart. Like most alcoholics I was living in fear, a fear brought about by the littlest things. Drinking seemed to solve the problems, but only for a short time. My wife and children looked on me with bewilderment, then disgust. I could see no hope or future and only one escape—that dim liquid tunnel of alcohol.

One day in January, 1971, I told Jody I was leaving on an assignment. Instead, I holed up in a New York hotel and drank heavily for ten days straight.

Somehow a friend located me and got me home to a frantic wife and frightened children where I collapsed in bed. It took me several days to recover enough to face facts. I really was an alcoholic and was about to lose my family and probably my life!

With trembling hands I picked up the phone and called the group of alcoholics Liz put me on to. Within an hour a man arrived and we talked. He invited me to attend a meeting with him that night. I did and found a wonderful group of people—honest, sympathetic, straightforward and willing to help anyone at any time.

In our group, each person had a sponsor, someone whom you phoned when you needed help and he'd come over and sit with you, encourage you and help keep you from falling back into the canyon. That, plus large quantities of tranquilizers, helped keep me going.

And then one evening I met Eileen Connally. She happened to be a guest of friends we were visiting, and both my wife and I were captivated by her beautiful personality. She was such an exciting, open person. And she had an elusive *something*.

Jody and I found ourselves opening up to her, confessing our problems, yes, even our marriage difficulties. And then Eileen told us her story. I was surprised to find out that she was a recovered alcoholic.

As she told us her story, time stood still for Jody and me. "And then," said Eileen, "two years ago I met the Lord and was filled with His Spirit."

Eileen told how even though she stopped drinking, she found no real deep peace or inner strength until "I gave my life to Jesus Christ."

Her eyes misted for a moment. "Something happened that I can't explain. But it was as if I had suddenly been infused with a strength I never knew before."

That night I did something I hadn't done since I was a small boy. I kneeled at my bed and prayed. Only instead of not knowing to whom I was talking, I spoke to the Person Eileen had met. I admitted to Him I was a complete failure. "Lord," I said, "I'll take anything You send me."

A peace came over me and I fell into a sound sleep. In the morning, I awoke with a sense of happy expectancy. *Something* had happened.

But I wasn't sure of what it was—only that, as days went on, the problems I faced somehow didn't seem as frightening or impossible to solve. I became closer with my family, and we began going to church together. Jody and I began to find meaning again in our marriage. However, I still puzzled. If Christ had come to me, why had I not seen a light, or heard a "voice," or something? I remembered that Eileen had said that the Holy Spirit comes quietly to some, compared to the dramatic way in which He comes to others.

A month passed before I saw Eileen again. When I did, I confessed my doubts to her. "When," I wanted to know, "will I be strong enough to receive this power?"

She asked me a strange question then: What had I done for others during the past month? I found myself telling her about a man I had met who couldn't stay away from alcohol. This guy couldn't understand why I, who had been such a worrywart, seemed so calm and happy. Suddenly, I had found myself enthusiastically telling him about what God had done for me, how my worries had diminished and how so far I hadn't even wanted a drink. "With His help," I told him, "I feel that this will be the case forever."

Then I saw that Eileen was laughing joyfully at me. She leaned forward and put her hand on my arm: "Don't you realize," she smiled, "that you already have Him?"

Suddenly I saw what she meant. I had my Sponsor. Even though I knew my group would always be there, never again, through the grace of God, would I have to call anyone to help me out. I believe that the Holy Spirit is with me. And He is all the sponsor I need.

The Peace We Found in Forgiveness

by Jay Meck

This Pennsylvania farm couple turned heartbreak into a special kind of triumph.

As I finished the milking that Friday afternoon last October, I was glad it was done early, for now I would have time to do some other chores before supper and we'd be able to make the pet parade at the New Holland Fair.

I knew how the boys yearned to see that parade, especially our youngest, little Nelson, seven, who'd be home from school any minute. I poked my head out of the barn door. No sign of Nelson yet, but I did see my wife Ruth coming out of the basement. She had been storing sweet potatoes for winter. Now she would be preparing an afternoon snack for Nelson, most likely some of that gingerbread he liked so much.

Putting away the milking pails, I thought how nice it was that as a farmer I could be at home during the day to enjoy my family. I loved it when Nelson bounded up our farm lane from school. He'd come back into the barn to tell me what happened that day, his freckled face beaming. Then he'd scurry over to the house to get a nibble from Ruth and dash back down the lane to wait for his older brother Johnny to come home from school. When Johnny appeared, Nelson never failed to say, "Ha-ha, I got home before you. What took you so long?" Then the two of them would race back up to the house.

The routine was always the same and never failed to give me pleasure. How blessed I was, with a wonderful wife and three boys to share the farm.

Just then I heard someone running up the lane. Expecting Nelson, I came out of the barn only to be faced with his school-bus driver, Mike.

"Nelson's been hit by a car!" Mike yelled frantically. "Call an ambulance!"

My head suddenly felt light. Ruth yelled from the kitchen door that she would call one.

I tore off wildly down the lane to the road. My heart was racing like a tractor in the wrong gear. My mind was in a tailspin. *Please, Lord, not Nelson!* I thought. *Who could have done this? Who?*

When I reached the road I pushed my way through the crowd already gathered near the school bus. There on the blacktop of Highway 340 lay my son. I bent down and touched him softly. He didn't move. As I brushed back a fold in his hair, tears stung my eyes.

Just down the highway a car was pulled over and I saw the license plate—the orange and blue colors of New York.

The area where we live—the Dutch country of southeastern Pennsylvania—attracts a goodly number of tourists and some of them don't have a very good reputation among us natives.

I stood up over Nelson and in a choking voice asked, "Who hit him?"

There was silence until finally a young dark-haired man and a woman who looked to be his wife stepped forward. They seemed frightened and dazed.

"He just ran out in front of us," the woman said, clutching tightly to the man's arm.

I walked over to them. I'm not a man of violence—in fact I've never so much as laid a finger on anyone. Yet my arms felt heavy and my hands tingled. I took a deep breath, unsure of what I should do. "Jay Meck's my name," I said finally.

The man flinched, but shook hands with me. Just then the ambulance pulled up and its driver urged Ruth and me to follow. As we drove away, I looked back to see the couple holding on to each other, staring after us.

On our way to Lancaster Hospital we passed an Amish family, preserved in tranquility in a horse and buggy. The New Yorkers, I thought, had intruded upon that kind of peacefulness. They had come here where they didn't belong.

At the emergency room, Dr. Show, the man who delivered all our boys, met us immediately and said what I'd suspected all along. "Nelson's gone."

The next hours, even days, became a blur. We were besieged with cards and letters. Scores of friends and neighbors dropped by to help with the milking. They brought pies and casseroles. But even surrounded by all the sympathy, Ruth and I found we just couldn't keep little Nelson from our thoughts. He meant too much to us.

Nelson had come into our lives late, almost as if he were a special gift from God. Being the youngest, I suppose we held him precious and delighted in him more. But, oh, how much there was to delight in! The Sunday-school librarian called him "Sunshine" because he always had a cheerful disposition and a smile that never seemed to go away. What was most extraordinary about our son was his understanding of Christianity. He had an uncanny sense of caring for others.

In school, for instance, he was the little guy who made friends with all the unfortunates—the cripples, the shy children, the outcasts. In the evenings when I'd go to his room to tuck him in, Nelson would be lying in bed with his hands folded. "Boy, Pop," he'd say, "there's sure a lot of people I've got to pray for tonight."

Like other small children, Nelson would squirm in church, but he would then startle Ruth and me by marching out after services and announcing, "I have Jesus in my heart." Later, he'd come in with a sick bird he'd found and wanted to help or he'd bring a stranger to our home, some poor soul seeking farm work.

Though older, Bob, 18, and Johnny, 15, were extremely close to their brother. The following Tuesday, when the funeral was over and we were sitting in our kitchen, Johnny recalled Nelson's daily vigil at the lane after school. "I'll bet Nelson's up in Heaven right now and when I get there he'll say, 'Ha-ha, Johnny, I got home before you. What took you so long?'"

Johnny's words tore into my heart. Ruth's and my grief was compounded when we discovered how senseless our son's death really was. Nelson didn't die through a car's mechanical failure or by natural causes. Perhaps we could have accepted that. No, Nelson died because someone had not stopped his car for a school bus that was unloading children.

Much to our dismay, the man turned out to be a New York City policeman, a person we thought would know the law about stopping for buses with blinking lights. But he hadn't. Both he and his wife had been taken to the police station here where he had then been arrested. After posting bond, trial was set for January 17, 1975, three months away.

Why, Ruth and I agonized, hadn't this man been more careful? Why couldn't he have waited? The whole thing was so pointless. The more we thought about it the more it filled us with anguish. And our friends' and neighbors' feelings only seemed to add fuel to our torment.

"I sure hope that guy gets all that's coming to him," a man told me one day in the hardware store.

"You're going to throw the book at him, aren't you?" another asked.

Even the school authorities, hoping to make a case out of stopping for school buses, urged us to press charges.

Ruth and I were beside ourselves. As Christians, we had received the Lord's reassurance that Nelson was now in eternal life. But how, we cried out, were we to deal with the man whose negligence caused so much heartache?

A few weeks after Nelson's funeral, an insurance adjustor called on us to clear up matters concerning the accident. He mentioned he'd visited the New York couple shortly before.

"They seem broken up," he added.

They're broken up? I thought. *What about all the tears we've shed?*

Yet a certain curiosity—perhaps a desire for an explanation—led Ruth and me to ask if it would be possible for us to meet with them.

The insurance man looked at us oddly. "You really want to see them?"

"Yes," I said.

He agreed to act as intermediary, and to our surprise, the couple, whose names were Frank and Rose Ann, accepted our invitation to come for dinner the Monday before Thanksgiving.

As the day drew closer, I became more dubious. *Could I really face them again? Why were we putting ourselves up to this?*

Ruth and I prayed long and hard about it. Night after night we asked the Lord to provide us with His strength and guidance when they arrived.

When the day came—just a month and a half after our son's death—I looked out the kitchen window to see a car coming up our lane through a light rain. My hand trembled as I reached for the kitchen door to let them in.

We gathered in the living room and the conversation was forced. After comparing country life to city life, everything we talked about seemed to be an outgrowth of the tragedy.

But in talking with them, I began to notice something strange. A feeling of compassion came over me.

Frank was a policeman who'd been on the force eight years. He had a spotless record, but the accident, he said, might cost him his job. As a member of the tactical force in a high crime area of Brooklyn, Frank put his life on the line for others every day. He worked hard at his job, certainly as hard as I did on the farm.

And Rose Ann, like Ruth, had three children at home. She had looked forward to their vacation last October—their first trip away from the city since their marriage. But now she was worried. The New York papers had printed an account of the accident and because of it, they were staying with Rose Ann's parents, fearful of facing their neighbors.

"I just don't know what's going to happen," Frank said. His eyes, like his wife's, seemed vacant. Both had lost a great deal of weight.

At dinner, we ate quietly. It was while we were having coffee that they noticed a picture that hung on the kitchen wall, a chalk drawing of Jesus and the lost sheep.

"Nelson loved to look at that," Ruth said. "His faith, like ours, was important." She went on to explain how she and I had grown up in a local church and how we both were long-time Sunday-school teachers at our Mennonite church.

"But it's more than a church," Ruth said. "You've really got to live out your beliefs every day."

Frank and Rose Ann nodded. After dinner we drove them around for a while, showing them a wax museum and a schoolhouse, sights they'd meant to see on their first trip here.

After they left, Ruth and I faced each other at the kitchen table. We had suffered, we knew, but surely not as much as that couple was suffering. And the strange thing was, I could now understand their suffering. Frank, like me, was human. Though he came from a different background—a big city that I didn't understand—he was a human being, with all the faults and frailties I had. He had made a mistake that anyone could have made. Jesus Christ was a man too—the Perfect Man—and through Him I could see that hatred or vengeance was not the way to handle that mistake—certainly not if Ruth and I professed to live out our faith every day.

Frank and Rose Ann, I could see now, were those lost sheep in the picture, and that's why they were brought back to our house. Only through Ruth's and my compassion—only through our employing the kind of love Jesus stood for—could we find peace and they find their way home.

Realizing that, on January 17, at the trial, I did not press charges. Except for a traffic fine, Frank was free.

Ruth and I still correspond with the couple. We hope to visit them in New York City someday soon, for we want to see the city, see them again and meet their three children.

Though Nelson is gone, even in death he continues to teach us something about life. Not long ago I found a little pencil box of his. As I emptied it, a scrap of paper fell out. On it was "Jeremiah 33:3," a verse Nelson was to memorize for a skit. "Call to Me and I will answer you and will tell you great and mighty things which you have not known."

I have to believe that Nelson, in his brief life, discovered some of those mighty things, especially the greatness of God's love and how we must spread it around to others.

When Ruth and I called out to God, His message was just as powerful. No matter how deep the wound of sorrow is, forgiveness and faith in God will provide the strength to "occupy till Christ returns," (Luke 19:13) and the broken pieces of our lives will be made whole in Him.

8.

Hope for People Seeking a Deeper Faith

Now faith is the substance of things hoped for, the evidence of things not seen.

HEBREWS 11:1

The Prayer of Praise
by Catherine Marshall

"Step by step, I was led on an exciting spiritual adventure."

Not too very long ago I reached a low point in life in which everything seemed to go gray. It wasn't all psychological or spiritual grayness, either. Events in the exterior world seemed to be going against me—things like a Hollywood studio purchasing my novel *Christy,* then deciding not to produce it; the fiction manuscript on which I was working was presenting problems so great that I began to see that after pouring myself into it for three years I was going to have to suspend work on it.

An almost wild succession of small, vexing personal inconveniences came on in waves—the dishwasher broke; the bathroom plumbing went awry; a truck driver backed into our mailbox and demolished it; the lawn developed chinch bugs; the car kept stopping cold on us.

I thought about the Bible passage in which the Apostle Paul says, "In every thing give thanks; for this is the will of God in Jesus Christ concerning you." (I Thessalonians 5:18) It's one with which I have always had trouble.

I prayed about it in puzzlement. "You mean," I asked the Lord, "that even in the midst of difficult or tragic circumstances, by an act of will I'm to thank You? Wouldn't it just be words, almost hypocritical?"

God's answer was just as direct: "Obedience means turning your back on the problem or the grief and directing your eyes and attention toward Me. Then I will supply the emotion to make the praise real."

So I decided to try to obey. Early one morning I

went out on the patio to begin. I had my long list of disappointments, some minor, some deeply tragic. As I stood in the early morning coolness, birds sang in the trees. The sky was still gray-white with the faintest suggestion of blue. I began that first time hesitatingly, woodenly.

"Lord, I think I'll begin with the small irritations first—for example, the truck driver who demolished our mailbox yesterday. Surely I'm not supposed to thank You for *that!* However, I can see as I talk to You that the mailbox is of no consequence. Looking at You puts petty problems into perspective in a hurry."

I persisted on down my list. But as I approached the major problems and griefs that had been troubling me, I again rebelled.

"Lord, I can see praising You for bringing good out of all these things. But I still don't understand how I can praise You for the bad things themselves."

"I am Lord over all—good and evil," He seemed to answer. "You start praising. I'll supply the understanding."

Step by hesitant step, in the months that followed, I was led on an exciting spiritual adventure.

My first discovery was that I knew almost nothing about praise, neither what it was, nor how to do it. Aside from some joyous hymns and a few we-adore-and-worship-Thee's, most of us churchgoers sit so properly in our pews staring straight ahead, how can we know how to praise? Praise is mentioned occasionally as a nice worship exercise; but as a key to answered prayer? That to me was a new concept altogether.

In my adventure, I began to see that God steps in to change unhappy or even disastrous situations in our lives when we thank Him for the situation itself. That makes sense only when we understand that God is "in" every circumstance—good or bad—that He allows to come to us. Growth comes at the point when we take an active step toward God, Who stands waiting for us at the center of the problem, and thank Him for it.

The Bible gives us many illustrations of praise being the hinge upon which great events turned. There was the time that Paul and Silas were cruelly beaten at Philippi and jailed in chains. They gave themselves to prayer, which is understandable. But also to joyous praise.

Praise for what? we might ask cynically. That their backs were raw and bleeding? That they were chained fast in prison with all the city authorities against them? Thanking God for *that?* From any human point of view it seems like foolishness.

But Paul says that anything about Christ's cross, or the crosses you and I bear in life, is "foolishness" to the world. Paul learned that God allows us to have disappointments, frustrations, because He wants us to see that our joy is not in such worldly pleasures as success or money or popularity. Our joy is in the fact that we have a relationship with God. Few of us ever understand that fact until circumstances have divested us of any possibility of help except by God Himself.

When Paul and Silas, though bruised and bleeding, turned their minds from self and sang their thanksgiving to the Lord, an earthquake rocked the city of Philippi, shook the prison, burst the gates and wrenched the chains from the walls. Two other miracles followed quickly. The jailer and his entire household became followers, and when morning dawned, the city authorities withdrew all charges, saying, "Go in peace." (Acts 16)

Here is another incident, one from today. The Redeemer Temple in Denver, Colorado, is an unusual church attended by people of many denominations. On Sunday, May 17, 1970, the sanctuary was crowded. Suddenly a young man stumbled up to the altar. He was obviously drunk. "My name's Clarence," he said. "I'm proud not to be white, proud to be a Black Panther."

Waving a black beret aloft, he began a rambling speech filled with clichés and hate talk. The pastor walked over to the intruder and put one arm around his shoulders. "Clarence, see all those people out there? They love you because they know how much Jesus loves you."

Finally Clarence sat down. But as the pastor began the morning prayer, the drunken man's voice was heard again.

Then a strange thing happened. All over the church, people began softly praising God aloud. "Thank You, Lord" . . . "We praise You for what is happening." When they stopped, Clarence was gone.

But not long afterward, in the same church, Clarence rose and made a public apology for his behavior that day. Then he asked for prayer for himself and for the Black Panther organization. Even in the minor emergency of an interruption of a worship service, praise had wrought its own miracle.

I have begun to see that as we begin praising in each circumstance, ever-fresh insights follow. When we praise, we are letting self go by deliberately turning our backs on the problem or grief where self has been most involved. We stop fighting the evil and less-than-good circumstances. With that, resentment goes. Self-pity goes. Perspective comes. We have turned our back on the problem and are looking steadily at God, at His goodness, His love. The power this gives us in solving our problems and overcoming our obstacles is undeniable.

Soon I also made the discovery that—as nothing else does—thankfulness enables us to live in the present moment. Not often do any of us grasp one shining moment, live fully in its "presentness," and consciously enjoy it. I shall not forget one such moment.

After dinner one evening my mother and I were comfortably settled in our living room. Around us flowed the music of a fine recording, the London Philharmonic playing Mendelssohn's *Violin Concerto in E Minor*. As we listened, our hands busy making some table mats to be a gift, the singing, soaring melody was a delight.

All at once my heart overflowed with praise. Silently I lifted all of it to God: *This quiet room, the comfort and peace of it. . . . By Your mercy and grace, Lord, mother is still with us. Isn't it great that we have such rapport that often conversation isn't even necessary? . . . This music, so glorious. Work for my hands to do, work that I enjoy. This moment—what delight—in the midst of a busy life.*

Later I marveled that such a quiet, unassuming moment had meant so much. *Why?* I wondered.

The word "consciousness" is probably the key. The thankful heart raised in praise and adoration, verbal or silent, becomes the vessel to capture the distilled essence of the presentness of life.

Yes, we gain in many ways when we deliberately plunge a negative situation into the positive Presence of God. The longer I ponder this matter of praise, and experiment with it, the more evidence I see that here is the most powerful prayer of all, a golden bridge to the heart of God.

What is hope? Hope is wishing for a thing to come true; faith is believing that it will come true. Hope is wanting something so eagerly that—in spite of all the evidence that you're not going to get it—you go right on wanting it. And the remarkable thing about it is that this very act of hoping produces a kind of strength of its own.

—NORMAN VINCENT PEALE

Hope for People Reaching a Deeper Faith   275

radio. I met a lovely girl who was doing educational programs. We were married and she has been the Angel—
but that I call her—ever since.

I Found My Quiet Heart
by Paul Harvey

---

*One of America's most-listened-to broadcasters
shares the discovery that made his life complete.*

Newsmen are said to have tough hides, cold hearts, "printer's ink in their veins." We see so much of tragedy, disaster, the mud and blood that makes news. Understandably,
we can become insensitive, cynical, hard.

That's why I'm grateful for what happened to me just
about a year ago. It took place up a little mountain road
in Cave Creek, Arizona. I think today that all the experiences in my life had been building up to this one.

First, the Christmas Eve when I was three, a gun-
man's bullet took the life of my policeman father. To
provide an income for my sister and me, mother had
apartments built in our house. As soon as I was old
enough, I, too, looked around for ways to earn money.

Radio was just coming into its own; by age nine I
was making cigar-box crystal sets which I sold for a dollar. A few years later I took part in a seventh-grade class
play presented over Tulsa's KVOO radio station. After
that I spent every spare minute hanging around that
studio. Finally they put me on the payroll. I was 14 and I
did everything from sweeping, to writing commercials,
with a little announcing on the side. I kept remembering
what one of my teachers had said, "Paul, in this wonderful land of ours, any man willing to stay on his toes
can reach for the stars."

Radio became my star. At 17 I did some of everything on a local station in Salina, Kansas; then came jobs
in Oklahoma City and St. Louis. In St. Louis at KXOK

radio I met a lovely girl who was doing educational programs. We were married and she has been the Angel—
that's what I call her—in my life ever since.

Together we worked hard. By 1945 I had my own
network news program. By 1968 I was on television and
doing a newspaper column as well.

Seemingly, I had achieved everything for which a
man could ask. Everything, that is, except for a quiet
heart.

Something was missing. There was a vague emptiness
in my life, an incompleteness that I could not define.

This emptiness was still with me in March of last
year when Angel and I were vacationing near Cave Creek,
Arizona. We noticed a small church on an isolated hilltop.
On impulse one bright Sunday morning Angel and I decided to attend a service there. We drove up the mountain
road and as we rounded the last turn, the little steeple
pierced an azure sky, and white clapboard siding reflected
the morning sun.

Inside were a dozen or so worshipers on wooden
folding chairs, a scene reminiscent of ones I had seen
many times as a youth. During those formative years,
there was one scripture verse I learned that had stayed
with me throughout the years: "For God so loved the
world, that He gave His only begotten Son, that whosoever
believeth in Him should not perish, but have everlasting
life." (John 3:16)

Sometimes I would get to thinking about that—how
wonderful it was. I never made it to the altar in any
church, but I liked that promise of "everlasting life." So
one night, alone in my room, kneeling at my bed, I offered
my life to Christ.

Now, as the upright piano sounded a familiar melody
in this unfamiliar little Arizona church, I was reminded of
my long-ago expression of "belief." I did indeed "believe."

The minister mounted his pulpit. As his eyes swept
the congregation, he said, "I see we have visitors here." He
paused for a moment, then added, "I don't often talk
about baptism, but today I'm going to talk about baptism."
Inside I yawned. But then, for some reason, my attention
began to focus on the simple eloquence of this country
preacher.

He talked about how alone man is without a heavenly

Father, how much we needed to surrender our lives to Him to find any real purpose for living.

But, I thought, *hadn't I done this?*

"Now I'm going to assume," continued the minister, "that most of you here this morning have already made this commitment. But the giving of your life to Jesus is just the first step in your life as a Christian. There is another step: baptism—the way Jesus experienced it, by immersion in water. This becomes the outward expression of your inward commitment.

"This baptism," he continued, "through the symbolic burial of your old self and the resurrection of a new one, is your public testimony to your commitment." He quoted supportive scripture, paused, let it sink in.

"There is no magic in the water," he added. "One's immersion is simply an act of obedience, a sign of total submission to God."

Submission to God.

I twisted on my chair, new understanding discomfited me. Long years ago I had asked to be saved but had I offered to serve? I began to realize how much of me I had been holding back. I thought of my prayer time each morning driving to my Chicago studio at 4:30 A.M. Often on the dark, deserted expressway I would seem to hear God's plan for the day. But by the time I was halfway downtown, I'd be arguing with Him, making exceptions, bending His directions.

Could this be the source of my uneasiness, the inconsistency within me?

Now the minister was looking over his spectacles at the congregation. "If anyone here agrees with me about the importance of this and wants to be baptized, step up here and join me beside this pulpit."

I found myself on my feet, down the aisle, by his side.

The preacher had said there was nothing magic in the water. Yet as I descended into its depths and rose again, I knew something life-changing had happened. A cleansing inside out. No longer did there seem to be two uncertain contradictory Paul Harveys—just one immensely happy one. I felt a fulfilling surge of the Holy Spirit.

Afterward, I cried like a baby, a kind of release I suppose. I remember looking at Angel and her eyes were shining. She knew well what this meant to me, for she had been blessed with the same experience as a girl.

The evolving joy has been escalating. Yesterday I was praying for guidance and not really meaning it; today the difference is in a genuine desire to know what He wants and an eagerness to *do* as He says. Though I had learned John 3:16 early in life, it took me till last year to learn John 14:15 as well: "If you love me, keep my commandments." The Christian life is one of obedience, not partnership.

Sometimes I see a similar eagerness in the faces of young people caught up in the growing Jesus movement so prominent in the news today. I can identify with their joyous expressions as they rise up out of the water after their baptisms. And I see their increasing number of baptisms as irrefutable evidence the Holy Spirit is everywhere He is invited, changing for good all those He touches.

The change this simple act has made in my life is so immense as to be indescribable. Since totally yielding to Him through the symbolism of water baptism, my heart can't stop singing. I've shaken off a lifelong habit of fretting over small things. A thousand little worries and apprehensions have simply evaporated.

Also, perhaps because baptism is such a public act— and because one's dignity gets as drenched as one's body—I've discovered a new unself-consciousness in talking about my beliefs.

The other evening, on a speaking trip, I was flying over west Texas into a beautiful sunset. My heart swelled with joy in my new surrender and I thought how wonderful: If this is no more than what the unbelievers believe, a sort of self-hypnosis, it nevertheless affords an inner peace which passes all understanding. And, if it is what we believers believe, then we have all this—and heaven too!

I am come that they might have life and that they might have it more abundantly.

JOHN 10:10

My Path of Prayer
by Duke Ellington

From the heart of an eminent composer comes the sound of praise.

When my mother died in 1935, I lost all ambition. I did nothing but brood. And when my father died a couple of years later, the bottom just dropped out. The grief was so great because I kept remembering everything my parents had left me. There was the memory of my mother playing the "Rosary" on the piano when I was four. It was so beautiful I burst out cryng. Afterward she had me take some piano lessons on a new upright. Later I worked and pounded the piano keys until I was all music.

My father was a caterer and sometimes worked at the White House. He later became a blueprint technician for the Navy Department. My mother, my sister, myself, we never wanted for anything. He was a good provider. He was also a man of rectitude and faith.

My parents loved us, fed us, cleaned us, took us to church. Two churches. Every Sunday we first went to my father's church, Methodist. Then my mother took us to her church, Baptist. Their respect for each other was a lesson itself. You don't forget that kind of teaching.

They left me such a heritage of belief that after they were gone it was natural I should turn to the Bible for help, again. I read it through four times. That took over two years. What did I get out of it? I thought that I knew something about life and living, about a good sound and grief and joy. But after studying the Scriptures, I found a new awareness of how to meet my problems, how to deal with my fellowman, and how to bring God further into my work.

There's really nothing new under the sun. "One generation passes away and another generation comes, but the earth abides forever." (Ecclesiastes 1:4.) So there's nothing to get uptight about. If you know that, you don't have to jump at every trouble. I wrote a piece, "There Ain't But the One," which said it all. So leave it to God.

One sure way I know to meet my problems is prayer. I pray regularly, when I arise, when I retire. I pray my thanks for whatever He gives me: a thought, a bar of music, food. I believe I am helped by prayer. It makes me aware of my total dependence on Him.

We all belong to Him in the first place. I figure that when we're born we are only given a lease, that's all. We're accountable to Him at the end of the lease time. We're not supposed to arrive at the end all scarred up by anger and hurt and self-pity. My grief left when it came to me that past a certain point, it's a sin to grieve.

The light that shows us how to deal with our neighbors and ourselves and God is easy to find: the Ten Commandments. Beautiful poetry, but they're a whole way of life, too. There's a natural inclination to break them, but we are shown the way back if we allow ourselves to be.

One of the great things the Bible gave me was to try and look inside a man instead of at the cut of his clothes. It makes you aware of what you lack. My manager has always said that my band has no boss. He's right. I won't argue with anybody, in the band or out of it. I accept my fellowmen. I love them, or try to. That gives me an inner peace of my own. Arguing with anyone brings me to the point of anger and then to judging others. I can't and won't do that. That's pitting my puny strength against the great Power that runs the universe.

My feeling is that God gives each of us a role to play in life. Mine is music. The first piece I ever wrote was "Soda Fountain Rag." I was 15 and jerking soda in the Poodle Dog Cafe in Washington, D.C., my hometown. Since then there have been many thousands of pieces, many of them called sacred music.

Where do they come from? God fills your mind and heart with them. All you have to do is believe and wait until they come and use them, whether it's laying brick a new way or writing a song. The ideas come to me anytime, anyplace. So I accept the blessings and write them. I write on trains, planes, ships, in cabs, buses—at

night, in the morning, in the din and fury of the music
world and the frenzy of a thousand one-night stands.

Way back, years ago, Mahalia Jackson did one of my
things, "Come Sunday" and my version of the 23rd Psalm.
Later, we did an album together. It attracted the attention
of various church people. Dean C. Julian Bartlett and the
Rev. John Yaryan, canon of Grace Cathedral in San Francisco, asked me to present a concert of sacred music there.
When you get that kind of invitation, you're not in show
business. You think to yourself, *It all has to be kind of
right. You have to go out there and make a noise that tells
the truth.*

I had to stop and figure out my eligibility. I prayed.

Every man prays in his own language, and I believe
there is no language that God does not understand. Every
time his children have thrown away fear in the pursuit of
His word, miracles have happened.

When I went out to Grace Cathedral in 1965, there
was a shout that it was all new. It wasn't. The sacred
music began a way back, in the Thirties, and earlier inside
me.

At that first concert in San Francisco I told the 2500
people present, "In this program you hear a statement
without words, but I think you should know that it is a
statement with six tones symbolizing the six syllables in
the first four words of the Bible, 'In the beginning
God. . . .' "

We opened and closed with "Praise God." It was
based on the 150th Psalm. In the program I tried new songs
and new instrumental works, "Supreme Being" and "Something About Believing" and "Almighty God." The trumpet
preached a solo. A fire-and-brimstone sermonette came
from the percussion section. When we reached the closing,
"Praise God," the audience was on its feet and stayed there
through a whole *a capella* rendition of "The Lord's
Prayer."

The response to that first sacred concert was completely unexpected. One news story began: "Duke Elling-
ton talked to the Lord in Grace Cathedral last night." All
of us, every listener, every member of the band and
chorus were talking to the Lord that night.

Since then we have done sacred concerts in more
than 50 houses of worship in American and Europe. When
the church is too small we go into a hall. One church

found the 200 voices in the chorus too much, so the church rented a ball park. The chorus need be only 20 voices. In a church the band and chorus are arranged in the sanctuary. The bishop, minister, priest or rabbi usually addresses the congregation before we begin.

The sacred concerts do not take the place of worship in the ordinary manner. But the music I write for them is and always was an act of worship. From the very beginning it was a response to a growing sense of obligation to myself in self-defense through the Almighty. It continues to be an expression of God in my life.

I am only saying in music what I have been saying on my knees for a long time.

———————————

Be of good courage and he shall strengthen your heart, all ye that hope in the Lord.

PSALM 31:24

Where Joy Found Me
by Lou Ann Loomis

"For the first time I knew that praise was not words; it was a living experience."

Visiting hours were over at the hospital in Houston, and attendants were getting me ready for the iron lung. They put on a rubber neck strip, pinned it tight enough to almost choke me, then lifted me gently from my wheelchair and laid me on the bed of the lung. Now they were sliding the great iron lid over me until only my head protruded. I heard the thud of the clamps along the sides of the lung. I was locked in for the night.

All over the ward other iron-lung patients were being readied for sleep. I tried to concentrate on the television program reflected in the mirror on the lung, but disappointment kept nagging at me. I'd felt so sure that my prayer would be answered today! Ever since I had first heard about the great moving of the Holy Spirit—how He was entering people's lives, filling them with joy, giving them strength to do His work—I had yearned to know more. I had written everyone I could think of who might teach me about it, besieging them with questions. And today I'd had the tingling feeling that I would get an answer.

But of course, I'd been wrong; there would be no more mail delivery or visits now. Nothing more could happen today.

I was in the hospital after one of my recent bouts with surgery. It was all so familiar now, the trays rattling past in the hall, the doctors' names coming over the loudspeaker. But as I lay there in my metal cage, my mind raced back, as it often did, to the first time I had come here—when it had not been familiar, but utterly strange and terrifying.

I was 11 years old then, a healthy, happy, active little girl who played second trombone in the junior high school band, practiced baton twirling and had a passion for acrobatics. Then came that terrible fever. I was rushed to this place and shut away in a great iron monster, my breathing, my legs, arms, hands, totally paralyzed with polio.

I spent months counting some holes in the hospital ceiling, over and over. Several times daily I was taken from the lung for self-breathing periods, three strangling moments during which I strained till sweat poured off me, but no breath came. With no air for speaking I would beg the nurse with my lips, "Put me in! Please put me in!" until my ears roared and the room turned black.

Many times during those early days I tried to pray, but the iron dome above me was like a barrier, shutting me away even from God. At last one dark, sleepless night when the strangeness and isolation seemed too much to bear, I cried out for the nurse.

Soon I heard footsteps approaching. "Do you know the Twenty-third Psalm?" I asked the white shape beside me.

"I'm not sure. I can try."

"Please! Say it with me."

And so, adjusting the words to the breathing of the lung, we began together: "The Lord is my shepherd; I shall not want." I waited for the next outrush of air, listening for the assurance of her voice merging with mine.

"He leadeth me beside the still waters . . ."

Even as we said the words, something of that stillness touched me. Those calm waters flowed about me, soothing, quieting me. It was my first experience of God.

There were many others in the ten years that followed. Out of pain and struggle came progress. I was able to go home. I still slept in an iron lung at night, but during the day I was able to sit in a wheelchair with only a corsetlike pneumo belt for breathing. Eventually I recovered use of enough muscles below my elbows to feed myself, use the telephone, write. But most wonderful of all was the growing awareness of Jesus in my life.

That was why I was so very eager to learn all I could about the Holy Spirit. For blessed as I had been, I was still so far from the Christian I longed to be. The child of

11 in me cried out for the healing of those memories of pain and terror which could still sometimes stand between me and the full joy of life in Christ.

"Lou Ann, you have a visitor." The nurse on duty was bending over me, breaking into my recollections, bringing me back to the present.

"A visitor? But—it's after hours."

"I know. But this man has come from so far that the floor nurse made an exception."

A minute later I was looking up into the face of one of the people to whom I had written my list of questions about the Holy Spirit. He had come to answer them in person!

We talked eagerly for a while; neither the ward attendants nor the other patients paid the least attention to us. And as we talked I began to realize that this Spirit-filled man was making no attempt to settle my various intellectual queries. After a while he simply laid his hands on my head—the only part of me outside the lung—and prayed that the Holy Spirit should enter into me.

What was it Jesus had promised to whomever would receive this Spirit? "Out of his heart shall flow rivers of living water." (John 7:38, RSV) My visitor departed as swiftly as he had come—but from my heart rivers indeed were pouring.

And the living water bursting from my lips, blessedly and unexpectedly, was purest praise. Words of thanks and adoration to Him flowed into my mind with such force that I could not complete one sentence proclaiming my love for God until another overwhelmed the first. For the first time in my life familiar phrases seemed not ritual but essential. "Praise God from Whom all blessings flow!" "Glory be to the Father and to the Son!" For the first time I knew that praise was not words; it was a living experience, the pouring through of something greater than myself. No, not something, Someone.

The water with which God had soothed me here in this very place so long ago had become a spring inside me, bubbling forth unto Him. Through the gift of praise the Holy Spirit was at last driving out that other, that fearful, childish spirit. Myself and my small problems were forgotten in the flood of love and worship. And here is how I later tried to put it down on paper.

*And I stood immersed
In the midst of the river—
Yet I was closed
And it cleansed me not.
Until one day, one thought, one hour,
The hard case of my inner self
Was broken loose.
And into that inner being
Flowed the very stream of God—
The river in which I had stood, unmoved,
Flowed in.
And out—
And I was a living channel, a life of His Love.
And still I stood immersed
In the midst of the river.
Yet I was open now.
And God and I were One.*

Hope will make thee young, for Hope and
Youth are children of one mother . . .

—PERCY BYSSHE SHELLEY

Communion in Space

by Buzz Aldrin

An astronaut tells of a little-known but significant event on the moon.

For several weeks prior to the scheduled lift-off of Apollo 11 back in July, 1969, the pastor of our church, Dean Woodruff, and I had been struggling to find the right symbol for the first lunar landing. We wanted to express our feeling that what man was doing in this mission transcended electronics and computers and rockets.

Dean often speaks at our church, Webster Presbyterian, just outside of Houston, about the many meanings of the communion service.

"One of the principal symbols," Dean says, "is that God reveals Himself in the common elements of everyday life." Traditionally, these elements are bread and wine—common foods in Bible days and typical products of man's labor.

One day while I was at Cape Kennedy working with the sophisticated tools of the space effort, it occurred to me that these tools were the typical elements of life today. I wondered if it might be possible to take communion on the moon, symbolizing the thought that God was revealing Himself there too, as man reached out into the universe. For there are many of us in the NASA program who do trust that what we are doing is part of God's eternal plan for man.

I spoke with Dean about the idea as soon as I returned home, and he was enthusiastic.

"I could carry the bread in a plastic packet, the way regular inflight food is wrapped. And the wine also—there will be just enough gravity on the moon for liquid to pour.

I'll be able to drink normally from a cup. Dean, I wonder if you could look around for a little chalice that I could take with me as coming from the church?"

The next week Dean showed me a graceful silver cup. I hefted it and was pleased to find that it was light enough to take along. Each astronaut is allowed a few personal items on a flight; the wine chalice would be in my personal-preference kit.

Dean made plans for two special communion services at Webster Presbyterian Church. One would be held just prior to my leaving Houston for Cape Kennedy, when I would join the other members in a dedication service. The second would take place two weeks later, Sunday, July 20, when Neil Armstrong and I were scheduled to be on the surface of the moon. On that Sunday the church back home would gather for communion, while I joined them as close as possible to the same hour, taking communion inside the lunar module, all of us meaning to represent in this small way not only our local church but the Church as a whole.

Right away questions came up. Was it theologically correct for a layman to serve himself communion under these circumstances? Dean thought so, but to make sure he decided to write the stated clerk of the Presbyterian church's General Assembly and got back a quick reply that this was permissible.

And how much should we talk about our plans? I am naturally rather reticent, but on the other hand I was becoming increasingly convinced that having religious convictions carried with it the responsibility of witnessing to them. Finally we decided we would say nothing about the communion service until *after* the moonshot.

I had a question about which scriptural passage to use. Which reading would best capture what this enterprise meant to us? I thought long about this and came up at last with John 15:5. It seemed to fit perfectly. I wrote the passage on a slip of paper to be carried aboard *Eagle* along with the communion elements. Dean would read the same passage at the full congregation service held back home that same day.

So at last we were set. And then trouble appeared. It was Saturday, just prior to the first of the two communion services. The next day Neil Armstrong, Mike Collins and I were to depart Houston for Cape Kennedy. We were scheduled for a pre-mission press conference when the flight physician arrived and set up elaborate precautions against crew contamination. We had to wear sterile masks and to talk to the reporters from within a special partition. The doctor was taking no chances. A cold germ, a flu virus, and the whole shot might have to be aborted. I felt I had to tell him about the big church service scheduled for the next morning. When I did, he wasn't at all happy.

I called Dean with the news late Saturday night. "It doesn't look real good, Dean."

"What about a private service? Without the whole congregation?"

It was a possibility. I called the doctor about the smaller service, and he agreed, provided there were only a handful of people present. So the next day, Sunday, shortly after the end of the 11 o'clock service my wife, Joan, and our oldest boy, Mike (the only one of our three children who is as yet a communicant), went to the church. There we met Dean, his wife, Floy, and our close family friend Tom Manison, elder of the church, and his wife. The seven of us went into the now-empty sanctuary. On the communion table were two loaves of bread, one for now, the other for two weeks from now. Beside the two loaves were two chalices, one of them the small cup the church was giving me for the service on the moon.

We took communion. At the end of the service Dean tore off a corner of the second loaf of bread and handed it to me along with the tiny chalice. Within a few hours I was on my way to Cape Kennedy.

What happened there, of course, the whole world knows. The Saturn 5 rocket gave us a rough ride at first, but the rest of the trip was smooth. On the day of the moon landing, we awoke at 5:30 A.M., Houston time. Neil and I separated from Mike Collins in the command module. Our powered descent was right on schedule, and perfect except for one unforeseeable difficulty. The automatic guidance system would have taken *Eagle* to an area with huge boulders. Neil had to steer *Eagle* to a more suitable terrain. With only seconds worth of fuel left, we touched down at 3:30 P.M.

Now Neil and I were sitting inside *Eagle*, while Mike circled in lunar orbit, unseen in the black sky above us. In a little while after our scheduled meal period, Neil would give the signal to step down the ladder onto the powdery surface of the moon. Now was the moment for communion.

So I unstowed the elements in their flight packets. I put them and the scripture reading on the little table in front of the abort guidance-system computer.

Then I called back to Houston.

"Houston, this is *Eagle*. This is the LM Pilot speaking. I would like to request a few moments of silence. I would like to invite each person listening in, wherever and whomever he may be, to contemplate for a moment the events of the past few hours and to give thanks in his own individual way."

For me this meant taking communion. In the radio blackout I opened the little plastic packages which contained bread and wine.

I poured the wine into the chalice our church had given me. In the one-sixth gravity of the moon the wine curled slowly and gracefully up the side of the cup. It was interesting to think that the very first liquid ever poured on the moon, and the first food eaten there, were communion elements.

And so, just before I partook of the elements, I read the words which I had chosen to indicate our trust that as man probes into space we are in fact acting in Christ.

I sensed especially strongly my unity with our church back home, and with the Church everywhere.

I read: "I am the vine, you are the branches. Whoever remains in me, and I in him, bear much fruit; for you can do nothing without me." (John 15:5 TEV)

These things have I spoken unto you, that my joy might remain in you, and that your joy might be full.

JOHN 15:11

Walking Where Dragons Live

by Keith Miller

In his book, Habitation of Dragons, *from which this excerpt is adapted this business-man-turned-author discusses some of the road-blocks of deeper spirituality.*

Several years ago when I was a new Christian, I decided I would try to be absolutely honest with my wife. We had just moved to a new town and had a good many extra expenses. This transition was making us a little nervous and frantic around the house. In the midst of everything, Mary Allen went out and bought a new dress on sale, which she could not return. Buying something new sometimes has a soothing effect on her nerves, and understanding this, I was not too surprised or upset.

But when she tried the dress on and asked me how I liked it, I told her I had seen a girl on First Street wearing one just like it that same day. First Street is a very unsavory part of the city. I said the dress was okay, but seeing a cheap-looking girl in one just like it spoiled it for me—which was all true. Mary Allen just glared at me and never wore the dress. I was furious. We could not afford it anyway, but to buy the dress and not wear it was really terrible.

But I learned something that day. Christian honesty does not mean that I am obligated to express every thought that passes through my mind. I must learn to hear the *real* question someone is asking and answer that question, not just the one phrased by the outward words.

This was the amazing genius of Jesus' conversation

with people. He always saw through their superficial conversation to the real questions they were asking and dealt with them. Mary Allen had been wanting to know, at a deep level, "Am I attractive to you? Is it all right that I impulsively bought this dress just because I feel dowdy right now? Do you love me?"

Those were the real "woman questions"; and the true answer to all of them was "yes." But because of my insensitivity, I had answered the superficial question correctly with legalistic honesty—but by so doing I had said "no" to her *real* questions.

Lord, help me not to give people my current medical history when they say, "How are you?" in order to be honest. Give me a sensitive ear to hear the secret needs and doubts behind the facade of words I will walk through today.

George, a real-estate developer in our community, recently had a conviction that he should do more to help minority groups. George is one of a group of us who meet at 6:30 on Monday mornings to pray and share together our struggles to grow in the Christian faith. When George took a stand on housing, it cost him plenty: about $100,000 the first year, he estimated, plus some painful rejections in our city. It was an unhappy picture he painted for us.

But something happened to several others in the group because of George. Two ministers granted use of their church educational wing for a Head Start program during the week. A free medical clinic was set up in one of those churches for poor people who couldn't qualify for help. Several of us began dialogues with black groups to learn more about the issues and to try to be helpful.

I do not know how much we can do and I admit that sometimes I am afraid of the hostility of people whose backgrounds and circumstances are different from my own. Sometimes the race and poverty situations seem so hopeless that I just want to run away and forget them. But I pray that I will not. Because as I get closer to people who appear to be different from me, I find that most of the real differences are in my mind. And as I take small specific steps to go and do things which need doing, I realize that Christ is probably not as concerned with measuring the magnitude of my effectiveness as He is with whether or not I go.

Lord, help me to learn the value to You of a "cup of cold water" where it's really needed and how to use a bucket to wash some tired smelly feet—without an audience.

Sometimes when one of our children feels rejected by a group, or thinks she is unattractive and unacceptable, my stomach tightens and I ache for her. I want to run and hold my little girl and protect her from the pain and rejection of the world. Then one night I learned something about handling such a situation from Alice.

I was in a small group of adults who were struggling together to learn how to pray and to live as disciples of Jesus Christ. We were getting acquainted by going around the room, each telling the others some things about his childhood. When it was Alice's turn, she spoke to us hesitantly.

"When I was a tiny little girl, I was put in an orphanage. I was not pretty at all, and no one wanted me. But I can recall longing to be adopted and loved by a family as far back as I can remember. I thought about it day and night. But everything I did seemed to go wrong. I tried too hard to please everybody who came to look me over, and all I did was drive people away.

"Then one day the head of the orphanage told me a family was going to come and take me home with them. I was so excited, I jumped up and down and cried. The matron reminded me that I was on trial and that it might not be a permanent arrangement. But I just knew it would be. So I went with this family and started to school in their town—a very happy girl. And life began to open for me, just a little.

"But a few months later, I skipped home from school one day and ran in the front door of the big old house we lived in. No one was at home, but there in the middle of the front hall was my battered old suitcase with my little coat thrown over it. As I stood there and looked at that suitcase, it slowly dawned on me what it meant—they didn't want me. And I hadn't even suspected."

Alice stopped speaking a moment, but we didn't notice. We were each standing in that front hall with the high ceiling looking at the battered suitcase and trying not to cry. Then Alice cleared her throat and said almost mat-

The Secret of Our Survival
by Capt. James E. Ray

A former Vietnam POW's story of faith.

"Psst."

I struggled upright on the damp pallet in my solitary cell to hear better. It had sounded like a whisper.

No, I must have been hallucinating. I slumped back, wondering how long it had been since my 105 Thunderchief had been shot down as we bombed a railroad bridge on the Hanoi-China supply line.

That was May 8, 1966. I tried to forget the weeks since, the endless interrogations, the torture which left me screaming in agony.

Now I wish I had gone down with the plane. Anything would be better than the desolation, the awful sense of guilt at writing a confession under torture, the aloneness.

There! I heard it again. Now an unmistakable, "Hey, buddy?"

I scrambled flat on the floor and peered through the crack under the door. I could see I was in one of many cells facing a narrow, walled courtyard. The whisper had come from the next cell. I whispered back. He introduced himself as Bob Purcell, another air force man. We waited as the guard passed and then began to converse.

Soon all the prisoners on that yard were secretly whispering. We started by learning about each other, where we were from, our families. One day I asked Bob what church he went to.

"Catholic," he said. "And you?"

"Baptist."

Bob was quiet for a moment, as if my mention of

church evoked deep memories. Then he asked, "Do you know any Bible verses?"

"Well, the Lord's Prayer," I answered.

"Everyone knows that."

"How about the Twenty-third Psalm?"

"Only a little."

I began whispering it. He'd repeat each line after me. A little later he whispered the entire psalm back to me.

Other prisoners joined in, sharing verses they knew. Through these contacts a fellowship grew among us. The others said that I shouldn't feel bad about "confessing" under torture. "We've all done it," they assured me. I didn't feel so alone anymore.

As the number of prisoners grew, two of us shared a cell. My first roommate was Larry Chesley, a Mormon from Idaho. Though we had a few differences of belief, our common denominators were the Bible and Jesus Christ, and we were able to share and write down a great deal of scripture.

For by now it had become vital to our daily existence. Often racked with dysentery, weakened by the diet of rice and thin cabbage and pumpkin soup, our physical lives had shrunk within the prison walls. We spent 20 hours a day locked in our cells. And those Bible verses became rays of light, constant assurances of His love and care.

We made ink from brick dust and water or drops of medicine. We'd write verses on bits of toilet paper and pass them on to others, dropping them behind a loose brick at the toilets.

It was dangerous to pass these on. Communication between cells was forbidden and a man unlucky enough to be caught passing a note would be forced to stand with his arms up against a wall for several days, without sleep.

But the urge to share developed inventiveness. One night I lay with my ear pressed against the rough wooden wall of my cell to hear *Thump . . . thumpety thump* as somewhere on the wall, cells away, a fellow POW tapped out in Morse code: "I will lift up my eyes unto the hills, from whence cometh my help." (Psalm 121:1)

He tapped out his name—Russ Temperly—and passed on the seven other verses in that psalm which I scratched on the concrete floor with a piece of broken tile. "My help cometh from the lord," the psalm assured us and with that assurance came His Presence, soothing us, telling us to fear not.

By 1968, more of us were squeezed together and for two years four of us lived in an eight-by-eight-foot cell. In this close proximity, even minor personality rubs could flare into violent explosions. For instance, one guy liked to whistle. Talk about getting on your nerves! Some of the verses that helped us bear with one another were from Romans: "Every man among you is not to think of himself more highly than he ought to think . . ." (Romans 12:3, 5)

Only by following Christ's teachings in constant forgiveness, patience and understanding were we able to get along together. The whistler? We recommended a schedule for when he should whistle.

Two and a half years went by before I could write dad and mother. A year later I was allowed to receive my first letter. In the meantime we subsisted on letters written 2000 years ago.

By late 1970, almost all of the American POWs had been moved to Ha Lo, the main prison in downtown Hanoi. Newspapers later called this the Hanoi Hilton; we called it Heartbreak Hotel.

Some 50 of us lived, ate and slept together in one large room. Thanksgiving came shortly after we moved in and we held a brief service. We all were surprised to find how many of the men knew scripture, learned from those verses passed along in whispers, bits of paper and wall thumpings. We immediately made plans for a Christmas service. A committee was formed and started to work.

Bits of green and red thread decorated the walls, a piece of green cloth was draped like a tree. Our crèche was made of figures carved from soap rations or molded from papier-mâché of moistened toilet paper.

We pooled the verses we knew and we now had a "consensus Bible," written covertly on bits of paper, some of it King James, some Phillips, some Revised Standard. But it served. It was the only Bible we had. As we sat in silence, the reader began: "In those days a decree went out from Caesar Augustus that all the world should be enrolled . . ." As he completed this verse, a six-man choir sang "Oh Little Town of Bethlehem."

He went on: "And she gave birth to her first born son and wrapped Him in swaddling clothes . . ." "Away in the manger no crib for His bed, our Little Lord Jesus lay down His sweet head . . ." sang the choir.

Once again I was a youngster in Sunday school at the First Baptist Church. Time had rolled back for all of us grizzled men in prison pajamas as, with eyes shining and tears trickling through beards, we joined in the singing. Glinting in the light from the kerosene lamp was a cross made of silver foil.

Occasionally the guards would knock on the door, ordering us not to sing, but they finally gave up. Our program continued into a communion service led by Air Force Lt. Tom Moe. A Lutheran, he sang his church's communion chants as Episcopalians, Methodists and men of other denominations bowed their heads together.

A Jewish prisoner told us about the Hanukkah tradition and entertained us by singing, "the eight days of Hanukkah" to the tune of "The Twelve Days of Christmas." Amid the laughing and singing, we looked up to find the prison camp commander and his English-speaking interrogators watching.

Later that night, after many months of our asking, the commander brought us a real Bible, the first any of us had seen in prison. He said we could keep it for one hour. We made the best of it. One of us read aloud the favorite passages called out by the others. We also checked some of our handwritten scripture. Amazingly, we weren't far off.

We didn't see that little clothbound King James version again for several months. Finally, after continual requests, one of us was allowed to go out and copy from it for "one hour" each week.

But when we'd start to copy, the interrogator would plant his elbow on the Bible for the first 15 minutes. Then, after he'd let us start, he'd ask mundane questions to distract us. I'd just ignore him and write as fast as I could. The next week we'd have to return the previous week's copy work. They seemed to be afraid for us to keep the scriptures, as if they sensed the spiritual help kept us from breaking.

From that we learned a most important lesson. Bible verses on paper aren't one iota as useful as scriptures burned into your mind where you can draw on them for guidance and comfort.

After five weeks we didn't see the Bible again. But

that had been enough time for us to memorize collectively the Sermon on the Mount, Romans 12, First Corinthians 13, and many of the psalms. Now we had our own "living Bible," walking around the room. By this time, too, we held Sunday worship services and Sunday school classes. Some of the "eat, drink and be merry" type fighter pilots took part; some of them contributing as much to the services as the guys who had always professed to be Christians.

We learned to rise above our surroundings, to overcome the material with the spiritual. In constantly exercising our minds, we developed teaching seminars in which we studied special subjects led by men experienced in various fields. These included learning Spanish, French, German, Russian. I particularly enjoy music and will never forget the music course.

Bill Butler, the leader of this program, drew a giant-sized piano keyboard on the floor with brick dust. Then, standing on a "key," one assistant would hum its note. Other assistants, up the keyboard, hummed each note of the chord which was being demonstrated, while Bill explained how chord progression works.

Two years passed this way at Heartbreak Hotel, years of continuing degradation, sickness, endless hunger and never knowing whether we'd ever see home again. But instead of going mad or becoming animals, we continued to grow as a community of men, sustaining one another in compassion and understanding.

For as one of the verses I heard thumped out on the wall one night said: "Man does not live by bread alone, but by every word that proceeds out of the mouth of the Lord." (Deuteronomy 8:3)

His Word became our rock.

The Yellow Kite
by Beverly Newman

*My son was my one reason for not giving up
on life completely—and it was his small request that changed it.*

I stood at the window and watched the neighborhood children flying their kites on the hill behind our house. My
four-year-old son Michael stood next to me with his face
eagerly pressed against the glass. Then, looking up at me
with pleading eyes, he again asked if he could have a kite
like the other children.

For days now, ever since he had first seen them con-
gregate on the hill, Michael had been asking the same
question, and had been given the same answer: "Wait until you are a little older."

It was easier not to go into a long explanation, but
actually Michael was too young to fly a kite all by himself,
and that meant that one of his parents would always have
to go with him to help. Because of my health I simply
didn't have the strength or energy, and my husband was
usually at work. Once again, Michael hid his face in my
skirt, something he always did when he was going to cry
and didn't want me to see.

As I turned from the window, I felt like crying myself. I looked around the room; the furniture was shabby
and worn, and the walls were badly in need of paint. You
could see the light places on them, the spots where previous tenants had hung their pictures. Even though we had
lived here for several months, I had not done very much
to fix the place up. We had moved so many times, and
each time it seemed like the neighborhood was a little
more run-down, and the house a little older, each one in
need of repairs.

My husband Bill worked long irregular hours at his job and earned a good salary. However, there was never enough money and we kept going deeper in debt. I had lost three children through miscarriages and the complications which followed caused me to make several emergency trips to the hospital and to be constantly under a doctor's care. As a result, a tension had grown between us and we found we could no longer get along with one another.

It all looked so hopeless; even God seemed to have forgotten us. I prayed so often about our problems, asking God for help, but things only seemed to get worse. I found myself thinking, *God doesn't care, and I guess I don't either.*

I walked over to the mirror and studied my reflection. It was almost like looking at a stranger. I looked pale and worn, much older than my years. I no longer bothered to fix my face or do anything with my hair. I stepped back and studied my whole image—the old dress that I had worn all week was wrinkled and torn at the pocket and there was a button missing at the neck.

As I stood there and stared at myself, a feeling of dread, almost panic, came over me, and it filled my whole body with fear. It was the realization that I was giving up on life. I had stopped caring about anything; I felt defeated. I could no longer rise above the depression that had taken hold of me.

In the last few months, my husband had grown rather quiet and we did not talk much. I was aware of his eyes studying me when he thought I was preoccupied with something. I used to be so particular about everything. Bill had not said a word about the change that had come over me, but his actions said a lot. He made a special effort to get me interested in new things, but I did not respond. In fact, I did not respond to him in any way, and he did not know quite how to handle me anymore.

Michael was the one spark of life left for me. He could make me smile, and when he hugged me, I would feel love. I clung to him much in the way one would cling to a life preserver. He needed me and I knew it—that kept me going.

As I tucked him into bed that evening, Michael said, "Mommy, may I pray to God to send me a yellow kite?" Then, fearing that I might again repeat what I had said so many times before, he added, "Maybe He doesn't think I'm too young."

"Yes," I said. "We will leave it up to Him to decide about it once and for all." I was tired of the whole thing and hoped that maybe this would make Michael stop talking about it.

Michael prayed his prayer and fell asleep with a smile on his face. As I stood there looking down at that beautiful child with the blond curls, so trusting in his faith that God would answer his little prayer, I found myself questioning God. Would He really answer such a small prayer when He had chosen not to hear any of my frantic pleas or send me any help to relieve my situation? "Oh, God," I prayed, "please help me! Show me the way out of this dark place."

The next morning as I raised the shade in the kitchen, I stared at the sight that met my eyes—a string hanging down in the front of the window. Not quite able to believe the thoughts that were being put together in my mind, I found myself running out the back door and into the yard. There it was, a yellow kite, caught on the roof with its string hanging down.

"Oh, thank You, God, thank You!" I repeated over and over again. I was thanking Him for the yellow kite, and I was thanking Him for the joy that was flooding into my soul. He had answered the prayer of a little boy, just a little prayer, but by answering that prayer, He had also answered my prayer for help.

Suddenly I remembered Michael. I ran to his room, scooped him up in my arms and carried him into the backyard. He was still half-asleep and didn't quite know what to make of this mother who was babbling about something on the roof and saying, "Wait until you see!"

He clapped his hands and bounced up and down in my arms when he saw the kite. "Mommy, Mommy, and it's even yellow!" he exclaimed. I smiled at him and added, "It's a miracle too." He hugged me and said, "I knew God would answer my prayer. I just knew He would."

I thought to myself, *This was why I had been so depressed. I had lost my faith. I had turned my back on God, and then insisted that He had stopped caring.* The yellow kite was not the only miracle that God sent to us that morning.

When Bill came home we took the kite to the beach and flew it. It went so high that it was almost out of sight for a while. Bill said he had never seen a kite fly as high. We asked all over the neighborhood but we never found a trace of the kite's former owner.

We moved several times in the years that followed, and the yellow kite always went with us. My depression left me and as my health improved, so did my relationship with my husband.

At each new place I would hang the kite in some corner where I could see it as I went about my duties. It served as a reminder that no matter how bad things may seem, we must never lose sight of the fact that God cares, that He hears our prayers. No request is too big or too small to bring before Him.

For thou art my hope, O Lord God: thou art my trust from my youth.

PSALM 71:5

The Plan for Your Life

Does God have a special place for you in the total scheme of things? If so, how can you find it? This Spiritual Workshop offers some answers.

Is it hard for you to believe that God has a plan for your individual life?

If so, you are missing the real adventure of spiritual life.

Look at it this way. If God is to heal the ills of our world, He can do it two ways: (1) through direct intervention, (2) through His children. Over the centuries God has mostly worked through people.

You can be one of His instruments for good—*if* you are willing to give yourself to Him and be a part of His master plan. The purpose of this Spiritual Workshop is to help you find new direction and new meaning in life by doing this.

Following are seven affirmations drawn from Glenn Clark's book, *The Divine Plan*. Try using one each day for a week. Can you find scripture passages to go with each section? Divide each paragraph into one-sentence meditations for daily use until the whole concept of God's plan for your life sinks deep into your subconscious mind.

One—I Believe

I believe that God has a divine plan for me. It is wrapped in the folds of my being as the oak is wrapped in the acorn. I believe that this plan is permanent, indestructible and perfect. When I relax myself completely to it, it will manifest itself through me. I can always tell when I am centered in the plan by the inner peace that comes to me. This peace will either bring on a creative surge of activity which will unfold the plan, or it will bring a patience and stillness which will allow others to unfold the plan to me.

Two—It Is a Part of My Daily Activities

I believe that God's plan for me is a part of a larger pattern, designed for the good of all. This larger pattern has interweavings that reach out through all the events that come my way. I can best put myself into harmony with the larger pattern by accepting with acquiescence all the events that I take part in. I shall see events as instruments for the unfolding of the plan for me.

Three—It Is in My Contacts with People

I believe that God has selected certain people to belong in His plan for me. I believe that I will continually be finding them; through proximity, mutual attraction or need, we will find one another. I believe in sending out a prayer to the Father to draw me to those people who are meant to help me and to be helped by me.

Four—The Good Coming My Way

I feel free to ask my Heavenly Father for that which He means for me to have—work, love, material goods, relationships. When the right time comes, these things will be made manifest. This realization enables me to look forward to receiving only that which is mine according to God's plan. This attitude brings the following advantages:

It allows me to accept joyfully those good things which do come my way.

It releases my mind from anxiety, fear, jealousy and uncertainty about the enjoyable areas of life.

It gives me courage and faith to do the things which are mine to do.

When my mind is attuned to the things which are mine, I become free from greed, passion, impure thoughts and deeds; but when I watch others to see what they are receiving, I cut myself off from my own source of supply.

Five—My Plan Is Always Expanding

I believe that the gifts of God are many thousands of times greater than I am capable of receiving. I therefore pray to increase my capacity to receive and to give. Any *thing* with which I find a natural harmony (and which does not interfere with anyone else's natural expression of life) is mine to enjoy. Any *work*—no matter how difficult—for which I feel a natural call is mine to do. When I am attuned to these ever-expanding gifts and calls of God, I find no barrier.

Six—When One Door Is Closed Another Will Open

When I am hindered from doing the thing I want to do, I believe that God has closed the door only to open another, and that upon every closed door there is a sign pointing the way to better and larger doors ahead.

If I do not readily see the door just ahead, I believe that it is because there is some blindness, deafness or disobedience within my life that walls me off from God. God is using the resulting trouble or failure to help me find guidance so I may see the right door.

Seven—My Plan Keeps Me Close to the Father

It lets the divinity that is within manifest itself through me. I believe that the whole world about me is full of beauty, joy and power. It is full of God. I can share it and enjoy it if I attune myself to God's divine plan for me.

I shall ask my Heavenly Father, who dwells within me, both to give me His help in my plan's realization, and to help me share the vision with others that it may bring peace and happiness to many.

Heartwarming Books
of
Faith and Inspiration

<table>
<tr><td>☐</td><td>12963</td><td>A SEVERE MERCY   Sheldon Vanauken</td><td>$2.50</td></tr>
<tr><td>☐</td><td>01184</td><td>HE WAS ONE OF US: THE LIFE OF
JESUS OF NAZARETH   Rien Poortvliet</td><td>$9.95</td></tr>
<tr><td>☐</td><td>12674</td><td>POSITIVE PRAYERS FOR POWER-FILLED
LIVING   Robert H. Schuller</td><td>$1.95</td></tr>
<tr><td>☐</td><td>13269</td><td>THE GOSPEL ACCORDING TO PEANUTS
Robert L. Short</td><td>$1.75</td></tr>
<tr><td>☐</td><td>13266</td><td>HOW CAN I FIND YOU, GOD?
Marjorie Holmes</td><td>$1.95</td></tr>
<tr><td>☐</td><td>13588</td><td>IN SEARCH OF HISTORIC JESUS
Lee Roddy & Charles E. Sellier, Jr.</td><td>$2.25</td></tr>
<tr><td>☐</td><td>13890</td><td>THE FINDING OF JASPER HOLT
Grace Livingston Hill</td><td>$1.75</td></tr>
<tr><td>☐</td><td>14385</td><td>THE BIBLE AS HISTORY   Werner Keller</td><td>$3.50</td></tr>
<tr><td>☐</td><td>14379</td><td>THE GREATEST MIRACLE IN THE WORLD
Og Mandino</td><td>$2.25</td></tr>
<tr><td>☐</td><td>14216</td><td>THE GREATEST SALESMAN IN THE WORLD
Og Mandino</td><td>$2.25</td></tr>
<tr><td>☐</td><td>14228</td><td>I'VE GOT TO TALK TO SOMEBODY, GOD
Marjorie Holmes</td><td>$2.25</td></tr>
<tr><td>☐</td><td>12853</td><td>THE GIFT OF INNER HEALING
Ruth Carter Stapleton</td><td>$1.95</td></tr>
<tr><td>☐</td><td>12444</td><td>BORN AGAIN   Charles Colson</td><td>$2.50</td></tr>
<tr><td>☐</td><td>13436</td><td>SHROUD   Robert Wilcox</td><td>$2.50</td></tr>
<tr><td>☐</td><td>13366</td><td>A GRIEF OBSERVED   C. S. Lewis</td><td>$2.25</td></tr>
<tr><td>☐</td><td>14406</td><td>NEW MOON RISING   Eugenia Price</td><td>$2.50</td></tr>
<tr><td>☐</td><td>14096</td><td>THE LATE GREAT PLANET EARTH
Hal Lindsey</td><td>$2.50</td></tr>
</table>

Buy them at your local bookstore or use this handy coupon for ordering:

INSPIRATIONAL FAVORITES

EUGENIA PRICE
St. Simon's Trilogy

☐	13682	Beloved Invader	$2.25
☐	14089	Maria	$2.50
☐	12835	New Moon Rising	$1.95
☐	14195	Lighthouse	$2.50
		and	
☐	6485	Don Juan McQueen	$1.75

HAL LINDSEY

☐	14096	The Late Great Planet Earth	$2.50
☐	13490	The Liberation of Planet Earth	$2.25
☐	14374	Satan Is Alive And Well On Planet Earth	$2.75
☐	11259	The Terminal Generation	$1.95
☐	14108	There's A New World Coming	$2.50

Bantam Book Catalog

Here's your up-to-the-minute listing of over 1,400 titles by your favorite authors.

This illustrated, large format catalog gives a description of each title. For your convenience, it is divided into categories in fiction and non-fiction—gothics, science fiction, westerns, mysteries, cookbooks, mysticism and occult, biographies, history, family living, health, psychology, art.

So don't delay—take advantage of this special opportunity to increase your reading pleasure.

Just send us your name and address and 50¢ (to help defray postage and handling costs).